PRAISE FOR *BETTER TOGETHER*

"*Better Together* has already become the go-to resource for smooth transitions and healthy growth when churches merge. Now Jim Tomberlin and Warren Bird have updated and expanded it to include church planting, multiplication as well as multisite congregations. This invaluable field guide has become even more relevant, helpful, and practical."

—Chris Hodges, senior pastor, Church of the Highlands, author of *The Daniel Dilemma* and *What's Next?*

"We are in a time when increasing numbers of congregations must ponder the previously unthinkable—merger. As someone who has overseen church mergers, I can testify that combining congregations is no easy matter. People like to believe there's no church like their church. In order to birth a new, merged congregation, there must be relinquishment of some things we love. But there can also be gains.

In this must-read book, *Better Together: Making Church Mergers Work*, Jim Tomberlin and Warren Bird, two of Christianity's most respected voices, give us practical help for how to lead congregations to be better together. Based on firsthand research, they develop a common language that subsequent conversations about church mergers can build upon and walk readers through the steps to a successful church merger.

Most important, the authors present congregational merger as a matter of remaining faithful to Christ's mission rather than merely ensuring institutional survival, giving us a very helpful book."

—Will Willimon, United Methodist Bishop, retired, Professor of Christian Ministry, Duke Divinity School, author of *Leading with the Sermon: Preaching and Leadership* (Fortress, 2019)

"*Better Together: Making Church Mergers Work*, an important book, is vital for this moment in time! Jim Tomberlin and Warren Bird have extensively updated and expanded their previous brilliant work with brand new research, current models and clear action steps for how church mergers work. This is a crucial guide for the new reality in which we live and as church leaders we should be profoundly grateful we have it to direct us."

—Dave Ferguson, visionary leader of *NewThing Network;* cofounder of Exponential Church Multiplication Network; author of *Hero Maker: 5 Essential Practices for Leaders to Multiply Leaders*

"Over the past few decades, church mergers have gone from being a novel idea to a necessary strategy for the continued expansion of the church. Jim Tomberlin and Warren Bird teach us that survival-based mergers are a thing of the past and missional mergers are the future. The church I serve has benefited greatly from their strategic thinking and pastoral insights. In a rapidly changing world, we are not only *Better Together—*we are *necessary* together."

—Terry Crist, lead pastor, Hillsong Church Phoenix, Arizona, and Las Vegas, Nevada, Director, USA Hillsong Network

"Our merger/adoption was helped greatly by the counsel highlighted in *Better Together*. Nearly every time we broke from their coaching, we paid the price. This book has time-tested wisdom that will help churches looking to go to the next level in being 'better together.'"

—Brian Tome, founding and senior pastor, Crossroads Church, Cincinnati, Ohio

"When two churches begin a conversation about merger, it is like undertaking a journey into the unknown. The potential for blessing is tremendous, and yet the obstacles are very real. Jim Tomberlin and Warren Bird are the essential guides in this journey. They have walked alongside faithful leaders of mergers, listened for experience and gleaned extraordinary wisdom. *Better Together* shares the fruit of this movement of God in our time. There is no resource for us quite like this!"

—Ken Carter, bishop, Florida Conference, The United Methodist Church; author of *Fresh Expressions: A New Kind of Methodist Church for People Not in Church.*

"What's the front edge of church merger insight? You're holding it. The wisdom distilled in this book helped me as a local church pastor, and currently as a movement leader. As church mergers continue to increase, this new edition of *Better Together* is a 'must' for the next generation of leaders."

—Scott Ridout, president, Converge (formerly Baptist General Conference)

"I am so grateful for the collective wisdom and encouragement that Jim Tomberlin and Warren Bird have given the global church in their work *Better Together: Making Church Mergers Work.* I have turned to this text time and again (and recommended others to do the same) as we have continually pondered mission and ecclesiology in our urban context. I deeply appreciate Tomberlin and Bird's voice in advocating the ways that churches can indeed be better together."

—Drew Hyun, pastor, Hope Church NYC, New York, New York

"*Better Together* is one of my go-to tools in my toolbox! It is a practical manual for church leaders, church planters and local churches as they navigate the opportunity of a church merger. Making church mergers work is essential for the advancement of God's Kingdom in the days and years to come."

—Greg Nettle, president, Stadia Church Planting

"In my work with church planters and multisite churches, I talk to so many who are attempting to merge with another church, and I always ask them, have you read *Better Together*? I believe that church mergers will continue to prove an answer to prayer and a key strategy for Kingdom advancement. This expanded and updated edition is a must read for anyone considering a church merger."

—Chris Railey, senior director of Leadership/Church Development, The General Council of the Assemblies of God

"Church mergers can open doors to powerful redemptive ministry or they can be a complete disaster. It is vital that any ministry leader considering a church merge do their homework before getting started. *Better *Together* is an excellent resource packed with research, insight and examples of churches successfully navigating the challenging waters of mergers."

—Mark Jobe, senior pastor of New Life Community Church, Chicago, Illinois; president of Moody Bible Institute, Chicago, Illinois

"Warning: never approach a church merger without an expert guide. I credit Jim Tomberlin and Warren Bird for teaching me the new math of mergers: 1+1=3! God used this game-changing resource to help our leadership team successfully navigate two church mergers. Now we're using the fresh insights from this updated edition in conversations with multiple congregations exploring potential mergers. The real-life stories, practical tools, and templates help create a roadmap that churches of any size can follow!"

—Tim Lucas, lead pastor of Liquid Church, lead author of *Liquid Church: 6 Powerful Currents to Saturate Your City for Christ*

"You have in your hands an outstanding resource with a well-developed merger process. Take your time and follow the procedures and principles outlined here, and you can avoid a lot of the problems that plague an unsuccessful merger."

—David O. Middlebrook, managing shareholder, TheChurch-Lawyers.com; coauthor of *Nonprofit Law for Religious Organizations: Essential Questions and Answers*

"As part of the Ginghamsburg team that engineered a merger to create a 'new,' thriving, urban congregation, I deeply appreciate the information, inspiration, and practical toolkit in *Better Together*. It will help your church navigate the pitfalls and potholes that we had to discover the hard way."

—Karen Smith, senior executive director, Ginghamsburg Church (United Methodist), Tipp City, Ohio

"New churches and church multiplication are center stage in this expanded and updated version of *Better Together*. I have seen time and again church planters benefit from acceleration through a God-directed merger. Church multiplication movements can often be furthered by healthy mergers. Mergers can also be a pathway toward the emergence of Level 5 churches!"

—Todd Wilson, cofounder of Exponential and author of *Made for More: Six Essential Shifts for Creating a Culture of Mobilization* and *Multipliers: Leading Beyond Addition*

"*Better Together* has become the go-to book on how to do mergers well—the kind of mergers that are about multiplication more than subtraction, and expansion more than elimination. Jim Tomberlin and Warren Bird provide invaluable help through research, great examples, practical guidance, and helpful language."

—Ed Stetzer, executive director, Billy Graham Center at Wheaton College, author and blogger, edstetzer.com

"Whenever a church indicates they are considering a merger with another congregation, there's only one book I recommend and that's Better Together. In the years to come, church mergers are going to become much more commonplace, and I'm grateful that Jim Tomberlin and Warren Bird have created the playbook to help ministries navigate this process in a helpful and healthy way."

—Tony Morgan, founder and lead strategist, The Unstuck Group; author of *The Unstuck Church: Equipping Churches to Experience Sustained Health*

"This is a must-read book for several reasons: It's the first of its kind on a new, increasing wave of church mergers built on vision rather than survival. It's based on real-life, first-hand research based on real church mergers by two of Christianity's most respected voices. It develops a common language that subsequent conversations about church mergers can build upon, and the authors walk the reader through the various steps to a successful church merger."

—Bill Easum, president, 21st Century Strategies, Inc., www.effectivechurch.com; coauthor, *Ten Most Common Mistakes Made by Church Starts*

"Jim Tomberlin and Warren Bird are on the front lines of a church world changing so rapidly most of us have a hard time keeping up. *Better Together* is the best kind of work: based on real-life facts, marked by thoughtful interpretation, and filled with a vision for the beauty and flourishing of the church. This book could open untold doors for your church and ministry."

—John Ortberg, pastor and author, *Water-Walking-Discovering-Obeying-Radical-Discipleship*

"Tomberlin and Bird have knocked the ball out of the park in this book. The research is incredible, the content is insightful, and the net results are invaluable. Considering the trends, this book is a must-read for church leaders serious about making the most of what God gives them."

—Dan Reiland, executive pastor, 12Stone Church, Lawrenceville, Georgia; author, *Amplified Leadership*

"The church merger process that has been instinctively used in the past . . . has failed. And it will continue to fail. If a merger is at all in your thinking, please read this book. There is a right way . . . and you'll find it here!"

—W. Charles Arn, president, Church Growth Inc., Monrovia, California; author, *Heartbeat: How to Turn Passion into Ministry*

"This book addresses the most common challenges related to church mergers. Having planted several churches as well as having experienced the complicated task of a church merger, this is a must-read. You can choose to travel this road alone, but take my advice, it's always easier, faster, and 'better together.'"

—Jaime Loya, senior pastor, Valley International Christian Center, San Benito, Texas

"An essential resource for any mission-driven church considering a merger. Practical, field-tested strategies that will help leaders avoid common pitfalls. I highly recommend it!"

—Jonathan Schaeffer, senior pastor, Grace Church, Middleburg Heights, Ohio

"We *need* this kind of win-win thinking in the church. I'd love it if denominational leaders were thinking this way. (I wonder if a challenge needs to go out to them explicitly!) I don't know of any resource like this in print. *Better Together* will stimulate a wave of kingdom impact that will make us all say 'Why didn't we think of this sooner?'"

—Mark Ashton, senior pastor, Christ Community Church, Omaha, Nebraska

"Today's congregational leaders often wonder whether 'going it alone' is their best option. Yet the 'm-word' (merger) can elicit tremendous fear, confusion, and disappointment—both when the negotiations succeed and when they don't. This book offers clear and thoughtful guidance about the how and the why (and even the 'Why not?') of merger initiatives. Serious study of this material will move leaders miles ahead in their thinking and will greatly increase the chances that a robust and renewed ministry will result from a merger initiative."

—Alice Mann, consultant, formerly with the Alban Institute; author, *Can Our Church Live?*

"Jim Tomberlin and Warren Bird have bent my mind again. Like many, I was mired in the old math of church mergers—and now I see that mergers, done well, offer a powerful way to expand God's kingdom. *Better Together* is ahead of its time. It's thorough and inspirational without being laborious. Thank you, Jim and Warren, for pushing me in this direction!"

—Tom Nebel, director of Church Planting, Converge Worldwide, Orlando, Florida

"*Better Together* is a practical and complete guide to an emerging opportunity to reclaim and maximize kingdom resources. Don't attempt to even consider a merger without taking advantage of their research."

—Steve Stroope, lead pastor, Lake Pointe Church, Rockwall, Texas; author, *Tribal Church* and *It Starts at Home*

"Opportunities for churches working together have never existed like they exist now, but only those who are alert and aware of these strategies will take advantage of this connection. Merging churches takes help and expertise, and this book is a powerful guide to jumpstart such an endeavor."

—Rick Bezet, lead pastor, New Life Church, Central Arkansas

"In a church I previously served, I initiated a merger. Ours was the joining church, and we became part of a stronger church in my community. We did many of the things this book recommends. It was the best thing to do for my church and for the kingdom of God. God really blessed the merger."

—Rod Layman, pastor, First Baptist Church, Mesa, Arizona

"When I began consulting twenty-four years ago church mergers were normally based on two dying churches coming together for survival. Not so anymore. Tomberlin and Bird show that today's most successful mergers are mission-driven as two (or more) churches come together around a compelling vision. *Better Together* will become a definitive guidebook. Out of a complex and emerging landscape, Tomberlin and Bird have distilled useful principles and provided a new vocabulary of family-related terms to use. We are speaking of our own merger as a 'marriage' because we envision 'having kids together' through new ministry sites in the future."

—Christopher M. Ritter, directing pastor, First United Methodist Church, Geneseo, Illinois

"Tomberlin and Bird rightly describe a growing movement among churches learning to walk, work, and worship God together as one; churches rejecting competition for cooperation and working smart not hard. As one who has both led and benefitted from church mergers, I invite you to prayerfully consider this practical guide."

—Mark DeYmaz, pastor, Mosaic Church, Little Rock, Arkansas; author, *Building a Healthy Multi-Ethnic Church*

International Praise for *Better Together*

"Jim Tomberlin and Warren Bird are on to something very important. As they point out, you don't have to use the word *merger*. Regardless of what you call it, the concept is similar to church planting and has tremendous potential to expand the impact of vibrant churches as well as revitalize declining churches."

—Nicky Gumbel, senior vicar, Holy Trinity Church Brompton, London, England; founder, Alpha Course

"God is rewiring his church to reach a new generation. *Better Together* is an invaluable resource to any church considering a merger. It is comprehensive, well researched, practical, and insightful. We pastor at a multisite church that has successfully grown through a merger and can say, 'Tomberlin and Bird get it!' Mergers have great potential. They also come with potential pitfalls. This book will help ensure both churches involved are truly better together."

—Bruxy Cavey, teaching pastor, and Tim Day, senior pastor, The Meeting House, Oakville, Ontario, Canada

"Jim Tomberlin and Warren Bird have always been exceptional at anticipating the next strategic phase in the development of the local church. With *Better Together: Making Church Mergers Work,* they have empowered a generation of pastors and leaders to navigate merger initiatives successfully. Church mergers have become a highly relevant subject for the church in Europe with tremendous implications for church-planting. It is a must-read book for every strategic church leader."

—Leo Bigger, senior pastor, ICF Church, Zurich, Switzerland

"Jim Tomberlin and Warren Bird have provided the church with a visionary and practical book from which, if many church leaders could embrace it with real humility, the kingdom impact could be huge.

Whether you lead a thriving church or are involved in one that is struggling, I commend this book to you."

—Steve Tibbert, senior pastor, King's Church, London, England; author, *Good to Grow*

"This book is a treasure trove of gems, practical tips on how to navigate the rough seas of merging a church and some small things that can have a major impact. If we had this book fifteen years ago when we had undergone such an endeavour, it would not have been so painful for a lot of people, and we would have been able to avoid many of the pitfalls we have found ourselves in. I can recommend this book to any church considering embarking on such a journey."

—Johan Geyser, cultural architect, Mosaïek Church, Johannesburg, South Africa

"The book is extremely helpful in understanding that good mergers actually increase the kingdom of God—including the total number of churches because they become vehicles of change, not preservers of the status quo. Mergers may not be what church leaders had in mind for their churches when they started them, but they may indeed be God's key to open doors to new opportunities of greater harvest. For those local churches considering a merger, *Better Together* contains lots of practical wisdom that would lead to peril if not heeded."

—Dietrich Schindler, executive director, Church Planting, Evangelical Free Church, Germany

"Much like blended families, church mergers are becoming more frequent in our generation. Thanks to *Better Together*, we now have an excellent guide to assist us in avoiding the land mines and maximizing the potential of this unfamiliar territory."

—Mark Conner, senior minister, CityLife Church, Victoria, Australia

Better Together

BETTER TOGETHER

Making Church Mergers Work, Expanded and Updated

Jim Tomberlin and Warren Bird

Fortress Press
Minneapolis

CONTENTS

FOREWORD

Craig Groeschel

On Thursday, December 7, 2000, two elders from a nearby church called and asked me if I'd consider becoming their pastor. Because the church I had started, Life.Church, was thriving and just about to celebrate our fifth anniversary, I didn't even consider praying about it and politely declined.

To my surprise, they didn't take "no" for an answer.

The men queried again, this time asking me if I'd at least pray about it. Trying not to sound rude, I explained that I was certain God wanted me to continue with the church we started. Sensing their deep desire to find a pastor, I offered to help them find the best person to lead their church. I was shocked when they declined my offer and asked me a third time to consider becoming the pastor of their church. "Is there anything we could do to get you to consider our church?" the men asked with genuine passion. "We really feel like God led us to you."

At this point I felt a little frustrated by their persistence and said somewhat flippantly, "Well, if you want your church to become a part of ours, I'll consider that."

I'm not sure if I expected them to laugh, scoff, or walk away. I do know that I never, ever expected them to say they were open to that idea. Exactly thirty days after that initial conversation, on January 7, 2001, 89.6 percent of their church voted to merge with our church, and we became one church in two locations.

At the time, I'd never heard of a church merger before. As the years unfolded, I discovered that many churches across the world are asking the question, "Could we do more for God's glory united with another church than we are doing alone?" Now, what was unheard of before is becoming a viable and strategic option for many congregations.

Since our first partnership with that local church, we've joined forces with eight other churches as part of our 38 campuses across 11 states as of late 2020. Even though these have all worked out well, we've also stepped away from dozens of similar merger opportunities.

Over time, we've discovered that two are often better than one—but not always. Sometimes $1 + 1 = 3$. Combining the right ministries can produce better outcomes than the individual ministries could accomplish alone. But other times, $1 + (\text{the wrong})\ 1 = 0$. Although healthy mergers can create a spiritual synergy greater than you can imagine, the wrong mergers are like cancer to a human body.

I'm so thankful that someone finally wrote a book to address the hidden challenges and unexpected opportunities of uniting two ministries into one. And I'm even more thankful that it wasn't just anyone, but two of the most knowledgeable men I know on this subject. Not only do I value Jim Tomberlin and Warren Bird as friends, but I'm also deeply grateful for their hearts to serve the local church. If you are considering joining forces with another church, you've picked up the right book. Read *Better Together* carefully. Read it prayerfully. And I know God will prepare you to make the right decision.

Craig Groeschel
Founding and senior pastor of Life.Church, Edmond, Oklahoma, and author of *Dangerous Prayers: Because Following Jesus Was Never Meant to Be Safe*

PREFACE

- 2% of congregations each year vote (or are required) to close, a number likely to increase due to the COVID-19 pandemic, but some of them could instead restart as a merger.
- 12% of senior pastors change churches in any given year—and some of those churches will choose to merge as a succession strategy.
- 20% of churches are growing, able to revitalize a struggling church.
- 40% of senior pastors are within a decade of retirement—and some of those churches will choose to merge in order to start a new chapter.
- 100% of church planters need a place to meet, and among those whose young congregations come to own a church building, 20% of the time it happens through a merger.

Bottom line: An increasing number of church leaders, both denominational and nondenominational, are seeking God for insight. They are asking, "Could there be a merger in the future of *our* church?"

For the past decade, we have been witnessing a swelling wave of mission-driven church mergers that is transforming the church landscape across North America. Mergers are occurring among churches of all sizes and types. They are happening in urban centers, suburban neighborhoods, and rural communities. They reflect a growing trend where two local churches at different life stages leverage their common DNA and complementary differences to generate greater synergy for a stronger regional impact.

These new kinds of merger are not what have been typical of the past, when two struggling churches made a last-gasp effort to survive. Church-merger conversations may begin because of financial difficulties; they may surface through local partnerships or denominational affiliations or initiated by a church planter or a multisite church. But these mergers succeed today largely because of a united and compelling vision that lifts a church, especially a church that's stuck or on a downward slope, into a new pattern of life and growth.

> *Mergers today succeed largely because of a united, compelling vision that lifts a church that's stuck or on a downward slope into a new pattern of life and growth.*

Want some specific examples?

- A church planting network leader told us of his desire to plant a church in a nearby community by partnering with an existing church that needs some revitalization and a pastor. What happened? "It seemed like a hugely unlikely pairing, but God continued to open conversations and doors and the 'unlikely' became a reality. The church has more than doubled in size, and new people are choosing Jesus and beginning the journey of following him."
- A United Methodist leader told us, "Currently the choices we offer to churches in long-term decline are to (a) become a legacy church where the property is sold and the proceeds are used for new churches, (b) be merged with another United Methodist church, or (c) struggle to remain open knowing that this option has an extremely low success rate."
- A Lutheran bishop told us, "I'm intrigued to think through this [mission-driven] lens. In our neck of the woods, merger is often a cost-effective way to manage existing realities of decline, not a strategy for growth. I'll be surprised if we have even one merger that has resulted in greater mission effectiveness . . . but I'd like to change that direction."
- A pastor who led the merger of his church of 25 with a church of 15, which two years later is a church of 85 members, says: "Unless you were part of the merger from the beginning, you would never know who was part of the two different churches today. We are truly one church."
- A joining church pastor said, "In prayer I believed that the Lord spoke that it was his will for the merger to take place. It wasn't what I wanted. Instead, I wanted to continue to lead the church, but once the Lord spoke, I had no choice but to obey. Our church became a campus, and it has continued to grow since then and now has more than 2,000 in attendance."

Do you sense a new embracement of mergers in each of those examples?

Roughly 80 percent of the 320,000 Protestant churches in the United States have plateaued or are declining, and many of them are in desperate need of a vibrant ministry. Among the 20 percent of growing congregations across the United States, many are in desperate need of space. These conditions present a potential win-win for forward-thinking church leaders who believe that "we can do better together than separate," and it is revitalizing church topography.

In essence, we believe that almost a 100 percent of today's Protestant churches could become a candidate for a merger. Figure 0.1 shows a client analysis by The Unstuck Group, the consulting group where lead author Jim Tomberlin serves as a consultant. It depicts various categories of the typical life cycle in a church. The 14 percent on the left are typically the best candidates for the lead church role in a merger while the 86 percent on the right are typically the best candidates for the joining church role in a merger (concepts we'll introduce in chapter 1).

For a detailed description of each phase of the life cycle, see *The Unstuck Church: Equipping Churches to Experience Sustained Health* by Tony Morgan.[1]

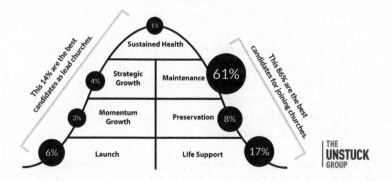

Figure 0.1

Why an Expanded and Updated Version?

When we published the original edition of *Better Together: Making Church Mergers Work* in 2012, it was the first book to focus entirely on church mergers. We wanted to document the emerging trend of healthy, mission-driven mergers as an alternative to the old, failure-prone mergers of two declining churches.

It was our intention to give common language to this growing phenomenon, to destigmatize the idea of merging with another church, and to provide a practical roadmap that churches could follow toward a successful, healthy merger outcome.

Better Together was also the first book to draw upon cross-denominational research projects, a national survey of merged churches, and numerous interviews to highlight common learnings and best practices.

A decade later our early observations about a church merger trend have been validated, and the embracing of church mergers as a viable option has become celebrated. Our terminology has been integrated into the church-merger conversation and the tools we introduced have proven effective. All of these developments and conversations are contained in this updated version.

Yet, there have also been dramatic shifts in cultural attitudes toward churches and a distinct decline in church attendance in the past decade. Also, the recent COVID-19 pandemic has put already economic fragile churches in greater jeopardy of surviving. In this expanded and updated version, we wanted to address the impact of these trends. In short, this new edition adds:

- 28 Merger Fact graphics, most based on a 2019 survey that drew 962 usable responses
- Several dozen new stories and updates to many stories from the first edition
- Additional insight on the biblical foundations of mission-driven mergers and church multiplication
- Three new chapters plus additional tools and templates you can adapt to your own merger context
- New applications of healthy mergers to church planters, mainline leaders, and more

Our hope is that all the new information, data, stories, and tools will be even more helpful in churches becoming *better together!*

Why Jim and Warren?

Both of us love the local church and believe passionately that God wants to use it to fulfill Jesus's command to make disciples of Jesus Christ (see Matt 28:19–20). We've each trained for ministry, pastored, and held other ministry roles.

In 2005, Jim began consulting and coaching churches in developing and implementing multi-congregation and merger strategies. In 2019, Jim merged his consulting company MultiSite Solutions with Tony Morgan's The Unstuck Group to expand their capacity to assist more churches, including their growing practice with church mergers.

Meanwhile Warren was bumping into mergers during his years of pastoring and teaching seminary. Then, while serving as research director at Leadership Network, Warren was able to conduct the surveys, interviews, and workshops that led to the original edition of *Better*

Together. Warren now serves as vice president of research and equipping at ECFA (Evangelical Council for Financial Accountability), who joined a coalition of other organizations to sponsor a 2019 national survey on mergers—see more details in appendix A, "Merger Research."

Flow of the Book

The book shows how to think about and complete a successful merger. The first section is introductory, the second is informative (descriptive), and the third instructional (prescriptive). Throughout the book we include factoids, charts, checklists, and we include a checklist of steps to take in a merger, examples of frequently asked questions (FAQs) from several actual mergers, as well as details of several dozen churches whose merger stories we tell in the body of the book.

To help with the conversation, we introduce the terms *lead church* and *joining church,* which we use from chapter 1 onwards. Our experience is that every healthy church merger involves a *lead* church and a *joining* church—a delicate dance in which one leads and the other follows. Some are almost equal in size and health, but most are vastly different. Regardless, one always *leads* and the other *follows.* More on that idea in chapter 1.

We also suggest a family-related set of terms: *rebirth mergers, adoption mergers, marriage mergers,* and *intensive care unit (ICU) mergers.* We explain and illustrate these models in chapter 5.

A Merger in Your Future?

If you're not already having (or hearing about) merger conversations, there is a good likelihood that you will soon, whether you're on paid church staff, a church planter, a lay leader, an active church member, a denominational leader, or a seminary student. As you do, we want you to bring far more faith and optimism to the discussion than what you find in the typically dismal newspaper headlines about two struggling churches forced to merge as a desperate, last-gasp hope for survival.

Instead, by reading this book, you'll see that mission-driven church mergers have tremendous potential to exponentially expand the impact of strong, vibrant churches, to generate momentum to young "homeless" churches, or to revitalize plateaued and declining churches.

> *Mission-driven church mergers have tremendous potential to exponentially expand the impact of strong, vibrant churches as well as to revitalize plateaued and declining churches.*

Yet the journey is not without danger. There are numerous land-mines to avoid by any who embark on a merger expedition with another church. We want to help strong and struggling churches alike to know that merging is a viable option for impact and revitalization. We want to show how it can be adapted to assist vibrant churches in reaching more people. We want to give hope to leaders of stuck or struggling congregations that their church might find a second life through a successful church merger.

We want you to be able to tell a story like this California pastor, a survey participant: "A church of thirty merged with our church of 125. The merger was the best thing for each church, and we became one body in an incredible way. Due to the merge, in less than four years, we have grown to a congregation size of over 750 people, with over 300 first-time decisions for Christ, over 200 baptisms, and so many amazing stories of God's faithfulness. We are now a healthy, thriving church that is seeing more fruit than we ever saw before the merger. We are debt-free and financially healthy; we have grown our staff to 15 and are making plans for expansion. One of the most exciting things is that twenty-five of the thirty individuals who remained in the "smaller" congregation are still part of our new church family—and more excited than they've ever been."

We want your church to consider how it might do ministry *better together.*

Notes

1. This graphic reflects the survey results of 1,564 churches who completed the leadership team version of The Unstuck Church Assessment during 2019. The survey incorporates objective metrics of church health along with the subjective perspectives of the church's leadership team members. You can take the assessment for free at https://assess.theunstuck-group.com/

PART I

THE NEW CHURCH MERGER LANDSCAPE

1

MERGERS ARE EVERYWHERE

Mergers are everywhere. Big and small churches, new and old ones, denominational and nondenominational, theologically diverse and geographically scattered.

You may not use the word *merger*. You may call the idea a *consolidation, federation, restart, replant, partnership, adoption, grafting, collaboration, satellite, unification, reunification*, or even something more indirect like *joining forces, repotting*,[1] or *becoming a legacy church*.[2] By the way, we notice the increasing usage of the term *legacy church* to signify declining congregations with a great past, but they are struggling to sustain themselves in the present (we'll say more about this idea in chapter 4).

Whatever label you use, the core idea is two or more churches becoming one—the combining, integrating, and unifying of people, structures, systems, and resources to achieve a common purpose: doing life and ministry together as a vibrant, healthy, local expression of Christ's body, the church.

However you describe them, mergers are happening with increasing frequency. And unlike the results in previous generations, many church mergers today are producing positive growth and admirable fruit. Increasingly, they are becoming a vehicle for unifying local congregations around a shared mission that is producing healthier churches that are making more and better disciples of Jesus Christ.

For troubled churches, a healthy merger is a far better outcome than for the church to close. As the book *Ending with Hope* observes, "By closing one congregation, energy is released for use in places where God is working in new ways." It changes the congregation's focus. It's no longer thinking "about failure but about redirecting resources for new ministry."[3]

Much More than the Multisite Movement

Our original edition of this book focused on an emerging trend of mission-driven church mergers, many of which were stimulated by the multisite church movement. While we still believe the multisite movement was the biggest catalyst for these new kinds of mission-driven mergers, the church merger trend has now spread way beyond the multisite outcome.

For the past decade we have been witnessing a swelling wave of mission-driven church mergers that is transforming the church landscape across North America. Mergers are occurring among churches of all sizes and types, and they are happening in urban centers, suburban neighborhoods, and rural communities. Such mergers reflect a growing trend where two local churches at different life stages leverage their common DNA and complementary differences to generate greater synergy for a stronger community impact.

These new kinds of merger are not what have been typical of the past, when two struggling churches made a last-gasp effort to survive. Church-merger conversations may begin because of financial difficulties, surface through local partnerships or denominational affiliations, or be initiated by a multisite church or a church planter. These mergers today succeed largely because of a united and compelling vision that lifts a church, especially one that's stuck or on a downward slope, into a new pattern of life and growth.

> *Mergers today succeed largely because of a united, compelling vision that lifts a church, especially one that's stuck or on a downward slope, into a new pattern of life and growth.*

Eleven Merger Contexts . . . And Counting!

It's definitely a new day for church mergers. According to Leadership Network research, 2 percent of US Protestant churches merge annually—that's six thousand congregations. More significantly, another 5 percent of churches say they have already talked about merging in the future[4]—that's fifteen thousand more. Plus, among multisite churches an amazing 60 percent see mergers as part of their future.[5] And among megachurches, 17 percent have merged with another congregation in the previous twenty years.[6] These churches—plus tens of thousands of others elsewhere around the globe—are sensing that they could fulfill their God-given mission better together than separately, and they're exploring new ways to join forces for the advancement of God's kingdom.

According to our 2019 research, the context for mergers today is much broader than most people realize. One example: we found that 20 percent of mergers involve a church planter! (See Merger Fact 1.) In short, mergers are showing up in a wide variety of contexts, each situation offering a slightly different benefit. Here's our list of eleven current top contenders:

1. **Stable but stuck churches** are experiencing renewal marked by fresh vitality, new spiritual energy, intensified community engagement, joyful momentum, and most important, an increase in newcomers, who are deciding to follow Christ and to be baptized.

2. **Struggling churches** in survival mode are being salvaged, and experience new life by merging with a healthy church.

3. **Historic churches**, often in urban centers that are facing dim prospects for the future, are delighted to discover that a merger can translate their considerable heritage into a terrific foundation for a new or next generation.

4. **Healthy church plants** that are growing and in need of facilities are finding them through a merger with a congregation that has facilities with perhaps room to spare. (Both Merger Fact 1 [page 7] and 2 [page 40] highlight how often this is happening!)

5. **Former church plants** are reuniting with their sponsored church by merging back onto the original campus or merging as part of a new multisite campus, believing they can be better and stronger together than apart.

6. **Separated churches** that had formerly broken away from each other are being reconciled and reunified through mergers.

7. **Denominational churches** are using a merger approach to revitalize, struggling congregations in their faith family, nurturing them back to health and vitality through temporary or permanent adoptions.

8. **Diversity-minded churches** with a desire to become more racially and ethnically diverse are seeing mergers as a way of intentionally diversifying their church and becoming more

multiethnic.

9. **Pastor-less churches** of all sizes are seeing mergers as a way of securing a new pastor or ensuring a smooth succession transition as their pastor retires.

10. **Multisite churches** have experienced significant growth with more than one out of three (40%) multisite campuses coming by way of a merger. A growing number of multisite churches have an intentional strategy that proactively initiates, encourages, and facilitates church mergers.

11. **Movement making churches** have developed an intentional merger strategy. Some churches—such as Crossroads Church in Cincinnati; LCBC in Lancaster, Pennsylvania; New Life Church in Chicago; or Sandals Church[7] in California—are developing regional or national networks mostly composed of church mergers.

For example, in Hutchinson, Kansas, five of the twelve campuses of Crosspoint Church have come from mergers. The church has had so many potential mergers knock on its doors that it's developed a roadmap to merging. A prospective joining church takes upon itself the task of becoming a Crosspoint congregation, working through several steps and evaluation points across the months. "We won't merge with anyone in less than a year," says lead pastor Andy Addis. "Mergers need to gestate. We need time to walk together to build trust."[8]

Future chapters will provide examples from each of these contexts. The health of churches across all spectrums includes strong, stable, stuck, and struggling congregations. Many are motivated by survival, but an increasing number identify "mission advancement" as their primary impetus for merging.

Merger Fact 1

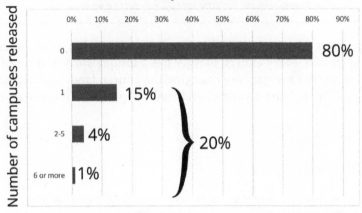

20% of Mergers Become a Location for a New or Replanted Church

2019 Survey: *How many of your geographical locations (campuses) have been released to become a new planted or replanted church?*

Two Key Terms: Lead Church, Joining Church

Every merger involves a *lead church* and a *joining church*. The merging of churches is a delicate dance where one leads and the other follows. The lead church represents the dominant or primary culture that will continue through the merger. The joining church is the congregation that will be lifted or otherwise shaped to become more like the lead church.

Sometimes the lead and joining churches are very similar in their look, feel, health, and approach to ministry, but usually, a distinct gap in *momentum* exists between them. Lead churches typically have growth momentum while joining churches seek new or additional growth momentum. For some joining churches, the merger process involves major transformation on the level of a death, burial, and resurrection as they grow into the identity of the lead church.

Sometimes a church will question, "Why should we be the joining church? We have a large facility, many assets, money in the bank, and no debt." The answer to who is the lead church and who is the joining church is not determined by the amount of physical assets or financial resources but by the state of health and forward momentum. A large but mostly empty facility can be more of a liability than an asset if the congregation is small and declining in size.

> *The answer to who is the lead church and who is the joining church is not determined by the amount of physical assets or financial resources but by the state of health and forward momentum.*

Regardless of whether you're a potential lead church or potential joining church, every church merger has a unique story and set of circumstances, but mergers are changing the church landscape across the body of Christ. Maybe your church will be part of a merger story as well!

Notes

1. One Southern Baptist group uses this term. See www.namb.net/namb1pbnewsarchive.aspx?pageid=8589994583.

2. See a United Methodist example in "Legacy Ministries to Dying Churches Give Congregations a Way to End Well," Faith and Leadership at Duke University, September 5, 2017, https://tinyurl.com/t2rqsl9; see a Southern Baptist example in Mark Clifton, "Introducing Legacy Church Planting," January 27, 2015, https://www.namb.net/send-network-blog/introducing-legacy-church-planting/. See also Gray, Stephen and Franklin Dumond, *Legacy Churches*, Carol Stream, IL: ChurchSmart, 2009.

3. Beth Ann Gaede, ed., *Ending with Hope: A Resource for Closing Congregations* (Lanham, MD: Rowman and Littlefield, 2002), vii.

4. See explanation in appendix A.

5. "Multisite Movement Continues to Grow: Latest Research from National Survey Reports Top Line Findings," Leadership Network, 2019, leadnet.org.

6. The question was asked in a 2015 study jointly conducted by Leadership Network and the Hartford Institute for Religion Research. This particular finding was not mentioned in the overall report about the study, written by Scott Thumma and Warren Bird, "Changes in American Megachurches: Tracing Eight Years of Growth and Innovation in the Nation's Largest-Attendance Congregations," available for free at www.leadnet.org/megachurch.

7. See Sandals Church's ROGO Foundation (ROGO stands for Real with Ourselves, God and Others), at http://rogofoundation.com/.

8. See http://crosspointnow.net for the church and http://crosseyedleaders.com/ for its materials on how new churches assimilate. The quote comes from personal conversation between Andy Addis and the authors.

2

GOD IS MOVING!

We love the idea of surfing the spiritual waves that Rick Warren describes in *The Purpose Driven Church*. He points out that near the community where he pastors in Southern California, people can learn a lot about surfing: how to choose the right equipment, how to use it properly, how to recognize a "surfable" wave, and how to catch a wave and ride it as long as possible. But they can't learn how to build a wave. Just like surfing is the art of riding waves that God builds, "our job as church leaders . . . is to recognize a wave of God's Spirit and ride it. It is not our responsibility to make waves but to recognize how God is working in the world and join him in the endeavor."[1]

In the pages ahead, we identify many logical reasons why church mergers make sense, why they are increasing, and why the results are increasingly positive. But those explanations are all secondary to our sense that God is clearly behind the momentum, especially in nations where Christianity has a long history and thus a need for revitalization of long-established churches whose life cycle is ebbing. In biblical terms, we believe mergers are another example of God doing a "new thing" (Isa 43:19), helping existing congregations to reach new levels of unity, of maturity, and "of the fullness of Christ" (Eph 4:13).

We believe this is congruent with God's desire for "divine makeovers" as expressed through the prophet Isaiah: "Your people will rebuild the ancient ruins and will raise up the age-old foundations; you will be

called Repairer of Broken Walls, Restorer of Streets with Dwellings"
(Isa 58:12).

Biblical Basis for Church Mergers

Where can you find mergers in the Bible? The word isn't there, but we
believe the concept is supported throughout Scripture. The apostle Paul
taught, "There is one body and one Spirit, just as you were called to one
hope . . . one Lord, one faith, one baptism; one God and Father of all"
(Eph 4:4–6). The Psalmist declared "how good and pleasant it is when
God's people dwell together in unity!" (Ps 133:1). The entire drama
of the New Testament is the story of God bringing diverse groups
together toward that divine reality.

Jesus talks of having "other sheep" (Gentiles) that need to be merged
into the flock (John 10:16). He said that the temple should be a house
of prayer for *all* nations, not just his own ethnic group (Mark 11:17).
The book of Acts says a wide variety of people were all brought into
one church to demonstrate the point, as Paul explains later, that in
Christ "there is no longer any distinction between Gentiles and Jews,
circumcised and uncircumcised, barbarians, savages, slaves, and free,
but Christ is all, Christ is in all" (Col 3:11 GNT). Paul explains how
Gentiles have been "grafted" into the same vine as the Jews (Rom 11:17),
and how God "brought Jews and Gentiles together as though we were
only one person . . . when he united us in peace . . . by uniting Jews and
Gentiles in one body" (Eph 2:15–16). The church is even likened to the
union of male and female when forming a marriage (Eph 5:22–32).

God is a champion for merging in the sense of bringing people
together, especially diverse people, into a beautiful mosaic that reflects
what heaven will look like on earth. Don't verbs like *grafting, reconciling,
uniting,* and *marrying* all convey the idea of merging? Jews and Gentiles,
men and women, rich and poor, slave or free, traditional and contemporary, old and young, denominational and nondenominational—all
are invited to join, *to merge* with God's family on earth and demonstrate
the power of the gospel to transform lives and to break down the walls
that divide us.

We affirm that healthy churches reproduce and multiply. That's why
we consult and write books on church planting and multisite ministry.[2]
We need more life-giving churches, not fewer. We are not saying that
every church should merge with another church, but we are advocating
that every church ought to consider merging if it would better fulfill the
biblically driven mission of your church and better extend God's kingdom in your community. Merging is congruent with the heart of God,

the principles of Scripture, and the ideal of more effectively stewarding the resources God has provided.

As one pastor in Atlanta told us, "The word *partnership* has changed the life of our church. The Bible tells how Peter caught so many fish that his boat was about to sink. He called over to another boat and they partnered together to capture all the blessings God was giving them. That's what happened as we came together to make a difference in this community." In his case, it was a cross-cultural partnership as his growing, predominantly African American congregation joined forces with a declining predominantly white congregation. The importance of bringing another boat alongside finds expression through many different values across Scripture, as summarized in table 2.1.

Table 2.1

Biblical Value of Churches Being "Better Together" through a Merger

Churches merge so that they can be more . . .

[all italics in Bible verses added by the authors]

Unified	"May they be brought to complete *unity* to let the world know that you sent me and have loved them" (John 17:23).
	"There is *one body* and one Spirit—just as you were called to one hope" (Eph 4:4).
Purposeful	"Being like-minded . . . *being one in spirit and purpose*" (Phil 2:2).
Collaborative	Paul views each city's church as one body, such as:
	"Paul . . . to *the church of God in Corinth*" (1 Cor 1:2) and
	"To *the church of the Thessalonians* in God the Father and the Lord Jesus Christ" (1 Thess 1:1).
Harmonious	"How good and pleasant it is when brothers *live together in unity*" (Ps 133:1).
	"If it is possible, as far as it depends on you, *live at peace* with everyone" (Rom 12:18).
Stronger	"Two are better than one, because they have a *good return* for their work" (Ecc 4:9).
Effective	"Now to each one the manifestation of the Spirit is given for the *common good*" (1 Cor 12:7).
Reproductive	"And God blessed them. God said to them, 'Be *fruitful* and multiply and fill the earth' " (Gen 1:28).

"This is to my Father's glory, that you *bear much fruit*, showing yourselves to be my disciples" (John 15:8).

Externally focused
"Seek the peace and prosperity *of the city* to which I have carried you" (Jer 29:7).

Healthy
"But to each one of us grace has been given as Christ apportioned it . . . to prepare God's people for works of service, so that the body of Christ may be built up until we all reach unity in the faith and knowledge of the Son of God and become mature" (Eph 4:7–13).

Reconciled
"Make every effort to keep the unity of the Spirit through the bond of peace" (Eph 4:3).

"Finally, brothers and sisters, rejoice! *Strive for full restoration*, encourage one another, be of one mind, live in peace. And the God of love and peace will be with you" (1 Cor 13:11).

"If you are offering your gift at the altar and there remember that your brother has something against you, leave your gift there in front of the altar. *First go and be reconciled* to your brother; then come and offer your gift" (Matt 5:23–24).

Humble
"Do nothing out of selfish ambition or vain conceit, but in *humility* consider each other better than yourselves" (Phil 2:3).

"Therefore, as God's chosen people, holy and dearly loved, clothe yourselves with compassion, kindness, *humility*, gentleness and patience" (Col 3:12).

Redemptive
To *redeem* those under the law, that we might receive *adoption* to sonship (Gal 4:5).

He predestined us for *adoption to sonship* through Jesus Christ, in accordance with his pleasure and will (Eph 1:5).

"Your people will *rebuild* the ancient ruins and will raise up the age old foundations; you will be called *Repairer* of Broken Walls, *Restorer* of Streets with Dwellings" (Isa 58:12).

Diverse
"After this I looked, and there before me was a great multitude that no one could count, from *every nation, tribe, people and language,* standing before the throne and before the Lamb" (Rev 7:9).

The Bible Teaches Multiplication

> And God blessed them. God said to them, "Be fruitful and multiply and fill the earth." (Gen 1:28 ESV)

The authors understand this verse as a reflection of God's desire for every living organism. If so, it involves growth by addition, by reproduction, and by multiplication. When God brought Eve to Adam, that represented growth by addition. Being fruitful by having children was growth by reproduction. When the children married and had children, that begins multiplication. It is the divine life cycle that God built into the human race and all of creation. Reproduction and multiplication are God's method for populating the earth with the human race.

Likewise, we believe this is God's desire for every local church. The local church is God's instrument on earth for making disciples of Jesus and populating heaven. And it's in the DNA of every local congregation to grow, reproduce, and multiply. God wants to bless *your congregation* so it can be a blessing in your community by growing, reproducing, and multiplying disciples of Jesus.

We see the principle of multiplication in the Great Commission Jesus gave his followers in Matthew 28:19–20: to make disciples who make disciples. The normal and natural outcome of disciple-making is church growth! Multiplication is not the end game; it's the means to an end. The end goal is making disciples who make disciples—both organically and exponentially. You can feel the exponential growth of the church through multiplication of disciples pulsating throughout the book of Acts (see table 2.2).

Table 2.2

Divine DNA for Local Churches: Exponential Growth

Acts 2:41	"So those who received his word were baptized, and there were **added** that day about three thousand souls." (ESV)
Acts 2:47	". . . praising God and having favor with all the people. And the Lord **added** to their number day by day those who were being saved." (ESV)
Acts 4:4	"But many who heard the message believed; so the number of men who believed **grew** to about five thousand." (NIV)
Acts 5:14	"And more than ever believers were **added** to the Lord, multitudes of both men and women." (ESV)

Acts 6:1	"Now in those days, when the number of the disciples was **multiplying** . . ." (NJKV)
Acts 6:7	"And the word of God continued to increase, and the number of the disciples **multiplied greatly** in Jerusalem, and a great many of the priests became obedient to the faith." (ESV)
Acts 8:4	"Therefore, they that were **scattered** abroad went everywhere preaching the word." (KJV)
Acts 9:31	"So the church throughout all Judea and Galilee and Samaria had peace and was being built up. And walking in the fear of the Lord and in the comfort of the Holy Spirit, it **multiplied**." (ESV)
Acts 9:42	"And it was known throughout all Joppa; and **many believed** in the Lord." (KJV)
Acts 11:21	"And the hand of the Lord was with them: and a **great number believed**, and turned unto the Lord." (KJV)
Acts 11:24	". . . for he was a good man, full of the Holy Spirit and of faith. And a **great many people were added** to the Lord." (ESV)
Acts 12:24	"But the word of God **increased and multiplied**." (ESV)
Acts 13:49	"The word of the Lord **spread** through the whole region." (NIV)
Acts 14:1	"Now it happened in Iconium that they went together to the synagogue of the Jews, and so spoke that a **great multitude** both of the Jews and of the Greeks **believed**." (NKJV)
Acts 16:5	"So the churches were strengthened in the faith, and they **increased in numbers** daily." (ESV)
Acts 17:4	"Some of the Jews were persuaded and joined Paul and Silas, as did **a large number** of God-fearing Greeks and **quite a few** prominent women." (NIV)
Acts 17:12	"Therefore, **many** of them **believed**, and also not a few of the Greeks, prominent women as well as men." (ESV)
Acts 18:8	"Then Crispus, the ruler of the synagogue, believed in the Lord with **all his household**. And **many** of the Corinthians, hearing, believed and were baptized." (ESV)
Acts 19:20	"The word of the Lord **spread widely** and **grew** in power." (NIV)

In 2 Timothy 2:2, you also see the multiplication process outlined in the apostle Paul's pastoral instruction to Timothy: "And the things you have heard me say in the presence of many witnesses (*addition*) entrust to reliable people (*reproduction*) who will also be qualified to teach others (*multiplication*)."

Multiplication and Church Mergers

Just as growth comes through reproduction, it can also come through adoption. Adopting a child is not reproduction, but it can lead to health and reproduction.

My (Jim) two oldest grandchildren (have I told you that I have eleven grandchildren?) were adopted from Ukraine. Their health and future in the orphanage was bleak. Being adopted most likely rescued them from an early death or a life of crime. Today they are flourishing and growing in a healthy family. Their future is full of hope and promise. One day they will marry and have children of their own. The Scripture affirms God's heart for orphans and God's redemptive purposes through adoption.

> Religion that God our Father accepts as pure and faultless is this: to look after orphans and widows in their distress . . . (James 1:27 NIV)

> To *redeem* those under the law, that we might receive *adoption* to sonship. (Gal 4:5 NIV, emphasis added)

> He predestined us for *adoption to sonship* through Jesus Christ, in accordance with his pleasure and will. (Eph 1:5 NIV, emphasis added)

Many church mergers are like adoptions where struggling churches with little hope for the future are rescued from decline and can become flourishing, reproducing congregations. The adopting church grows through adoption, and the adopted church can become a healthy, growing, reproducing church.

This is the strategy that Matt Chandler, lead pastor at Village Church in the Dallas metroplex area, has embraced. Under Chandler's leadership, Village expanded to six campuses, in most of the cases, adopting a struggling church as a multisite campus in order to infuse it with Village's life-giving DNA. Then starting in 2015, the campuses began to spin off as stand-alone churches, with the plan of spinning off the final one in 2022. The goal is that each will become a reproducing church.

Chandler emphasized that the multisite approach worked well for them for a season of church life. The structure alleviated the stress of overcrowding and allowed for healthy expansion when a half-dozen services at the original campus each weekend still couldn't fit all their attendees.

Now Village Church has a merger-multisite-replant multiplication strategy, "Our hope is that this vision will give us the opportunity to multiply out, planting more churches and sending out more missionaries in DFW and beyond."[3]

Merging Can Take a Church Closer to Multiplication of Disciples

Jesus instituted the church to be his vehicle for the good news of forgiveness, redemption, salvation, and eternal life. He declared, "I will build my church, and the gates of hell shall not prevail against it" (Matt 16:18 ESV). The local church is meant to be a prevailing church with the primary mission of making Christ-following disciples. Yet the majority of churches in North America are not prevailing and are struggling to make disciples who make disciples.

Exponential leaders Todd Wilson and Dave Ferguson have popularized the idea that churches function at one of five levels, as figure 2.2 illustrates. They break down the kingdom math simply—every church is either subtracting, stuck, adding, reproducing, or multiplying disciples of Jesus. From their analysis, the majority of churches today have a subtraction culture of scarcity and surviving; a small minority of churches are growing with an addition culture of gathering and accumulating, but very few churches today have a multiplication culture of releasing and sending.

Merging Can Help Any Church Move Toward Multiplication

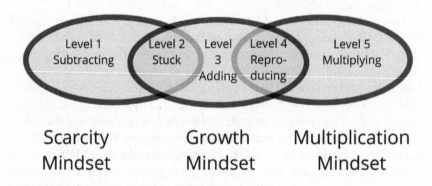

Figure 2.2

> *Very few churches today have a multiplication culture of releasing and sending.*

If a church is declining, it's Level 1. If it's holding even, it's Level 2. Those two groups comprise 80–85 percent of churches in North America.

If it's growing, it's Level 3. Many churches at Levels 1 and 2 aspire to become Level 3, but the reality is that the world will not be reached for Christ even if every church became Level 3 and grew. Billions of people would still remain untouched by the Gospel.

Level 4 churches reproduce themselves by planting other churches or by birthing campuses. That's certainly good but reproduction is not multiplication; but it is the *next step* toward multiplication. The only way for every man, woman, adolescent, and child to hear the gospel and see it demonstrated is through church multiplication. Multiplication is the only way the Great Commission will ultimately be fulfilled—by Level 5 churches that make disciples who make disciples, and likewise by churches that reproduce churches that, in turn, reproduce churches. Whether church reproduction is done through new church plants or new multisite campuses, reproduction to the third generation (and beyond) is true multiplication! [4]

Our friend Bill Couchenour at Exponential, a church-multiplication catalyst organization, often says, "Imagine if Noah had chosen to repopulate the world by fathering all the children—that would be an addition strategy. Instead, he fathered children who fathered his grandchildren who fathered his great-grandchildren and so on—that's a multiplication strategy."

How do church mergers fit into these five Levels? A Level 1 to Level 3 church can leapfrog from a declining or even growing status to become a Level 4 reproducing church or a Level 5 multiplying church.

Could merging with another church help your church move from struggling to surviving, from surviving to growing, from growing to multiplying? Yes! We believe every church regardless of its category could benefit from a merger—whether you're the lead church or the joining church. A merger can help both churches move toward multiplication.

Sandals Church in greater Riverside County, California, has been on a rocket ride. Founded in 1997 in the living room of Pastor Matt and Tammy Brown, it has grown to more than thirteen thousand weekly attendees across eleven locations. It started at Level 3 (adding), began moving toward Level 4 (reproducing) and is aspiring toward Level 5 (multiplying).

Of its twelve locations, eight have come by way of merger. Citing 2020 data, senior executive pastor Dan Zimbardi says, "Our eight mergers have grown on average of 847% pre-merge to post-merge with hundreds being baptized." In fact, the busiest campus for Sandals Church is one of its merger locations—one of the oldest churches in the area, located in the heart of central Riverside. "We are incredibly honored to be able to carry on the incredible work that Palm Baptist has been doing since 1941," the church's website says.[5]

The reason so many mergers have worked is that Sandals Church values kingdom-perspective multiplication. "At our core, we want to see churches thrive. We always come into potential merger conversations with the idea that we're there to help them, not necessarily merge," explains Jon Brown, executive pastor of the multisite development.

Due to the increasing number of conversations Sandals Church was having with churches that wanted to merge, they launched the ROGO Foundation. ROGO stands for Real with Ourselves, God and Others, the founding mission and vision of Sandals Church. The Foundation oversees the merger and launch of new Sandals Church campuses while also pursuing partnerships with church leaders and organizations that are passionate about the local church. The ROGO Foundation subscribes to an open-handed approach that supports other lead churches as they multiply—by training and freely sharing resources they have created from their eight mergers.[6]

God grows only so many megachurches, but every church of every size and stage can move toward multiplication. We believe that the Bible's message to us all is to see that as the ideal—to be blessed, be fruitful, and go multiply!

Notes

1. Rick Warren, *The Purpose Driven Church: Growth without Compromising Your Message and Mission* (Grand Rapids, MI: Zondervan, 1995), 14.

2. Jim Tomberlin, with Ben Stroup, *125 Tips for MultiSite Churches* (MultiSite Solutions, 2011), Kindle edition; and Jim Tomberlin and Tim Cool, *Church Locality: New Rules for Church Buildings in a Multisite, Church Planting and Giga-Church World* (Nashville: Rainer Publishing, 2014). To contact Jim, see Meet the Authors on page 270. Warren Bird is the coauthor of thirty-two books for church leaders including *The Multi-Site Church Revolution: Being One Church in Many Locations* by Geoff Surratt, Greg Ligon, and Warren Bird (Grand Rapids, MI: Zondervan, 2006); *A Multi-Site Church Roadtrip: Exploring the New Normal* by Geoff Surratt, Greg Ligon, and Warren Bird (Grand Rapids, MI: Zondervan, 2009); and *Viral Churches: Helping Church*

Planters Become Movement Makers by Ed Stetzer and Warren Bird (San Francisco: Jossey-Bass, 2010). To contact Warren, see Meet the Authors on page 270.

3. Kate Shellnutt, "Matt Chandler's Village Church Ends Multisite Era," *Christianity Today*, September 28, 2017, https://tinyurl.com/w822lwd.

4. For further explanation of the five levels, see "What's Next for the Multisite Church?" Interview of Dave Ferguson by Kevin Miller and Kyle Rohane, *Christianity Today*, November 2019, https://tinyurl.com/rduxahd.

5. https://sandalschurch.com/locations/palmavenue/.

6. For more information, see http://rogofoundation.com/.

3

WHY MERGE?

The previous chapter opened with a metaphor about surfing spiritual waves. God creates oceans, sends winds and builds waves. We can't do any of that. Our job begins with recognizing a wave that God's Spirit is making and then riding the wave, joining God's work.

That's where *Better Together* comes in: we help you recognize and join a "surfable" wave. We give you tools for understanding how "merger waves" work, but you can't ride a wave unless you get in the water. In this chapter, we share reasons to jump in the water and catch the wave.

Seven-Way "Win" of a Merger

We see the incoming waves of a healthy church merger as offering a seven-way win:

- *Struggling churches win.* Stuck and struggling churches get a fresh start in living out God's purpose for their church. One of our survey participants—the pastor of a joining church—had this to say of their 2009 merger: "Ninety-five percent of our people stayed through the merger and through the following year. Many became leaders in the new church over time." A survey participant from a different church defined "win" as: "Today, three years after our merger, most of us have to stop and think which church someone was a former member of."

- *Strong churches win.* Strong and stable churches gain momentum as stuck or struggling churches join them in a new chapter of life. A staff member from a church of two hundred that had a church of fifty merge with it said, "The number one reason we decided to join together was to reach our community faster and more effectively. In our opening month together, we had twice as many first-time guests than the two churches had separately before the merger. Within the first two months, twelve people had made decisions for Christ. We are on the road to reaching our next two hundred. I am sure we have made mistakes, but God is at work, and that's a huge win!"

- *The body of Christ wins.* The corporate testimony of the local church is stronger and better equipped to make disciples of Jesus Christ. The church's corporate witness is better for making more disciples. As someone in our surveys said, "We are reaching more people who are farther from God than either church was doing before the merger."

- *Local communities win.* Local communities are served better by strong vibrant congregations. As leaders of a church commented in our survey, "If it is God's plan, you can do no better. All leaders from the joining churches would agree that the mergers were the best thing that could have happened to our communities." A different survey participant said of a 2016 merger, "Although the merger was filled with difficult moments and relational conflict, the end result is that our church influence has increased in our city, and our attendance has more than doubled in size since after the merger."

- *The kingdom of God wins locally.* The kingdom of God advances and grows through vital, life-giving congregations. In one church, during the first weeks after its merger, nine people were baptized. "That's more than our church baptized in the last ten years," the pastor told us. The new church also saw ten other members join in those same weeks.

- *The kingdom of God wins regionally.* The kingdom's win becomes even greater when reproduction happens. Commenting on their two-year old merger, one survey participant said, "We took on the church plant as a campus and it's thriving to date." Another church reported, "The church is continuing to make positive impacts in the community. There is growth in salvations and baptisms as well as in Sunday morning attendance. New churches are being planted as a result." And one very gutsy church told us this in a survey: "Our merger is thriving because it was so clearly a God thing. An older church in 'hospice' merged with a young church plant. They sold their four million-dollar facilities for one dollar. The elder church totally integrated with a younger church to reach the younger community." This was a church of twenty welcoming a church plant of 120. Today, one year later, the church draws two hundred people weekly.

- *The kingdom of God wins globally.* Some churches are seeing mergers as a way to extend their reach beyond local and regional impact. Christ Fellowship in Miami is a multisite church with seventeen campuses regionally and globally. Two of their regional congregations and four of their global congregations in their network came about through a merger.

Everybody wins in a successful merger. With testimonies like these (and we could cite many more), isn't the idea of mergers—by whatever term you use—something worth prayerfully and seriously exploring? If these "wins" excite you for the church you serve—or a church you know, it just might be a potential candidate for a church merger as a means of building God's church overall and extending God's kingdom in new ways in this generation.

Top Ten Benefits of a Church Merger

Another way to summarize the "wins" of a merger is through a list of potential results. Table 3.1 summarizes our "top 10" reasons for why churches consider a merger:

Table 3.1

Why Merge?
1   To be better together than each church is individually
2   To begin a new church life cycle
3   To reach more people for Christ
4   To make a greater difference for Christ
5   To multiply your church's impact
6   To better serve your local community
7   To leverage the legacy and good reputation of the past

8   To maximize church facilities

9   To be stronger as a local church

10   To further expand God's kingdom

Old Math Mergers

How are today's mergers different from those of yesteryear? They represent two completely different paradigms that we could call "old math" and "new math" of church mergers. Old math mergers were more survival driven, whereas today's new math mergers are more mission driven. Also, old math mergers worked toward equality between the merging churches while today's focus is on aligning with the stronger church culture.

> Old math mergers were more survival driven, whereas today's new math mergers are more mission driven.

Sadly, the old math of mergers was too often 1+1 = 1. The combination rarely worked to produce a vibrant, healthy, larger, or growing church. As veteran church consultant Lyle Schaller explained, the newly merged church typically shrinks to the approximate size of the larger of the two former congregations because no one has made any effort to alter the congregational culture. Members were more comfortable in the smaller size environment that they knew before the merger, so they keep dropping away until the culture gets back to what it was. As a result, the typical merger of two smaller, no-growth churches "has had a spectacularly poor record in attracting new members."[1] This situation commonly occurs, he said, even when there's a good cultural fit between the congregations.

One reason for failure is that the old approach often embodied little more than a goal to survive. It was seen as a way of preserving as much as possible. It was not portrayed as a vehicle that could bring significant change. These "intensive care" mergers of two struggling churches were a last-gasp effort to stay alive but often ended with both going down together like two drowning people trying to survive, each unwittingly at the expense of the other. The final equation too often ended in 1+1=0.

At best, merging was wrongly perceived as a way of making the church work better without making any other needed changes. Two struggling churches (or sometimes three) would take what they thought were the best elements from each of them and combine them into a merged congregation.

By contrast, today's successful mergers tend to be missional in focus with one church embracing the vision and strategy of the other church. The new math has a synergistic effect. The merge represents far more than an action taken to survive. Such churches are motivated by a strong, future-oriented sense of mission and expanded outreach rather than by a desire for institutional survival. They are often preceded by four exploratory questions to determine a merger possibility:

- Would our congregation *be better* by merging rather than remaining separate?
- Could we *accomplish more* together than we could separately?
- Would our community be *better served* if we joined together?
- Could the kingdom of God be *further enlarged* by joining together?

Those questions represent the heart of a mission-driven merger. Though many of today's merger conversations begin when a struggling congregation acknowledges its precarious circumstances, those conversations are not only motivated by survival but by the dream of a renewed or greater mission.

What else can make the difference needed for success? According to Schaller,

> The critical component is a minister who is an effective transformational leader and possesses the skills, including the essential people skills, necessary to create a new worshipping community with a new congregational culture, a strong future orientation, a new set of operational goals, a new sense of unity and a new approach to winning a new generation of members.[2]

What's the most practical way for that to happen? The best merger success stories, according to Schaller, tend to be when *three* congregations—rather than the more common pattern of two—come together to create a new congregation that constructs a new building at a new site under a new name with the strong leadership of a new minister who is comfortable and competent in the role of being the pastor of a middle-sized (or large) congregation.

A typical successful development, which is positive according to Schaller, occurs within a few years: at least one-half of the governing board becomes composed of people who have joined since the merger

and who want to be part of a large and numerically growing congregation.[3]

> The best merger success stories, according to Schaller, tend to be when three congregations . . .
> come together to create a new congregation.

Indeed, that is happening. Gary Shockley, a former executive director
for new church starts in the United Methodist Church,[4] told us, "One of
the strategies we see working in our denomination is the 'vital merger'
where two or more churches sell all their assets, relocate, get a church
planter assigned to them and begin anew."[5]

Church mergers today are also different from those in the past in that
at least one of the partners is healthy and vital. Usually the healthy and
more vital partner is larger in attendance. Sometimes it's the same size
as the church merging with it. On rare occasions it's smaller than the
church merging with it.

Whatever the size comparison, successful mergers are rarely a fifty-
fifty deal of equals coming together. One church typically takes the lead
role, expanding its culture of growing, replicating, and multiplying. If
the merger is successful, far more than survival happens for the joining
church in the years after the merger. Instead, it's a clear gain. The joining church is revitalized as the lead church's healthy momentum continues, with evidence of more changed lives, more conversions, more
baptisms, and more signs of spiritual vitality.

> Successful mergers are rarely a fifty-fifty deal of equals coming together.

New Math Mergers

The old mergers were about trying to preserve an old way of doing
ministry, but the new mergers are about embracing a shared vision for
the future. The old mergers were fueled by survival; the new mergers
are driven by mission and vision.

> New mergers are about embracing a shared vision for the future . . . driven by mission and vision.

Successful mergers today operate with a new kind of math. These kinds
of mergers tend to have an exponential outcome greater than 1+1 = 2.

Arizona pastor Justin Anderson illustrates our point. He experienced
a three-church merger in late 2010 and early 2011. The merger tripled

the size of his church and left the congregation with a new structure, new leadership, and new name—Redemption Church (www.redemptionaz.com). Though the transition was painful at times, Anderson insists it was the right pathway to pursue. "We are better together than we were apart," Anderson says. "When it comes to vision, ideas, leadership, resources, and prayer for the three-church merger, 1+1+1 = 10."

This new math of mergers had such a positive outcome that a year later, Redemption Church did a fourth merger. Today there are ten Redemption congregations across Arizona under a team leadership model structured to support and help unique, contextualized local congregations "make disciples who make disciples who make disciples."

Anderson's experience with church mergers is only one of many people who report it as a big win. In our surveys, one Ohio pastor said, "The question the merger hinged upon for us was this: 'Could we reach the next two hundred people in our community faster together or separate?' When both pastors answered 'together,' it seemed unfaithful to do anything but merge." After praying, fasting, discussing with a pastoral coach, and then obtaining highly supportive votes by both congregations and their boards, these two churches from the same denomination merged—one with an attendance of 150 and the other with 55.

The survey also asked how the merger went for that church. The pastor of the joining church, who filled out the survey, ranked the experience an eight out of a possible high of ten, stating, "Our focus was on a greater impact on our community, and we achieved that. Both churches were stronger after the merge than before." For this merged church, 1+1 = far more than 2.

As these two churches illustrate, new-math mergers are working across many different church sizes. Premerger attendance at the first Arizona example was two thousand.

Premerger attendance at the Ohio merger was 205. But church growth, though an important barometer, is not the primary measure of a merger's success. Sometimes taking strategic steps may actually lower attendance for a season as a church becomes healthy. Sometimes the Divine Gardener has to prune the branches for future growth: "He cuts off every branch in me that bears no fruit, while every branch that does bear fruit he prunes so that it will be even more fruitful" (John 15:2). Instead, the most important measure for success is whether the merger can better achieve God's call of making disciples of Jesus Christ. *Success is more fully expressed by the outcome of a prevailing local church where lives are being changed, disciples made, and communities transformed as a result.*

> *Merger success is . . . where lives are being changed, disciples made, and communities transformed as a result.*

Serial Mergers and Church Networks

Research affirms that there is a definite trend since the 1990s toward a greater number of mergers. This is happening among churches of all sizes, with the typical example being in the attendance range of one hundred to two hundred after the merger.[6]

However, large churches are rapidly becoming new players in mergers, especially in multiple mergers. Some are even pursuing a pathway of intentionally adding merger after merger as a way of reaching more people and extending their impact. Other very large churches have created large networks of merger churches. Oklahoma-based Life Church, where Craig Groeschel (who also wrote the foreword to this book) is lead pastor offers three levels of how it welcomes other churches to partner with it. The broadest level is called *Open*, and it makes a wide range of the church's resources available at no cost to anyone who will use it in a noncommercial application to lead people to Christ. The next level is called *Network*, in which churches connect with Life Church through recurring weekend experiences that feature free video teaching messages. The most closely aligned level with Life Church is called *United*.[7] Churches that practice this level of partnership join with Life Church in reaching people around the globe. They become a Life Church campus. Their pastor becomes a campus pastor of Life Church. By late 2020, the church has thirty eight different campuses, eight of which came as mergers.

North Point Community Church, a church based in greater Atlanta, where Andy Stanley is senior pastor, does not use the word *merger.* Leaders there prefer instead the term *partners.* Their idea is to share best practices and encourage leadership development.[8] Two local partners became campuses of North Point, which means they link themselves to the other campuses financially and organizationally. The strategic partners beyond Atlanta are autonomous congregations who share North Point's philosophy and are licensed to use North Point video sermons and other materials.

For New Life Community Church in Chicago, where Mark Jobe is pastor (and is also president of Moody Bible Institute), fourteen of its twenty-eight campuses to date have been mergers, which they call *restarts.* Four were congregations that had been established over one hundred years previously. New Life is now training other churches, especially urban ones, in how the legacy of faith can be powerfully honored and given fresh passion through a Restart.[9]

Other churches actively solicit merger partners but do so regionally. The Chapel in Grayslake, Illinois, has built a hub of five merged churches around the suburban-rural outer edge of Chicago.

Granted, megachurches like Life Church, North Point, The Chapel represent less than 1 percent of North America's churches. Yet the innovations they introduce and popularize often have a ripple effect across churches of all sizes. "One factor in the spread of new ideas is what *Diffusion of Innovations* author Everett Rogers calls their observability,"[10] says Dave Travis, former director of Leadership Network and coauthor of *Beyond Megachurch Myths.*[11] "Some people hear an idea, grasp it, internalize it, and immediately start implementing it, but an even greater number of people have to *see* it first to understand. Once they see the model and its favorable results, they may decide that it has merit and value for them. Larger churches, due to their visibility and influence, often platform new models of ministry, which are then spread and adapted across the social ecosystem of smaller churches."

Clearly, larger churches are blazing a trail of extending their reach and multiplying their impact through intentional merger strategies that many other churches will follow in the days ahead.

Five Reasons Not to Merge

Church mergers happen due to a number of motives, wrong and right, immature and healthy. Some circumstances are not questionable in themselves, but they can lead to inappropriate motives or to mergers laced with distrust. Improper or unhealthy motives include the following:

- **Preservation.** Sometimes people view the merger as a vehicle to perpetuate the current church culture or save a building with more hope in preserving the past than in developing a new future. However, if a church is not willing to really change, a new name and a few more resources won't save it. Church leaders need to remember they are not in the "church-building" business but in the "disciple-making" business. We are not called to save buildings, but to save souls! None of the churches the Apostles started in the first century exist today. None of the buildings the first-century Christians congregated in are still standing, but the impact of those churches continues to the present. That is the legacy worth preserving!

- **Maintaining the Status Quo.** Other people use the merger as a tactic to avoid or distract from addressing deeper problems or systemic issues. Their focus is to maintain the status quo (Latin for *the mess we are in*). That's like a troubled marriage deciding to adopt a child to save the marriage and avoid dealing with the marital problems. Mergers are not a strategy for maintaining the status quo. They are a strategy for dramatic change.

> Mergers are not a strategy for maintaining the status quo.

- **One-Sided Retirement Plan.** Some use the merger as a strategy to create a co-pastor or multi-staff role as job security for a church leader or to help out a friend whose church is in trouble. Perhaps an underpaid pastor wants a steadier salary, or someone wants to provide a retirement or golden parachute exit strategy for an aging senior pastor. Though mergers can be a favorable option for a retiring pastor, it also needs to be a favorable option for the church.
- **Steeple-jacking.** Some target declining congregations for the sole purpose of taking over their facilities. Not caring about the people, they just want the assets. Likewise, they use the merger as a strategy to raise cash for an endowment, deferred maintenance needs, or personal gain.

The key is for the church that might acquire such valuable properties to keep right priorities and pure motives. As our friend Craig Groeschel says:

> If the stronger church doesn't believe it can truly help the weaker one and serve them with integrity, the stronger church should not move forward. I've seen stronger church leaders make unrealistic promises all in an attempt to get a building from a struggling church. Remember—it is not all about buildings! It is all about people! At Life Church, we have declined far more merger possibilities than we've accepted because we didn't think it would be in the best interest of the other church.[12]

- **Denominational Pressure.** A good number of mergers are within the same denominational family, such as two Evangelical Lutheran Church in America congregations coming together. Others come from similar church families, such as two independent Baptists merging or a Presbyterian Church in America church merging with one affiliated with the Evangelical Presbyterian Church. Or perhaps two nondenominational churches with similar doctrines and styles will merge. But when churches are pressured to merge by denominational authorities it is a setup for disappointment or failure.

Decades ago when several US denominations were merging and the ecumenical movement was still in its idealism stage, around the early 1900s until about the 1960s, there was no doubt more pressure on even unwilling churches to merge, causing the high failure rate that Lyle Schaller and others observed in their writings.

Today hierarchical denominations still have the same power to require a merger, but they tend to exercise it more collaboratively with the involved churches. Typical is the observation Jorge Acevedo, lead pastor of Grace Church, Cape Coral, Florida, expressed to us in our 2019 interviews:

> My experience and what I hear from fellow United Methodist leaders, is that more pastors of prevailing United Methodist churches are taking the initiative to begin conversation with lagging and failing congregations in their community. They see the potential of "transfer of DNA" from a stronger church to a declining church. Strategically, this transfer happens through leadership with clear mission, vision, values, strategy and structures as well as mutually agreed upon policies and guidelines. In our experience of adopting two declining churches, in one situation I initiated the conversation with the appropriate hierarchy and in the other my District Superintendent initiated the conversation. The church's fourth (and most recent) campus was a closed United Methodist church that Grace Church reopened.[13]

If Jorge's experience is typical, then denominational mergers are moving in a direction to allow trust to build with both congregations, who can then reach goal ownership and adjustments within areas of negotiable issues. The temptation to railroad a takeover is still present but the process rarely has to go that direction.

Nondictated, mutually desired mergers always have a higher likelihood of success.

Nondictated . . . mergers always have a higher likelihood of success.

We wouldn't make this list of unfortunate motives if we hadn't heard stories of most of these things happening. Scripture abounds with accounts of how God made good with any number of messes, selfish people, and even downright evil doings, but let us underscore that healthy mergers work best when they're birthed from healthy motives. Chapter 11 is devoted to how churches discern and hear God's leading. Obeying God fully is a nonnegotiable, and shady means are never a wise path to a God-honoring end.

> Healthy mergers work best when they're birthed from healthy motives. Shady means are never a wise path to a God-honoring end.

Right Motives + Risk

If you want to catch a wave you must be willing to take a risk. You must be willing to get wet, to get in the water!

The "why" of mergers can't be fully processed without also understanding that all parties in the merger have to take a risk—a step of faith with no guarantee of success. Our research on church mergers drew many sobering comments. They affirm that mergers can be hard, and many don't work out. This book does not announce that all mergers now work; rather, it affirms that an increasing number of churches have found a way to make mergers work and with many experiencing amazingly good results.

Are you up to exercising faith? People are inspired by contests that fight against the odds. We love it when the underdog makes it. We're drawn to success stories of people going against the odds and winning.

Many of us likewise believe that we can be the exception, entering marriage with every good hope of a meaningful, lifelong relationship, even though we know the reality is that too many marriages don't make it. We take long shots on other dreams—maybe of owning our own business or rising to the top of our field even though we know that only a few will actually make it in the final outcome.

Challenges are still present for today's mergers, but as Jesus told us, with God all things are possible (see Matt 19:26). Jesus also taught that we as his stewards sometimes need to take risks (see Matt 25:14–30). We believe some churches are using mergers to fulfill Christ's great commission (see Matt 18:19–20) in ways that God is eager to bless. Is that something for you to explore? Is it the "new thing" (Isa 43:19) that God might want to do for you? Ready to catch a wave.

Notes

1. Lyle E. Schaller, *Growing Plans: Strategies to Increase Your Church's Membership* (Nashville: Abingdon, 1983), 56.

2. Lyle E. Schaller, *Reflections of a Contrarian.* (Nashville: Abingdon, 1989), 148. See also 141–145.

3. Schaller, *Reflections of a Contrarian*, 148. See also Chapter Five, "Should We Merge?" in Lyle E. Schaller, *The Small Church Is Different* (Nashville: Abingdon, 1982).

4. Gary Shockley's current role and contact information is available at sandartistry.org.

5. For more on this approach for United Methodists and beyond, see Dirk Elliott, *Vital Merger: A New Church Start Approach That Joins Church Families Together* (Fun and Done Press, 2013).

6. This information is based on secondary analysis of the data from FACT 2005 (Faith Communities Today) https://faithcommunitiestoday.org/faith-communities-today-2005-study/, much of which is publicly available at ARDA (The Association of Religious Data Archives), www.thearda.com and then in the search box, enter the words *faith communities today.*

7. See church website at www.life.church/ or see locations at https://tinyurl.com/y5mddc2u.

8. See the website for North Point's strategic partners at https://northpoint-partners.org/. See also Sheila M. Poole, "North Point Ministries Spreading Its Reach," *Atlanta Journal-Constitution*, Lifestyle section, April 8, 2011, https://tinyurl.com/wyvufan.

9. See www.multiplicitynetwork.com. The website for New Life Community Church is www.newlifechicago.org.

10. From personal interview with Dave Travis who referenced Everett Rogers, *Diffusion of Innovations*, 5th ed. (New York: Free Press, 2003), 16, 258, 264.

11. See Scott Thumma and Dave Travis, *Beyond Megachurch Myths: What We Can Learn from America's Largest Churches* (San Francisco: Jossey-Bass, 2007).

12. Craig Groeschel, "What to Do During Merger Talks," *Swerve*, October 29, 2008, http://swerve.life- church.tv/2008/10/29/what-to-do-during-merger-talks.

13. Personal correspondence between Jorge Acevedo and Warren Bird. The church's website is egracechurch.com.

4

NINE MERGER DRIVERS

In many ways, this chapter is a continuation of the ideas in the "Why Merge?" chapter. In the previous chapter we focused primarily on the benefits of merging. Here we explore some of the common drivers or specific motivations that move church leaders to consider a merger. Each can have a healthy impetus behind it.

1. Mission-Driven Mindsets

The dominant message we hope you see in this book is a then-now comparison: most successful mergers today are mission-driven rather than the survival-driven mergers of the past. They occur when churches discern that their synergy could lead to a greater impact for the kingdom of God. The synergistic benefit of joining with like-minded churches on a similar mission affirms the wisdom of Solomon, who said, "Two are better than one, for they have a good return for their work" (Eccl 4:9). Some are struggling churches, but many are not. Many mergers are made possible because of a multisite strategy but not all mission-driven mergers are or become multisite churches.

2. Economic-Driven Pressures

Culture Shift. From the beginning of the American story, local churches were seen as an asset to the community and church attendance was an expected cultural value. The twenty-first century has seen a dramatic shift in cultural attitudes toward local churches and a distinct decline in the value of church attendance. Once desired as a valuable member of the community, local churches are increasingly seen as a liability that burdens rather than helps: they do not pay property tax, they monopolize key real estate, and they sometimes create traffic problems and noise issues. Having lost the attendance boost that came when American culture affirmed church attendance as a preferred value, many churches can't survive. As a result, the American landscape today is filled with declining congregations unable to sustain, much less maintain expensive facilities on valuable property.

> The American landscape today is filled with declining congregations unable to sustain, much less maintain expensive facilities on valuable property.

Warren used to attend a church that was initially based in the Times Square area of New York City. Today the church building is a restaurant, and Warren recently had pizza there. The facility that at one time hosted his denomination's flagship church has only a wall plaque newspaper clipping about the era when it focused on nourishment for the soul rather than serving food for the body.

That situation is not unique as each year at least four thousand Protestant churches in the United States close their doors forever. In fact, Warren has amassed a collection of photos he's taken of former church buildings. The majority have become residences or restaurants. Others have become businesses and breweries.

In one study, Washington DC's Capitol Hill neighborhood lost just over 40 percent of its religious properties over a ten-year period and an additional 6 percent are currently for sale.[1] A different national assessment concluded, "every year, over one thousand religious buildings become vacant in the United States." In fact, an entire book has been written with the stated goal "to increase the ease with which . . . developers can . . . acquire, redevelop, and profitably market religious buildings."[2]

Churches represent a lot of valuable real estate, often worth millions, sometimes ideally located, and usually zoned with favorable conditions that the surrounding community would no longer grant today. Not only do real estate developers see great potential in these sites but faith groups do too, such as would-be suitors for a church merger. Although good organizations exist for churches that decide to permanently close, helping them distribute their assets to a new generation of churches, merger talks may also begin directly between two churches or perhaps through a denominational mediator.

Inability to Adapt. Certain financial challenges are almost predictable, with or without a recession—or a worldwide pandemic. Many churches hit a stage in their life cycle when they cannot go forward without a totally new start. The early days of most churches are marked by growth, conversions, young families, and different forms of innovation such as a fresh worship style or a new way of serving the surrounding community in Jesus's name. Over the years, a triple whammy factor can develop: the average age within the congregation becomes ten to twenty years older than that of the people in the surrounding community, making it harder to attract new people; the pastor tends to be more senior in age, again adding challenges to efforts to attract younger newcomers; and the church facility grows older and needier in terms of costly maintenance, which adds more burden to the existing members.

A church like this can slowly lose its appeal to newcomers, especially younger generations, causing the congregation to decline further in attendance and to struggle further in its ability to go forward. As the cycle spins downward, corporate discouragement often sets in. Eventually a crisis—sometimes as simple as the need for major facility repair or the retiring of the current pastor—triggers a church to prayerfully consider, "Maybe we should merge with a like-minded, healthy congregation that's doing the job we want to be doing."

We believe an increasing number of churches are opting for mergers due to the economic recession of recent years that has forced many churches to reassess their long-term viability. Under prosperous times many churches were propped up by artificial life support that no longer exists for many of them. In addition, many churches that were already financially vulnerable before the COVID-19 pandemic are at even greater risk of surviving. As a result many church leaders are concluding that a merger may be a way to have a "second life" instead of closing the doors of the church permanently or limping along into a doubtful future. Of the roughly 320,000 Protestant churches in the United States, most church experts say that nearly 80 percent are stuck, struggling, or in decline.

Think about the scope of those numbers: 80 percent of 320,000 churches means nearly a quarter million churches across the country have room in their facilities to fill with additional vibrant ministry. Meanwhile, there are a few thousand dynamic, growing, vibrant churches in desperate need of facilities. Many of these strong churches experienced explosive growth as a result of the COVID-19 pandemic. Can you imagine the win-win here? Certainly some of these struggling churches may find new growth and vitality on their own as they pursue Jesus's mission to "seek and save what was lost" (Luke 19:10). But there will also be many more who are willing to join with a vibrant church in the days ahead. That means many are strong candidates for a merger.

A Church Redemption Story. Central Baptist Church was founded in 1896, two days before the City of Miami was founded. It grew with Miami into a prominent downtown church in the 1930s with an eleven-hundred-seat auditorium near the business district of Brickle. The ornate, four-storied, one-hundred-thousand-square-foot facility became a historic landmark in the center of Miami.

Yet, like many downtown churches of the twentieth century, it fell on hard times. This once-flourishing congregation that numbered in the thousands dwindled down to a handful of people who could not sustain their church ministry or maintain their facility.

As a Southern Baptist church, it reached out to one of its many church plants. Christ Fellowship had started in 1917 under the name Perrine Baptist Church on the outskirts of Miami. It was one of several Southern Baptist church plants out of Central Baptist Church of Miami. Under the leadership of Dr. Rick Blackwood from 1996 to 2020, the church had become a successful multisite church reflecting the diversity of Miami.

In 2008 Central Baptist offered their building to Christ Fellowship who absorbed the remnant, cleared up its financial woes, and relaunched a vibrant congregation back in the heart of the city.

A few years later a high-rise developer offered to buy the church parking lot in exchange for additional parking in a brand new high-rise apartment building. This generated the needed resources to upgrade the historic building as well as fund Christ Fellowship's expansion across Miami.

The story of Central Baptist Church continued, but as a new chapter under its daughter church from a century before! As long-time Central Baptist church member Jenisu Ansley, today in her eighties, shares, "There came a time when the church began to go down in membership, but fortunately God had a plan. That plan was for us to merge with Christ Fellowship. It was one of the best decisions our church has ever made." What a great story and another hopeful example of how a church merger can make a difference in a community.

3. Multisite-Driven Momentum

The congregation known today as Sunrise Church started in 1956, grew steadily, going from one to several weekend services, and relocated several times in and around Rialto, California. Today it is one church on multiple sites, each location becoming part of the church under different circumstances.

The first offsite campus came in 1996 through a merger and was the result of a dying congregation in the same denomination that approached Sunrise for assistance. That church is now a Sunrise Church campus and enjoys the benefits of being part of a much larger church beyond its campus.

The second offsite location was the result of two congregations a mile apart that had discussed a merger among themselves prior to becoming a part of the Sunrise Church family. One of the churches approached Sunrise to merge and then the other church wanted to merge as well. The process was first a merger of these two churches with Sunrise Church, and then combining them to become the Sunrise Church Ontario campus.

The third offsite location was a Grace Brethren Church, which was composed of a small group of people. They had worked very hard to grow and reach out to the community in middle Rialto for many years with little long-term result. After a few church facility makeovers, the pastor approached Sunrise Church seeking guidance. The merger was successful, and it is now a fourth Sunrise campus although still in the Grace Brethren denomination of churches—a campus with dual-denomination membership.

Sunrise East Valley (thirty-five miles way) was started in part to provide a campus for church members who moved east of the Sunrise Church Rialto campus and to reach out to the unchurched in the East Valley. It has been from inception a Sunrise campus rather than a separate new church.

In every case Sunrise Church staff and key ministry coordinators provided the following:

- Training for the pastoral staff and ministry counterparts
- Curriculum for use in the teaching ministries
- Outreach strategies
- A spiritual growth process
- Aspects of intentionality to promote multiethnic, multicultural ministry

According to Art Valadez, who today serves as the church's pastoral coach for multiplication ministries, "Multisite has worked well for us for many reasons. It has enabled us to reach out to people far beyond our immediate community and city. It has also provided localized congregations within our church for those who move out of Rialto and still want to be a part of Sunrise Church. Multisite has been a great tool for discipleship on many levels and has challenged us to stretch beyond our comfort zone in developing new leaders. Even though all our buildings are now built and paid for and we enjoy a beautiful, newer 2,000-seat worship center, multisite helps us to partner with others and continue a healthy outward focus."

Sunrise Church is not alone. The multisite church movement has definitely contributed to the recent rise in church mergers. According to Leadership Network research, 40 percent of multisite campuses are the result of a church merger—that's more than one out of three.[3]

> According to the latest research, over 40 percent of multisite campuses have been acquired through a merger.

The multisite phenomenon continues to grow with no end in sight. Every week over seven million people attend one of eight thousand–plus multisite campuses across the United States. There are more multisite churches than megachurches. Many multisite churches have two, three, or more campuses. Multisite has truly become the "new normal" for healthy, growing, large outreach-oriented churches, and it has transformed the church scene across the nation.

The modern multisite movement began in the late 1990s, mostly as a band-aid approach for megachurches that were out of room or limited by zoning restrictions. It quickly evolved into a growth strategy for healthy churches of several hundred people and larger and is increasingly becoming a revitalization strategy for stable but stuck churches. It is also driving a new kind of church merger that is more mission and strategy driven than survival oriented.

Multiplying through mergers is a fast track way to multisite when the conditions are right for a successful merger.

> Multiplying through mergers is a fast track way to multisite when the conditions are right for a successful merger.

Just over 60 percent of multisite churches see mergers as a part of their future, according to the 2019 Leadership Network survey of multisite churches:[4]

- 44% see mergers as a viable path for the future of their multi-site strategy
- 9% more view it as a "central part of our strategy moving forward"
- 7% more indicated, "we are exploring mergers but not sure how to start"

Multisiting through church mergers is clearly increasing.

Chicken or Egg First? Has multisite fueled mergers or have mergers fueled multisite? It works both ways, but we see the first option as the larger motivator. Successful church mergers have become one of the unintended but good consequences of the multisite movement. It's like the interview Warren had with a reporter who pointed out the rise in available commercial real estate in a certain city. The interviewer asked if it meant a bunch of churches would decide to open or relocate there. Warren explained that churches don't work that way in most cases. Most church plantings and expansions start with a leader who finds spiritual need among receptive people. Finding a good roof to put over their gatherings usually comes later.

But sometimes it does happen that available facilities lead to a church going multisite. Perhaps one church is struggling and is drawn to the fruitfulness God seems to be granting another church's ministry. Usually some kind of relationship is already present, either through a common denomination, network, or local ministerial fellowship. Discussions sometimes lead to the question, "How could we partner or collaborate together?" The answer, if the church isn't multisite already, sometimes is, "Well, it would work if we become multisite." Often as local church leaders share their lives with one another, trust develops, and the merger possibilities surface as an option to consider for serving their surrounding community in better ways.

Merger Fact 2

Multisite Merger Momentum Shows No Sign of Slowing

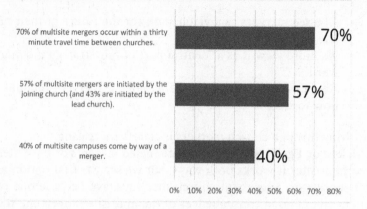

70% of multisite mergers occur within a thirty minute travel time between churches.
70%

57% of multisite mergers are initiated by the joining church (and 43% are initiated by the lead church).
57%

40% of multisite campuses come by way of a merger.
40%

0% 10% 20% 30% 40% 50% 60% 70% 80%

2019 Survey: *What was the travel time of the churches prior to the mergers—1 to 15 minutes, 16 to 30 minutes, 31 to 60 minutes, more than 60 minutes? Who initiated the merger—the lead church, the joining church, or other? Is your church multisite (one church in two or more geographic locations), monosite (one church in one geographic location), or multipoint (two or more different churches under one pastor)?*

Our surveys of church mergers have documented many examples in which all these situations happened. The surveys also revealed that multisite mergers have a higher rate of success and satisfaction than churches that merge into one location. Here are our key survey findings about multisite mergers.

Nationwide the multisite population is very large: over eight thousand multisite churches with over seven million people in weekly attendance. The latest survey indicates that 60 percent of them see mergers as viable for the future (as we mentioned already). Merger Fact 2 shows a few multisite-specific stats.

Though most multisite churches do not start out because of a merger, some multisite churches have developed a church merger strategy as part of their multisite strategy. In chapter 3 we introduced New Life Community Church in Chicago, which multiplies campuses through a merger strategy called Restart. New Life Community Church represents a small but growing number of multisite churches that are intentional in approaching other congregations about becoming one of their campuses.

When Scott Chapman at The Chapel, also in greater Chicago, learned that in any given year 1 percent of US Protestant churches close, it broke his heart but spawned an idea. "That closure rate means thirty-five to forty churches in the Chicago suburbs may be in danger of shutting down each year," said Chapman. "Finding them before that happens could be a huge Kingdom win." Mostly from personal contacts, The Chapel proactively experienced five mergers between 2005 and 2011. Although The Chapel is nondenominational, one merger church came from a denomination. When that congregation asked permission from their bishop, he released them saying, "That's now one less problem for me." After the merger, the church began to grow. A founding member of the joining church was found crying after one of the services. They were tears of joy. "Pastor," she said, "This is the church I always knew we could be."

However, in the new era of mergers described in this book, the process more often starts with a growing church, one that embodies a big heart toward reaching new groups of people and an effectiveness at doing so. It is multisite already—or it's becoming multisite. Typically, a multisite church targets a community where a significant number of attendees are already coming from, and it is on the lookout for a potential meeting site in that area. It's actively praying and asking around about possible site options, including churches that might benefit from a merger. Some of those discussions lead to mergers as an additional campus for the multisite church.

4. Facility-Driven Opportunity

Whenever followers of Jesus gather together in his name, they meet in a place. They are the *ecclesia* or "assembly," a tangible expression of the body of Christ. These assemblies meet in a place. This place becomes sacred space not because of location or architecture but because Jesus is present with them in a spiritual and corporate sense. These locations include:

- A new church meeting in a portable location needing a building.
- A multisite church looking for a venue in the next community.
- A historic facility needing a congregation.
- A declining church that can't sustain its property.

Merger Fact 3

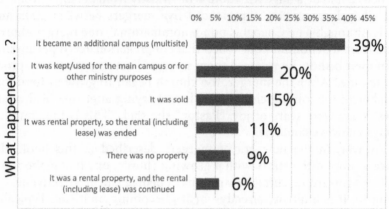

Almost 6 in 10 (59%) of the Joining-Church Facilities Continue to Be Used

What happened . . . ?

It became an additional campus (multisite)	39%
It was kept/used for the main campus or for other ministry purposes	20%
It was sold	15%
It was rental property, so the rental (including lease) was ended	11%
There was no property	9%
It was a rental property, and the rental (including lease) was continued	6%

2019 Survey: *What happened to the facility/property of the joining church?*

All of these are real scenarios with a common denominator—a place to do church, a place to gather for worship, teaching, and fellowship.

As we shared earlier, there are nearly a quarter million plateaued or declining churches across America. Most of them have underutilized facilities and many cannot be sustained. Yet the twenty-first century has seen a surge in new churches starting in temporary or portable venues who are looking for a permanent facility. Today there are more new churches being started each year than there are churches closing,[5] and an entire industry of "portable church" organizations has emerged in recent years. At the same time, as Merger Fact 2 and Merger Fact 3 illustrate, a number of existing church facilities are being used by church planters. In fact, during our 2019 survey, we were surprised at how many mergers followed the sequence of the lead church moving to the joining church's property—either because the lead church didn't have a permanent location, or the joining church's facilities had better long-range possibilities, often after the lead church did a face-lift, upgrade, or expansion.

In 2006, Brad and Christina Jenkins started The Gathering Church in downtown Tulsa, Oklahoma. Over the next several years their young church grew to a couple hundred people meeting in a school, but they were looking for a permanent facility.

Five minutes down the street from the school was Liberty Church, an established thirty-five-year-old church of 250 congregants, and with a twenty-six-acre campus, no debt, and a senior pastor approaching retirement.

Pastor Paul Taylor at Liberty Church became connected to the young church planter by a denominational leader. They became friends—a seasoned pastor with a young pastor, like Paul and Timothy. As their friendship developed, the senior pastor said, "I'm looking to retire, and you need a building. Why don't we just join together? You can become my successor and bring your people with you. You get a building, we get a pastor, and both churches get a brighter future."

In 2016, after several months of conversation, prayer and consideration, both congregations overwhelmingly approved the merger. Both congregations decided to change their names because they sensed that this was the best way for them to move forward with unity and momentum. Brad Jenkins became the senior pastor of the newly merged Anthem Church, and Paul Taylor continued on as a teaching pastor for another year before retiring.

Together they came up with something new. The newly merged church benefited from additional financial resources, a strong combination of young and old, and an increase in the number of dedicated volunteers serving their community. The church grew, ministries were added, and the facilities were expanded. Today Anthem Church is a flourishing congregation with more than five hundred attending every week and a strong vision to reach their community.

5. Denominational-Driven Strategy

Wherever churches have existed for more than a few decades, there is a potential for healthy and fruitful church mergers.

Every denomination has more churches in decline than growing, but they all also have healthy, growing churches. Increasingly, denominational leaders are seeing mission-driven mergers as a way to help their struggling (or stuck) congregations have better outcomes than the survival-driven forced mergers of the past. Recent years have seen an increase in denominational proactivity in brokering mission-driven mergers and making church facilities available to new churches or growing multisite churches. A merger can bring revitalization to a declining church and at the same time expansion to a growing church.

Since starting in 1985, Bay Hope Church, a United Methodist congregation in the Tampa area of Florida, has grown to more than two thousand in weekend attendance under the pastoral leadership of

Matthew Hartsfield. It represents a big vision and mission. "We felt God calling us to multiply campuses . . . across Tampa Bay, to reach every neighborhood with a vital, local congregation of Bay Hope Church," Hartsfield said. With a large vision to "mobilize 30,000 disciples of Jesus Christ in Tampa Bay by the year 2030 for the transformation of the world," Hartsfield found an eager partner and ally in his denomination.[6]

In 2017 Hartsfield was contacted by the district superintendent of the Gulf Central District, Candace Lewis, regarding a potential adoption of a "legacy church" in the nearby community of Westchase. As we explained at the beginning of chapter 1, legacy churches are declining congregations with a great past but who are no longer able to sustain themselves in the present. Too often they are closed down, the property sold, and the proceeds used for new churches.

Lewis helped both congregations through the merger conversation. The 168-seat Westchase congregation overwhelmingly approved the merger and was relaunched as Bay Hope Westchase, with expanded facilities (for children's ministry and office space). By the end of its first year as a merged congregation, attendance had grown from 165 to 250, and it was financially self-sufficient. By contrast, before the merger, the church was unsure if it would be able to afford a pastor for the coming year.

What a kingdom win! A legacy church was saved from extinction, a growing church extended its reach, the denomination turned a loss into a win, and a great role model was established that has inspired conversations among other United Methodist districts.

How to Increase Denominational Mergers

Unlike Lewis, too many denominational leaders today still think of mergers as a loss to their district, region, association, or denomination. Others force mergers to happen that neither church wants. Here are some suggestions on leveraging mergers for denominational and kingdom gains.

- **Embrace the tool.** See mergers as a viable option for strong *and* struggling churches under your oversight.
- **Reframe the merger conversation.** Move the conversation from a lose-lose or win-lose to a win-win possibility. Help both congregations see the mutual benefit of joining together.
- **Work both ends of the spectrum.** All denominations and networks have strong and struggling churches. A merger can

bring rebirth to a dying church or revitalization to a stuck church and at the same time expansion to a growing church.

- **Redefine metrics and rewards.** Change the scorecard. It's not about how many churches you have but how many disciples you are making. Shifts of metrics might include the following from-to patterns: from denominational focus to kingdom mindset, from legacy churches to prevailing churches, from number of overall churches to percentage of growing churches, from size of district (or association or denomination) to percent growth of baptisms, disciples, and attendance.

- **Facilitate Mergers**. Virtually every merger needs a trusted third party to help broker and navigate the merger possibilities. Instead of preserving the status quo, denominational leaders can be proactive in bringing two churches together. Instead of resisting the idea, seize the opportunity.

6. Succession-Driven Strategies

For 29% of joining churches, succession issues played a major role in the decision to merge.

In summer 2006, senior pastor Gary Kinnaman announced to his church his plans to retire and to begin a nationwide search for a co-pastor who would become his successor. Kinnaman had served Word of Grace in Mesa, Arizona, for twenty-five years and attendance had grown to over four thousand under his leadership, but in recent years attendance had been plateaued around three thousand.

A few weeks after his announcement, Kinnaman had a previously scheduled breakfast with Terry Crist of the smaller but growing CitiChurch, which had twelve hundred in attendance in nearby Scottsdale. At breakfast Kinnaman shared with Crist that he was looking for a younger but seasoned and successful pastor who would follow him at Word of Grace: "Someone a lot like you." Kinnaman then asked Crist, "Can you recommend anyone?"

Crist's response took Kinnaman by surprise. "I have someone to recommend—me." Kinnaman responded incredulously, "You would leave your church in Scottsdale to pastor mine?" "No, I would become the pastor of both congregations," Crist responded.

That initial conversation developed into a prayerful, nine-month, intense interaction between the senior leadership teams of the two congregations. It culminated in a unanimous decision of both teams to become one church in two locations under one vision, a new name, and a new senior pastor.

Under Crist's leadership, the newly renamed church, City of Grace, experienced explosive growth with thousands worshipping across two locations. The success of the succession merger then inspired yet another merger, a mission-driven merger. In 2016, Crist led the church to merge with the international Hillsong church out of Australia, becoming the sixteenth international campus (at the time) and later the US headquarters for the Hillsong church movement. Today Hillsong Phoenix is a flourishing regional multisite church with six campuses stretching across Arizona and Nevada. As Crist summarized the value of the merger on the church website, "It positions our church to reach more people with the gospel . . . reproducing campuses with greater strength, greater focus, and greater ability."[7]

Kinnaman continued as a member of the church but moved into a role of leading a citywide network of pastors, government officials, and marketplace leaders to serve the Phoenix area. His leadership led to his appointment as chairman of the Governor's Council on Faith and Community.

What began as a succession-driven strategy became far more than either pastor imagined when they had a game-changing coffee in Scottsdale! Who would have imagined that one healthy merger would lead to yet another healthy merger with a global church movement?

The biggest elephant in church boardrooms in the United States is the topic of senior pastor succession.[8] It is a difficult conversation for most aging senior pastors to have with their boards and staff, so usually it is ignored until too late. Many are predicting a tsunami of church turnovers during the next decade as the aging baby boomers turn over the reins of US churches to the next generation. According to William Vanderbloemen, founder and president of the Vanderbloemen Search Group, senior pastor succession "might be the biggest unspoken crisis the church in the US will face over the next twenty years."[9]

> The biggest elephant in church boardrooms in the United States is the topic of senior pastor succession.

Often when a pastor retires or leaves a church due to health reasons, the church is thrown into a tailspin to find a successor. The search is usually led by lay leaders who do not know how to find or interview senior pastor candidates. Meanwhile, the church stalls or declines in the interim period while the pastor search is in process. Often a new pastor comes and begins all over again with a new vision, abandoning all the vestiges of the previous pastor's philosophy.

There's got to be a better way! As these two pastor succession stories illustrate, a church merger could be a vehicle for a seamless senior pastor succession that keeps the church moving forward without losing momentum and upsetting the equilibrium of a healthy church.

Succession by merging with a respected local church pastor with a proven track record who is already culturally acclimated is far less risky than the traditional nationwide pastor search process.

7. Reconciliation-Driven Hope

Mariners Church, Irvine, California, held its first service as a church in a home in 1965. The church continued to grow over the years, and then in 1980 the church split because of a leadership conflict. The pastor who broke off created a new church with a new name only a few miles away. Even though the two churches were separated by only a few miles, they ministered independently. This situation generated a lot of pain and sadness.

Then in 1995, when Mariners Church was under the leadership of Kenton Beshore, God began to guide the paths of these two churches toward each other once again in an amazing reunion and mutual commitment to serve Orange County as one church body. In 1998, the two churches came back together as one. To this day, Mariners Church has continued to spread the gospel, transforming ordinary people into passionate followers of Jesus, courageously changing the world.

In another example, Christ Community Church was launched in 1984 in Ruston, Louisiana as a plant of Fellowship Bible Church in Little Rock, Arkansas. In 1995, Christ Community Church experienced a deep and painful split following a prolonged leadership conflict. The founding elders left the church along with a number of other families, and the senior staff remained along with a new elder board and continued shepherding the large number of families that stayed.

Six years later, in 2001, two of the founding elders who had left Christ Community began meeting with a small group of people to explore the potential launch of a new Fellowship Bible church plant in Ruston. In 2003, Crossroads Church was officially launched just a few miles away from Christ Community. For five years, these two church plants, both tracing their roots back to Fellowship Bible Church, coexisted in the same small college town.

By 2008, Crossroads had grown to three hundred adults plus two hundred college students in worship. They met in multiple services in a gym that holds only 375 chairs. Meanwhile Christ Community had an attendance of 350 in a new worship space that was built in 2005 to hold six hundred seats.

That same year, Wade Burnett, the executive pastor of Crossroads

Church at the time, initiated a dialogue with the pastor of Christ Community Church. Wade explained in a local newspaper interview, "We met for coffee and ended up having a three-hour conversation. We apologized to one another for having been so prideful and foolish for all those years. That meeting led to similar conversations with the other leaders," which culminated in a public reconciliation service in 2010. The elders from both churches—including those who were involved in the split in 1995—publicly shared the full forgiveness and grace they had extended to one another. The service concluded with the leadership from Fellowship Bible Church serving communion to all of the reconciled elders, and the elders in turn serving communion to the body who was gathered together.

Because the whole community had been affected by what Wade called this "bitter conflict," they posted their powerful story of reconciliation and healing online. A year later the two churches voted overwhelmingly to reunite under a new name and a reorganized leadership team incorporating staff and elders from both congregations. Wade Burnett, who initiated the reconciliation as the executive pastor of Crossroads Church, became the directional leader, and the two senior pastors became teaching pastors of what was renamed as The Bridge Community Church. Building on the momentum of coming together, the merged church is now meeting in two locations while pursuing a new and much larger vision of serving as a multisite, church-planting church for its entire region. Teaching Pastor Chris Hanchey reported ten years later in an email update to author Jim Tomberlin:

> Because of the 2011 merger, we are more missional, more diverse, and able to invest more resources in serving our community. We are seeing wonderful stories of growth, redemption, and life change, and we are excited about the future.
>
> We are also continuing to discover that being together is better, but it's also harder. More than a third of our church has come since the merger, so neither is a part of Christ Community or Crossroads. There are still many people who are healing from past wounds, and others who are grieving the loss of a church that they loved as a result of the changes brought by the merger.

What began as a reconciliation effort ended in a church reunion merger and a stronger corporate ministry with the potential to reach an entire region with the gospel. The rebirth and recasting of a much larger vision never would have happened without the fruits of a deep and very personal reconciliation.

The Takeaway. Church splits are always painful, especially when they involve disagreements that could have been resolved or conflicts that were ungodly or inappropriate. These less-than-noble church splits give the church a black eye in their communities and foster cynicism about our failures to walk our talk and genuinely live out our faith. But what better public statement could there be than for churches who have split from one another—and specifically the leaders of churches who may have been involved in these kinds of conflicts—to come back together in biblical restoration and reconciliation? Many times, this kind of spiritual transformation provides a foundation for much greater kingdom impact.

Unfortunately, too many churches were born unintentionally as the result of a church split. It is the authors' hope that this book will encourage potentially thousands of churches across the United States that were birthed out of conflict to seek reconciliation, whether or not those dialogues result in a reunified congregation.

Many of these conversations could develop into a reconciliation-based merger. In such mergers, typically a leader from one of the congregations initiates a reconciliation conversation. One phone call can put in motion a healing of relationships that could result in a reunification of two estranged congregations. One meeting over a cup of coffee could transform the church landscape in your community. Sometimes reconciliation mergers become one church in two locations (multisite) and other times they come back together in one location. Regardless, the driving motivation is healing and can result in reconciliation.

Is a reconciliation merger in your future?

8. Multiethnic-Driven Mergers

US churches are becoming increasingly multicultural. Although the most segregated hour in the United States historically has been the eleven o'clock church service on Sunday mornings, "the times are a-changing." Those who lead the Mosaix Network, which is committed to greater intentionality in developing multisite churches, are convinced that churches today are being marked by greater multiethnicity. Consider that in 1998, only 7 percent of evangelical churches in the United States could be described as having at least 20 percent racial or ethnic diversity in their attending membership. As of 2019, 23 percent could be so described.[10]

A growing number of emerging church leaders desire to see their congregations reflect on earth what we will all experience in heaven—a sea of diverse races, languages, and colors all worshipping Jesus *together*.

Those leaders work hard at being inclusive by preaching racial equality, building multiracial staffs, integrating worship teams, and serving their communities across racial and ethnic divides.

Some immigrant churches are merging together so that all generations can be under one roof. For example in 2007, the English-only ministry of a predominantly Hispanic church merged with a Spanish-only ministry formerly known as Centro de Restoration (Restoration Center), making it possible to accommodate the needs of multiple Hispanic generations in one church.[11] Others are finding that one of the most dramatic and accelerated ways to become a truly multiethnic church is by incorporating a minority congregation through a church merger.

> One of the most dramatic and accelerated ways to become a truly multiethnic church is by incorporating a minority congregation through a church merger.

One example of this mission-driven merger is beautifully illustrated by the healthy multiethnic and economically diverse Mosaic Church of Central Arkansas in Little Rock. In 2008 its directional leader, Mark DeYmaz, invited a struggling Hispanic church with two full-time pastors to join his leadership team, share his facility, and provide a third service of Mosaic Church. The pastors agreed to work on their weekly sermon together with the intent that each would communicate roughly the same message as the other. The third service then featured the message in Spanish by the Hispanic pastors, and Pastor Mark delivered the same sermon in English at the other two services. This arrangement provided a service for immigrants who speak Spanish only, and it also offered additional options to those Hispanic attendees and their spouses who would prefer English services over Spanish. DeYmaz solved a problem of many ethnic churches that start in the native language of a first-generation immigrant, but typically the second and third generations of an immigrant family prefer an English service as they move into the mainstream of US culture. Both options are now available to all Hispanic attendees, all under one roof and one church.

As in any successful merger, it was important to clarify for both congregations what this new relationship would look like. Leading up to the official merger with Mosaic, the pastors of the two congregations distributed a document defining the new relationship. Here is what they published on the day of the merger:

Merger of Iglesia Nazareno del Samaritano and the Mosaic Church of Central Arkansas

What It Is

1. It is an official merger between Iglesia Nazareno del Samaritano and the Mosaic Church of Central Arkansas whereby from now on we will all be known as the Mosaic Church of Central Arkansas.
2. It is an opportunity for expanded, more effective evangelism of first-generation Ivia Mosaic.
3. It is an opportunity for more effective evangelism of second and third-generation Latinos via Mosaic.

What It Is Not

1. We are not two churches under one roof. We are one church, now with multiple service options.
2. It does not in any way change our DNA. Rather, it eliminates a barrier we unintentionally established through the years, namely, one that made it difficult for many first-generation Latinos to find Christ and/or a church home with us at Mosaic.
3. It is not an exclusive or intentional segregation of people by ethnic heritage or language, etc. Anyone and everyone is welcome to attend any of Mosaic's worship services or program options![12]

This merger was driven by both pastors' passion and mission to build a truly multiethnic church. DeYmaz described the benefits to us in this way:

> Such a merger, when rightly conceived and executed, will be beneficial to both churches. On the one hand, homogeneous churches that are pursuing the multiethnic vision will immediately benefit from the addition of diverse staff and people to the mix, and the merger provides a visible sign of their commitment to transformation. On the other hand, the 1.0 (first generation) congregation will often benefit from the additional ministries provided, including children's or student ministry more in line with the integrated schools their kids are likely attending.[13]

DeYmaz insists that his motive was not to seek out a merger but to support whatever God was doing. "Our attitude and mind-set was to have an open hand with helping churches," he told us, "and when it led to the idea of merging, we were open to it." But to no one's surprise, when an opportunity came up in 2011 for another merger, and the mission fit was good, DeYmaz and the church's leadership enthusiastically explored and followed it as well. As of 2020 the church remains healthy and vibrant.

9. Pastor Search-Driven

One fall afternoon in 2015, Pastor Mike Meeks of EastLake Church of Chula Vista, California, received a letter from Torrey Pines Christian Church thirty miles away in La Jolla, California.

This letter detailed their ongoing involvement in a pastoral search, but after going through five pastors in four years it stated they were also considering a merge with a healthy, growing church in the San Diego area. Having recently read our book *Better Together: Making Church Mergers Work*, the pastor search team included in their letter an extensive questionnaire that could be filled out and emailed back. (The questionnaire was based on the twenty-five church merger issues described in chapter 15 of this book!) The team tasked with pursuing the merger option would review the information received and get back to them.

The list of the twelve churches who were receiving this letter was a bit intimidating. They were all healthy, growing churches and several were larger than EastLake Church. Three had a national profile. As a multisite church EastLake had seen God open surprising doors of opportunity over the years through their involvement in four previous church mergers. Meeks had seen facilities refurbished, programing refreshed, and congregations reinvigorated. So, they completed the questionnaire and pressed "send."

Torrey Pines Christian Church had a long history of healthy Christian community and several gifted and loving pastors had served faithfully in previous decades. However, their more recent history was one of slow decline in attendance and short-tenured pastors. Their bylaws made it difficult to gain congregational consensus regarding their mission and vision.

The present lay leadership was divided about how to move forward. "Do we find a new pastor or merge with a thriving church?" So, they decided to explore both tracks at once. After reviewing and interviewing the responding churches, they narrowed their potential choices to three. Then Torrey Pines contacted me (Jim Tomberlin) to help them decide what would be the best church merger choice. EastLake's experience with church mergers and the easygoing style of Meeks made East-Lake the obvious choice. Multiple meetings with various EastLake team members followed. Eventually the search committee was ready to recommend a merger with EastLake Church to the congregation.

They then moved into Q & A sessions with various constituent groups within Torrey Pines Christian Church. Several "town hall" gatherings with all interested members and attenders were scheduled. They answered questions about possible changes in name, worship style, and liturgy; about women in ministry, property ownership, congregational voting, and many other subjects. Each of these topics had passionate opinions attached to them.

Over the next several months, Meeks and his team met, prayed, and attempted to alleviate fears while answering all questions honestly and clearly. A merger would involve change. In some cases, significant change. To ratify a merger, the Torrey Pines Christian Church bylaws required a 3/4 affirmation of all members. The voting rosters had not been reviewed and purged for many years. Some voting members were dead. Many no longer lived in the area. And a significant number no longer attended Torrey Pines Christian Church.

Prior to voting, the Torrey Pines Christian Church team worked tirelessly to contact every "member" in order to affirm current membership or remove them from the voting rolls. Meek admits "I was surprised when the first vote was announced to be in favor of merging, having passed with five votes over the required 3/4 majority."

Of course, that meant there were some unhappy members at Torrey Pines campus; however, the real work of earning trust and delivering on their commitments was able to begin. The first service of the merged churches was Easter Sunday of 2016. Since then, Meeks explained, "It has been challenging at times, and we haven't achieved all we believe is possible, but today, Torrey Pines Christian Church is once again a healthy, growing congregation."[14]

Prior to this merger, Torrey Pines Christian Church was running approximately two hundred in weekend attendance and was in decline. EastLake Torrey Pines now averages over five hundred weekly attenders and has seen consistent, healthy growth. Many new attenders have made the decision to follow Jesus, be baptized, and become active members of this faith community. Many on-going members have continued serving and some have stepped up into growing levels of leadership. Meeks concludes, "We look back with gratitude at the miracle of this merger, and we look forward with excitement to what God will do in the decades to come." (We tell more about this story in chapter 14.)

Pastor Search Crisis. The majority of churches today are pastored by aging baby boomers who are approaching retirement with a small number of next generational pastoral candidates available. In addition, the traditional pastor-search process is loaded with fatal thinking like . . .

> If we could just find a young pastor who could attract younger people.

The reality is that many churches are not willing to make the changes to attract young families. As the chairman of one church board told me at the end of a long board meeting, "if young people start coming to our church, we will change the worship."

> What we need around here is a turn-around pastor who can lead us out of our downward spiral.

The reality is that there are very few pastors who are turn-around leaders, less than 10 percent according to church consultant Gary McIntosh.

> Let's find the best candidates within our denomination from across the country and move them here.

The reality is that there is more risk in bringing someone across country than going with a locally known and proven pastor with a good track record. Will the new pastor from out of town fit culturally with our community? Will the spouse and family be happy in our community? These unknowns are greatly reduced with a local pastor.

It is common church lore that every pastor goes through three phases in their tenure at a church. It can happen over three months or three years.

The first stage the pastor can do *no* wrong.

The second stage the pastor can do *no* right.

The third stage somebody *leaves* and it's usually the pastor!

At the end of the day, a church merger is really a vehicle for choosing a pastor. A congregation may be voting to approve or dis-approve a legal merger, but what they are deciding is who will be their next pastor.

After going through five pastors over four years the traditional way, Torrey Pines Christian Church found their pastor through a merger. Perhaps your next pastor may come through a merger.

Rarely a Single Motive

In most cases, a merger represents a blending of many of these motives at different levels.

A case in point is a wonderful ceremony that took place in downtown Baton Rouge, Louisiana. On that day in April 2010, Winbourne Avenue Baptist Church's one-thousand-seat sanctuary was the fullest it had been in decades. The church, established in 1947, had declined in recent years to fewer than twenty-five elderly people on a typical Sunday, but on this day over four hundred came, many from different parts of the country. They celebrated all God had done over the years as they now offered their church facilities as a gift to become the Dream Center campus for Healing Place Church. This was their final service with their own pastor, and the legal paperwork for the merger would be finalized two months later.

Meanwhile, since 2008, the Dream Center had been holding its own worship service there, drawing up to two hundred people from the community and launching numerous ministries including free groceries for those who need it, child care for all ages, a free clothing center, re-entry programs for ex-offenders, a street outreach for homeless and at-risk youth, and after-school programs including computer and GED courses for teenagers. On Sunday mornings, a van would drive around the neighborhood, picking up families for a free meal served from the church's large kitchen before the Healing Place's noon service began.

In this merger of Winbourne Avenue Baptist and the Healing Place Dream Center, the missional motive showed up strongly in both churches, whose congregations were enthusiastic about continuing the mandates of Scripture into the future. "You could say we are passing the torch," Eugene Coffing, chair of the Winbourne Baptist deacon board, told a local newspaper. "Healing Place is reaching out to the people in the surrounding neighborhoods for Christ, and they are doing it effectively."

"From my perspective, Winbourne Avenue Baptist was given a vision and a dream to start a church here in 1947, and they have been shining the light of the Gospel here ever since," added Craig Boutte, Healing Place pastor at the Winbourne Dream Center. "They are passing the torch to us because we also know God has a purpose for this area." Melvin Hardnett, a local businessman who coordinates the Dream Center's more than one hundred volunteers, agreed with his pastor. "They (the Baptist group) started the race and now we are going to cross the finish line," Hardnett said.

The lead pastor at Healing Place Church agrees, saying, "The great hearts of a group of people at Winbourne Baptist Church followed what they felt was God's lead to give us their facility to use for spreading the Gospel through the Baton Rouge Dream Center."

The economic pressure was primarily with the Winbourne Avenue congregation as their dwindling numbers could no longer fund the property costs. But Healing Place also faced economic challenges, wanting to do ministry but not being able to build or purchase something like the Winbourne Avenue facility, valued at $2 million. They too were looking for a win.

The multisite factor was only on Healing Place's side. It was founded in 1993 and just nine years later opened its first offsite campus. By the time the Winbourne Baptist opportunity opened up, Healing Place already had eleven different campuses, two of them overseas. The US campuses were already drawing over seven thousand people each weekend. Although this was its first Dream Center campus, the church clearly understood how to do effective ministry as one church in multiple locations.

The reconciliation factor was minimal. The two churches, one Baptist and the other nondenominational charismatic, had not previously been partnered together. Nor had there been any division in which a contingent from one church was now attending the other. However, reconciliation did occur at two other levels. First in 2007, the pastor at the time, after learning as much as possible about Healing Place Church, initiated contact, inviting its leadership to come on the Winbourne Avenue property and begin using some of the facility for ministry in that area. His hope was that the Winbourne Baptist congregation would eventually turn the property over to Healing Place. Second, through the Dream Center, bridges were built from the church, which was largely white as the community once was, to the community that is now racially mixed.

Of all six merger motivations, perhaps the strongest affirmation of all was a six-word message displayed on the day of the special service. Up on the sanctuary platform, just below the baptistery, a wide-screen TV declared the Healing Place theme in bold yellow letters: "Jesus is here, anything can happen."

A Dream of Greater Kingdom Ministry

There can be multiple, overlapping motivations for a church merger. You could be a church leader searching for a pastor, a church planter needing a facility, a retiring pastor looking for a successor, a denominational executive trying to rescue a declining church or help a healthy church within the denomination go multisite. You could be a member of a congregation wanting to heal and reconcile a church split or church board member not wanting to lose kingdom ground or community presence through church foreclosure. Regardless of the reasons behind a merger what drives church men and women forward is a compelling aspiration for their church to be something more, to do something significant, to make a difference and fulfill the purpose for its existence.

A Colorado pastor told us how he had become the pastor of a small church that had met in a school for five years without effective growth. "Members were tired of trying to push the boulder up a hill with only limited success in all areas," he said. "They were definitely exhausted by setting up in a school every week for five years."

Elders in the congregation raised the topic of a potential merger, looking for the right circumstances. They found a growing, "unleashing" kind of church in Bear Valley Church and asked their pastor to approach its leaders.

According to the pastor, by all counts, the merger went well.

It was successful because both churches understood there is no such thing as an even-steven merger. One church must assume the other. As the pastor explained, "We helped our folks see that what mattered most wasn't 'the church of us' but 'the church of Jesus.' In other words, we rightfully portrayed this as a way to maximize our kingdom impact—just the opposite of a corporate take-over. We further helped those in the joining church transition into the larger body by forming a large Sunday adult class, which helped maintain their close fellowship. Eventually most of the new people assimilated into the ministries of the lead church."

The joining church gave away its old facility to another church that is still using it to this day. "We merged because we could accomplish more kingdom ministry together than by remaining separate," he concluded.

This pastor personally modeled a humility and kingdom mind-set by joining the lead church in an assistant pastor role with only occasional preaching opportunities. Other than wishing he had asked to preach a little more often, he says he has no regrets about the merger.

This is the kind of story we suspect we'll all hear more about in the years to come.

Notes

1. See https://sacredspacesdc.org/dc-places-of-worship.

2. Robert Simons, Gary DeWine, Larry Ledebur, *Retired, Rehabbed, Reborn: The Adaptive Reuse of America's Derelict Religious Buildings and Schools* (Kent, OH: Kent State University Press, 2017), i.

3. "Multisite Movement Continues to Grow: Latest Research from National Survey Reports Top Line Findings," Leadership Network, 2019, https://leadnet.org. See also Warren Bird and Kristin Walters, "Multisite Is Multiplying: Survey Identifies Leading Practices and Confirms New Developments in the Movement's Expansion," Leadership Network, 2010, https://tinyurl.com/v5d2ryf.

4. "Multisite Movement Continues to Grow."

5. See Stetzer and Bird, *Viral Churches*.

6. B.C. Manion, "Bay Hope Plans Big Expansion," Laker Lutz News, March 22, 2017, http://lakerlutznews.com/lln/?p=44830.

7. Video announcement, Terry Crist speaking, February 21, 2016, https://videopress.com/v/u44VUaRC.

8. For two helpful resources, see Carolyn Weese and J. Russell Crabtree, *The Elephant in the Boardroom* (San Francisco: Jossey-Bass, 2004); and William Vanderbloemen and Warren Bird, *Next: Pastoral Succession That Works, Expanded and Updated Edition* (Grand Rapids, MI: Baker, 2020).

9. William Vanderbloemen, "Six Trends in Staffing," *Church Executive*, August 1, 2011, http://churchexecutive.com/archives/six-trends-in-staffing.

10. From the latest research of Dr. Michael Emerson, as presented and explained in his plenary talk at Mosaix's National Multiethnic Church Conference, November 5-7, 2019, Dallas, TX.

11. Daniel Rodriguez, *A Future for the Latin Church: Models for Multilingual, Multigenerational Hispanic Congregations* (Downers Grove, IL: InterVarsity Press, 2001).

12. Mark DeYmaz, *Ethnic Blends: Mixing Diversity into Your Local Church* (Grand Rapids, MI: Zondervan, 2010), 133.

13. Personal communication between the authors and Mark DeYmaz.

14. Personal correspondence between the authors and Mike Meeks.

PART II

HOW HEALTHY CHURCH MERGERS WORK

5

FOUR MERGER MODELS (BUT ONLY THREE THAT WORK)

This book debunks a bunch of persistent myths about mergers. One myth says, "A merger is just a takeover." No, in successful mergers, the joining church is involved because it *wants* to merge. Successful mergers today involve a lead church and a joining church. The merging of churches is a delicate dance where one leads and the other chooses to follow.

Another myth says that mergers are always between a big church and a small church, or a strong church and a declining church. While many are, certainly not all are. Instead, the new "always" for healthy mergers is that the healthy, successful merger is mission driven. Successful mergers today are more mission-driven and future-focused than the failed mergers of the past that were more survival-driven and focused on preserving the past.

Although all mergers involve a lead church and a joining church, not all mergers are the same or look alike. They vary by many factors including size, whether they change or keep their name, whether they remain single site or become multisite as part of the merger, and whether they function as a new church plant.

Perhaps the most important way mergers differ is in the model they follow. As chapter 1 explained, not everyone uses the term *merger*. For many people, the word *merger* contains a lot of emotional baggage, mostly negative. Instead, we'd like to introduce a set of family-related terms to describe the various ways churches can merge.

Here's a quick summary of the terms. Then the rest of the chapter offers a more in-depth description, profile, and pros and cons of each one:

- **Rebirth mergers.** A struggling or dying church gets a second life by being fully absorbed and restarted under a stronger, vibrant, and typically larger church
- **Adoption mergers.** A stable or stuck church is fully integrated under the vision of a stronger, vibrant, and typically larger church
- **Marriage mergers.** Two churches, both strong or growing, realign with each other under a united vision and new leadership configuration
- **ICU (intensive care unit) mergers.** Two churches that know they're in trouble try to turn around their critical situation but are survival driven. Such mergers often fail.

Figure 5.1 visualizes these four models, and then tables 5.1 and 5.2 compare them. The narrative that follows explains each model in more detail.

Four Models of How a Merger Happens

Rebirth	Adoption	Marriage	ICU
(Absorption)	(Integration)	(Realignment)	(Survival)

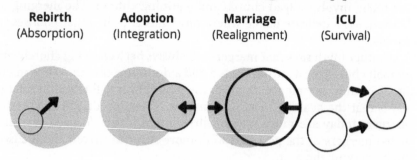

Figure 5.1

Table 5.1

What Is Your Merger Profile?

Merger Model	Health Level	Avg. Adult Age in the Congrega- tion	Worship Attendance	Church Budget
Marriage	Strong	30–50	Growing	Growing
Adoption	Stable	40–60	Static	Static
Rebirth	Struggling	50–80	Declining	Declining
ICU	Dying	50–90	Declining	Declining

Table 5.1 cont'd

Number of First-Time Guests as Percentage of Weekly Attendance [1]	Number of New Members in the Past Year as Percentage of Weekly Attendance	Number of Annual Baptisms as Percentage of Weekly Attendance	Primary Benefit of the Merger	Primary Challenge of the Merger
2% or more	5% or more	5% or more	Synergy	Alignment
0–2%	Less than 5%	Less than 5%	Revitalization	Integration
0%	0%	0%	Salvage	Absorption
0%	0%	0%	Life Support	Survival

How do these "family" terms relate to each other? Each has distinctive elements but they're not exclusive from each other. If placed on a spectrum, an adoption merger is in the middle between a rebirth merger and a marriage merger. An ICU merger is usually a merger of two near equals, both on life support. These are more reflective of the typical failed mergers of the past.

Every church merger introduces potential gains and losses. There are no guarantees. There are pros and cons to be prayerfully evaluated with every merger type.

> *Every church merger has potential gains and losses. There are no guarantees.*

The potential gains are dramatic. Church mergers can multiply church impact, increase outreach, produce synergistic ministries, revitalize churches, restore facilities, offer facilities to new churches, serve communities better, and revive new hope for the future. These potential gains are driving the church merger movement today.

The potential losses can be equally dramatic. A church can lose its name and facilities. The pastor, staff, and favorite ministry may not survive the transition. Not all members will stay, and some good friends may leave. What is most painful is the potential for the heritage and identity of a church to get lost in the merger process. These are all very real and very difficult possible outcomes of a church merger.

Merger Fact 4

Not All Declining Churches Are Financially Struggling

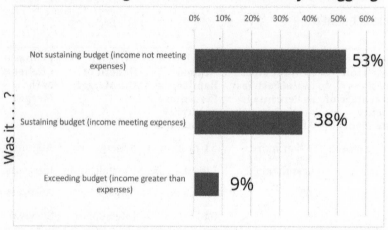

2019 Survey: *How would you describe the financial condition of the joining church at the time it decided to merge?*

In the following section we share examples of each merger model followed by commentary describing the pros and cons of that particular model. But first, we need to make an observation about finances. Being financially stable isn't the same as being healthy. Sometimes churches that are financially stable are in a more precarious situation because their financial strength gives a false sense of security. Thus, not all declining churches are financially struggling; many are actually financially strong. In our consultations, we've seen far too many churches that have been lulled into a false sense of security and a lack of urgency, as Merger Fact 4 documents.

Rebirth Model

Rebirth mergers occur when a struggling or dying church gets a second life by being restarted under a stronger, vibrant, and typically larger church. In our view, the majority of mergers are rebirths, even though they might not use that term.

> *The majority of mergers are rebirths, even though they might not use that term.*

Example

In fall 1917, a small group of residents in Fairbanks, Louisiana, gathered in a one-room schoolhouse built of rough lumber to organize a church. Three years later a local business built a small structure to be used as a community building. Over time it came to be known as Union Church as different denominations took turns on Sundays leading church services in it. In more recent times it became Fairbanks Baptist Church. Members bought additional property, built newer facilities, and called various pastors over the years. Attendance peaked in the 1990s at around three hundred.

In March 2011, after Fairbanks Baptist Church had declined for years, its leadership called a membership meeting, which about twenty-five people attended. They discussed where they would be in a year. They decided that they could be proactive about their church or they could let circumstances determine the church's future. After discussion, they voted unanimously to ask First Baptist Church of West Monroe, Louisiana (known today as First West), to enter into what they called a "partnership" with them.

A feasibility committee was created composed of representatives from both churches. Together they recommended a plan in which Fairbanks Baptist Church would dissolve and rebirth as a multisite campus of First Baptist Church of West Monroe, Louisiana.

The recommendation was approved twenty-eight to one by a congregational vote of Fairbanks Baptist Church in August 2011. The church was immediately dissolved, the assets were deeded over to First Baptist Church of West Monroe, and the plans for relaunching the campus began. During the renovations, the members began attending the First Baptist Church of West Monroe and were part of the launch core team of the new First West Fairbanks campus in January 2012. By 2020 First West Fairbanks has grown to a flourishing campus of three hundred people. The success of the merger inspired First Baptist to birth a third campus and create a strategy for church multiplication across Louisiana.

The dying church of twenty-five had been rebirthed with new hope and the adopting church of a couple thousand was reenergized with new vision!

Pros and Cons

Candidates for a rebirth merger can come from the nearly quarter million Protestant churches across the United States that are struggling, in decline, or dying. The majority of these churches have fewer than two hundred people in attendance—a good portion fewer than seventy-five people weekly.[2] Too many of them are more focused on maintenance or survival than on making disciples and transforming their communities. Roughly four thousand of these churches (1 percent of all Protestant churches in America) will close their doors permanently nationwide in the next twelve months.

These congregations in decline have underused facilities in need of repair that could be infused with the life-giving DNA of a healthy, growing church. Their empty seats could be filled again. The dream of the founders could be resurrected and extended through a merger with an effective, successful church. They can celebrate the past but not be stuck there. All of these congregations started with hope and a vision. Today, most of them are discouraged and barely hanging on.

Like Fairbanks Baptist Church in Louisiana, most of these churches possess land and facilities that are currently underutilized. Like Fairbanks Baptist, they can be reborn and find a second life through merging with a dynamic and vibrant church. They don't need renewal; they need a rebirth.

The most successful rebirths occur when the joining church is smart enough or desperate enough to be willing to relinquish everything to the lead church—its name, facilities, staff, ministries, and glorious past—all in exchange for a second life. The decision to merge usually does not happen until church leaders conclude that the pain of not changing is greater than the pain of changing. Their attitude becomes, "If we do nothing, we die. If we merge, we live." Then the odds increase for a successful merger with a strong church.

> *The decision to merge usually does not happen until church leaders conclude that the pain of not changing is greater than the pain of changing.*

Most church mergers include a name change. Our research confirmed that the majority of mergers involve a name change, usually by the joining church. Sometimes both churches come up with a new name altogether.

Sometimes, because of stewardship or strategic reasons, a merger will result in a sale of the joining church's building.

Even if a church loses its building through a merger, it does not have to lose its heritage or give up its identity. Though it may be necessary to sell the facilities, wise church leaders recognize that a church's heritage and identity are built around a place. A lot of blood, sweat, and tears of the joining congregation have been invested in their facility. A lot of emotion is tied to that place. People poured not only their resources but also their lives into the building that is now being sold. Many found Christ in that building, many were baptized or dedicated their children to God there; some were married in that place. Savvy church leaders are sensitive to the grieving process that comes with the loss of that building. They learn the history, culture, and identity of the joining church and discover the healthy traits to build on in creating a new future together.

Mergers are not really the beginning of new work in the community but are more of a rebuilding on the good work that had begun years ago, sometimes decades earlier. Instead of erasing the past, smart church leaders bless the past and communicate how the merger carries on the mission of the former days. Pastor Mark Jobe says it well in the Restart video, available online. In it, he explains the merger strategy of New Life Community Church in Chicago, which has been involved in nine restarts to date: "God has been at work in that neighborhood long before we came on the scene. God has been working sometimes a hundred years before we ever got there and it's on our hearts to say, 'Can we cooperate with what God is already doing [in this neighborhood]?"[3] Healthy rebirth mergers don't reject or erase the identity of the joining church but incorporate it into the new identity.

Unfortunately, it is easier to give birth than to produce a resurrection. Most declining churches would rather hang on to their control rather than turn the wheel over to someone who knows how to steer it out of a death spiral. Some will die this year—on average 1 percent of the Protestant churches in your community will be gone by this time next year. Most that are dead already in terms of mission and outward focus will hang on for years but will make little difference, if any, in their community. Their focus is on surviving and preserving rather than embracing a new vision for the future with a stronger church. They would prefer to have a "partnership" with a stronger church that allows them to survive, but not really have to change. But these churches don't need a partner; they need to be absorbed by a strong church, which is what the rebirth idea conveys.

> Their focus is on surviving and preserving rather than embracing a new vision for the future with a stronger church.

Rebirth mergers can be a wonderful win-win for both churches when the joining church correctly understands its current reality, but it can be a huge drain of time, energy, and resources when the declining church doesn't fully embrace the future under new leadership of the lead church.

The temptation for a lead church is to pour a lot of time and resources into a declining church that has no intention of changing. Jesus warned about people who pour new wine in old wineskins, "If they do, the new wine will burst the skins. The wine will run out, and the wineskins will be destroyed. No, new wine must be poured into new wineskins" (Luke 5:37–38).

An Atlanta pastor who went through a merger summarizes well the challenge and opportunity of rebirth mergers: "When understood as a vehicle to change rather than to conserve, to displace rather than protect, to shatter the old rather than restore, mergers can be a powerful tool for advancing the congregation's God-given mission."[4]

Adoption Model

Adoption mergers are typically stable or stuck churches that integrate under the vision of a stronger, vibrant, and typically larger church.

Example

It took a lot of hard work and prayer for a core group of families to keep Grace Baptist Church in Bountiful, Utah, viable through the years. So when the chance came to merge with one of Utah's Protestant churches with the largest attendance, Washington Heights, twenty miles north in Ogden, the faithful at Grace Baptist were both relieved and wary. But they explored the merger idea because, as one of the members told a local newspaper, "We just felt like God gave us an opportunity to blend these two church families together and that together we could do a lot more for the community."[5]

The two churches, sister congregations in the Conservative Baptist Association, voted overwhelmingly in 2010 to join forces. The joining congregation, renamed as Bountiful Heights, became a second site of Washington Heights Church, appointing Josh Knight as the campus pastor.

Handling administrative tasks in Ogden means the pastors are freed for ministry when they are in Bountiful, says senior pastor Roy Gruber, who now keeps an office at both campuses. "It really allows us to focus on ministry and the people." Since the alliance, Gruber notes, attendance is up at Bountiful Heights from seventy to over two hundred, mostly from word-of-mouth advertising about the changes under way. A children's ministry is rolling, and ten to fifteen youths regularly gather on Sunday nights now. According to Gruber, "That's a large part of what we're about. We do want to share our good news with our community, but mostly that happens life to life and people inviting their friends and neighbors."

Bountiful Heights has neither the parking nor the building to grow as large as Washington Heights, which exceeds two thousand people on a typical Sunday. "We're great with that," Gruber says. "It isn't about how many folks we can get in one location. It's about reaching out as much as we can. This merger was a real opportunity for like-minded churches to work together and do good for the community."

Six years after establishing a viable multisite campus the Bountiful Heights leadership expressed a desire to be released as a church plant of Washington Heights. It made sense to everyone and the Bountiful Heights campus became Flourishing Grace Church under the leadership of the former campus pastor, now lead pastor Josh Knight. As Gruber affirmed at the release, "Our goal all along has been to establish strong gospel-preaching, disciple-making churches across Utah in whatever way makes the most sense. We celebrate it whether it is through multisite campuses, church plants or mergers that become re-plants." As the two pastors expressed on an announcement video to both congregations, "the dream is to help people meet and follow Jesus."

What Washington Heights did in releasing a multisite merger campus as a new church is a common experience, as Merger Fact 5 affirms.

Merger Fact 5

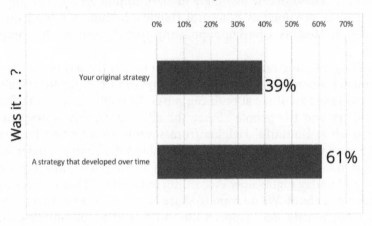

For Most, the Merger Strategy to Become a
New Church Developed over Time

2019 Survey: *For any of these campuses that became a church plant, was it . . . ?*

Pros and Cons

If limited to the terms in our book, most churches would describe their merger as an adoption, but in our view most "adoptions" are actually rebirths. Adoption mergers are not for desperate churches in danger of immediate extinction but more for stable or stuck churches who embrace the synergistic benefit of joining a stronger church. They recognize that their church's mission will be better fulfilled by submitting their name, ministries, and assets to a church that can multiply its impact beyond what it could do by remaining solo. Though the adopted church turns over everything to the lead church, it usually brings assets to the table in addition to a congregation of people: facilities, staff, and ministry programs that are often integrated into the lead church's overall strategy. Like an adopted child, they take on a new name and relationship, but they also add a dimension to their new parent that enhances the whole family.

As in rebirth mergers, there is usually a name change—and the potential loss of facilities, staff, ministries, members, and friends, but it does not have to be at the expense of losing the church's heritage and identity.

> *Most churches would describe their merger as an adoption, but in our view most are rebirths.*

There is also the potential for added disappointment, change resistance, and conflict post-merger because adopted churches, as they approach a merger, don't feel as desperate as rebirth churches. Therefore, they often don't feel the need to embrace the change as strongly.

Marriage Model

Marriage mergers occur when two comparable churches, similar in size and/or health, realign with each other under a united vision and new leadership configuration. Marriage mergers in churches are much like a marriage of two people coming together as one, bringing strengths and liabilities to the new entity. And like a lot of human marriages, churches coming together may have some difficulties, but they can work through them.

Example

Unlike most human marriages, church-marriage mergers often involve two churches at different stages in their life cycles.

In chapter 3 we introduced Redemption Church as a good example of a marriage merger—two healthy churches, each at a different stage in its life. Praxis Church was a growing church of twelve hundred meeting in two locations. It merged with the older and more stable, but plateaued East Valley Bible Church in the suburbs of Phoenix, a church that was even larger in attendance. Both congregations were healthy, bringing a lot of strengths and resources to the table, though at different life stages. The merged church took a new name together: Redemption Church. We'll explain their story in even more detail in chapter 16.

Pros and Cons

Marriage mergers have the greatest potential gains of all church mergers because both churches bring mutually beneficial, complementary strengths and assets to the merger. They create the greatest synergy because both churches are typically healthy, strong, and united under a compelling mission and vision that they have created together. Marriage mergers can also be a vehicle for a seamless senior pastor succession strategy, as described in chapter 5.

The greatest challenge in marriage mergers is when there is a sharing of the senior pastor role—such as the senior pastors from each church becoming co-pastors. It is an unusual senior pastor who is willing (or able) to share the leadership role with someone else. Two co-leaders under one roof usually produce some explosive outcomes!

Marriage mergers are rather rare because few mergers occur between churches where both bring a significant number of complementary strengths. Many mergers are described to the respective churches as a marriage merger but in reality, they are more of a rebirth or an adoption merger. Using marriage merger language can raise the egalitarian expectations in the joining congregation when in fact it is more of a hierarchical relationship. It can later feel like a bait-and-switch scenario, which often causes a lot of resentment and disappointment post-merger. Even in a marriage merger where the two churches are similar in health and/or size, there is always a lead church and a joining church. It is important to define that relationship early on in the exploratory conversations.

ICU Model (Which Usually Doesn't Work)

We titled this chapter Four Merger Models (But One Doesn't Work). The following is too often a final rally before death although exceptions do happen.

This, the least successful type of merger, comes from the joining of two or more churches that feel like they're in an intensive care unit. Typically, they've each faced many years of decline and have tried one or more interventions to start a new wave of life, none with success.

Example

In her book, *Can Our Church Live?*, former Alban Institute consultant Alice Mann describes two Massachusetts congregations, both part of the Evangelical Lutheran Church in America, that "beat the odds and gained significant vitality from the consolidation process."[6] The process involved a new pastor who was an entrepreneurial leader and change agent. She won the people's loyalty by listening, caring, and taking steps of faith with them. Through a multiyear series of intentional developments, the merged church took a new name and developed a whole new identity. The slow decline of both congregations was reversed, and the resulting new congregation entered a new era with hope and promise. In its first year, the "new" church had twenty-eight baptisms (which was about four times more than its predecessors). They also sponsored a faith-based day camp that included up to seventy-five neighborhood and congregation children.

Pros and Cons

Joining together may buy time and hope in order to figure out how to turn around the decline and make the changes necessary to experience health and growth. In rare cases, as in the previous example, ICU mergers do begin gaining ground again, especially if they get a new unified vision, new growth-minded leader, new location, and a new name. ICU units always contain hope that the patient will get better, and on occasion ICU mergers do make it.

On the con side, this kind of church merger represents the majority of failed mergers of the past because they are often unwilling or unable to change. It is a rare church leader who can lead these churches to turnaround. Church consultant Gary McIntosh concludes that only about five percent of pastors are turnaround leaders.[7] Thom Rainer, who has done years of research for the Southern Baptist Convention, notes that "there are not enough turnaround pastors to lead even one-third of America's churches in need of turnaround."[8]

> *ICU mergers typically fail because they are like two drowning men clinging to each other, neither letting the other take charge.*

ICU mergers typically fail because they are like two drowning men clinging to each other. Both trying to survive at the expense of the other, neither letting the other take charge.

They end up taking each other down. Instead of a recovery, they both end up side-by-side in the morgue. They often have good intentions, but without making other changes that infuse life, they are at best prolonging the inevitable.

The best explanation of why ICU mergers so often fail comes from Terry E. Foland, who has worked with about seventy efforts to merge churches over the past thirty years, mostly in the Disciples of Christ. He explains:

> When either the only or the primary motivation for merger is survival, most of the time, the merger only results in postponing the death of the churches that merged. Survival generally does not provide the motivation for leaders working to save a congregation to think in new ways about how to be the church. As a result, the

old patterns and habits of the churches continue, and the culture of the merged congregation contains the seeds for destruction. Putting together two congregations that have both been in serious decline and denial about why they have been in decline will not bring about the necessary changes to foster growth and generate new energy or vitality.[9]

Alice Mann's book *Can Our Church Live?* is subtitled *Redeveloping Congregations in Decline* because that is her focus. In it she strongly discourages what we're calling the ICU merger approach in which all parties are in the later steps of decline. "Why doesn't the consolidation of several weak congregations produce one strong one?" she asks. Partly because it encourages people to focus inward, she says:

> Often, merged congregations [of this type] spend a lot of time deciding whose candlesticks will be used at Christmas and not much energy asking: "Who lives in this community today, and how could we reach them?" The inability to answer that question creatively is part of the reason membership is declining in the first place. Even if members decide to take a new look at identity and purpose, the work becomes tougher, since two or more narratives are involved.[10]

Realistic Hope

All mergers, like all human beings, are messy and complicated with no guarantees. Every church merger has a unique pathway. There is no one-size-fits-all formula they all follow, yet all will wrestle with the same basic issues. How they address and manage those issues will vary from church to church but the first step is to understand what kind of merger is being considered and the pros and cons that come with each type of merger.

Notes

1. As Tony Morgan in the Vital Signs Report from The Unstuck Group explains, "The number of first-time guests over a 12-month period needs to be equal to or greater than their average weekly attendance. In other words, the number of weekly first-time guests should be 2% or greater than the annual average weekly attendance." For a research source to this 2 percent datum, and many other benchmarks, see Gary McIntosh and Charles Arn, *What Every Pastor Should Know: 101 Indispensable Rules of Thumb for Leading Your Church* (Grand Rapids, MI: Baker, 2013).

2. Anthony F. Buono and James L. Bowditch, *The Human Side of Mergers and Acquisitions: Managing Collisions between People, Cultures, and Organizations* (Washington, DC: Beard Books, 1989), xiv.

3. The video is found at https://newlifecommunity.church/restart/. The website for New Life Community Church is www.newlifechicago.org.

4. Richard Laribee, *Factors Contributing to Success or Failure of Congregational Mergers* (Pasadena, CA: Fuller Theological Seminary, 1998), 5.

5. Kristen Moulton, "Merger Makes Big Utah Church Even Bigger," *The Salt Lake Tribune*, December 7, 2010, https://tinyurl.com/suj39u7.

6. Alice Mann, *Can Our Church Live? Redeveloping Congregations in Decline* (Lanham, MD: Rowman and Littlefield, 2000), 70.

7. Gary L. McIntosh, *Taking Your Church to the Next Level: What Got You Here Won't Get You There* (Grand Rapids, MI: Baker Books, 2009).

8. Thom S. Rainer, *Breakout Churches: Discover How to Make the Leap* (Grand Rapids, MI: Zondervan, 2005), 214.

9. Terry E. Foland, "Merger as a New Beginning," in Gaede, ed., *Ending with Hope*, 65.

10. Mann, *Can Our Church Live?*, 67. See also *Congregational Resource Guide* at https://thecrg.org/about.

6

STAGES AND SPEED OF A MERGER

"The ten-week time between our announcement and the vote seems to have helped put most people at ease because they feel they have ample time to make an informed and prayer-based decision. As you would expect, comments have ranged from, 'It's about time!' to 'How could you?'" This comment came from our 2019 church merger survey.

Every church merger has a unique set of circumstances. No two mergers are alike. Yet we have found it helpful to frame the merger conversation around three primary questions happening in five different stages. Though the average time frame from the initial conversation to final approval is about eight months (see Merger Fact 7 on page 84), the unique circumstances of the merging churches affects the speed of the journey.

Three Questions That Frame the Merger Process

Almost weekly, I (Jim) receive phone calls from pastors or church leaders asking for guidance on how to proceed with a merger opportunity that is knocking on their church door. I explain that three main questions in the merger conversation frame the process going forward:

- Is this merger *possible*? They need to determine if a merger is possible through a conversation between the senior pastors or leaders and church boards. Is merging congruent with the mission and vision of our church? This discussion results in a decision to begin or end merger deliberations.

- Is this merger *feasible*? They need to determine the compatibility of the two congregations through due diligence in addressing the twenty-five issues to determine feasibility for every church merger (explained later in chapter 15). This results in a decision by the boards *not to merge* or a recommendation to both congregations *to merge*.
- Is this merger *desirable*? This becomes apparent as the churches go through a process of public meetings to discuss the recommendation to merge, culminating in a churchwide vote or poll.

If the senior leaders of two congregations conclude that the potential benefits of merging outweigh the drawbacks of going their separate ways, then the merger deliberation process can begin. Most happen quickly and are done within a few months, some can take longer. There are a lot of moving parts, but a church merger can be broken down into five basic stages analogous to courtship and marriage. The marriage analogy is helpful, but not perfect because it can imply equality of two partners, which is rarely the case in church mergers. As figure 6.1 shows, it is more like a dance where one leads and the other follows. Although this process is more art than science, each stage addresses a specific question. The time frames can vary but generally they fall into the following stages.

Mergers Are Like a Dance

1. *Is this merger possible?*
   Determine possibility by the two senior pastors and church boards.

2. *Is this merger feasible?*
   Determine compatibility by addressing the 25 issues of a church merger.

3. *Is this merger desirable?*
   Decided by a vote or poll of both congregations.

Figure 6.1

The Five Stages of a Church Merger

Every church is different in the speed it follows on its merger journey. We find it helpful to view the merger as happening in five different stages and then to estimate the speed of each stage based on your circumstances:

- *Exploration* is like dating as you assess the possibility of merging.
- *Negotiation* is like a courtship as you determine the feasibility of a merger.
- *Declaration* is like an engagement as you make a public announcement recommending a merger.
- *Consolidation* is like a wedding as the union takes place and begins with a ceremony and a name change.
- *Integration* is like a marriage as the two congregations begin the hard work of learning to live together as one church.

Exploration Is Like Dating (One to Two Months) Where We Ask, "Is This Possible?"

As we previously mentioned, every merger involves a lead church and a joining church. It is a delicate dance where one church leads and the other one follows. Should two congregations consider merging? Here are four questions in the Exploratory stage to help you make that decision:

1. Would our congregation *be better* by merging rather than remaining separate?
2. Could we *accomplish more* together than we could separately?
3. Would our community be *better served* if we joined together?
4. Could the kingdom of God be *further enlarged* by joining together?

Merger deliberations usually begin between the two senior pastors or acting church leaders. In some situations, this begins with denominational leadership. In other situations, during this stage, the denomination is the final approval on whether to proceed with a merger conversation.

In this stage, if the joining church has a senior pastor at the joining church (and the majority do, according to Fact 16 on page 125), the first and most important question to address is "what will happen to the senior pastor?" Will the pastor be retained, offered a new role, or replaced? This is a delicate issue that will determine whether to proceed or not and will set the tone and trajectory of the merger process.

Church Comparison Profile Exercise

A merger can be a great opportunity for both churches, if it's something that God is bringing about. If a merger is not right, the process can be a great diversion of time, money, and energy. Helping church leaders discern this decision is the primary reason we wrote this book!

> *If a merger is not right, the process can be a great diversion of time, money, and energy.*

I (Jim) encourage senior church leaders to assess the merger possibility by making a side-by-side comparison profile of the two churches. Often when the two church teams see the comparisons, the similarities and differences stand out. This initial exercise also helps the leaders to determine whether to proceed with the merger conversation as well as who is the lead church and who is the joining church.

Here are the areas we look at to help churches see their own reality. A template and an example of this profile are provided in chapter 15:

- Mission, vision, and values. Reveals how close or how far the two churches are in their overall purpose and philosophy of ministry
- Staff. A quick snapshot of the number of paid staff at both churches
- Budget and debt. Reveals financial health and challenges
- Worship center seating. Determines capacity and use
- Worship service times. Determines if the facility is being fully maximized
- Average weekend attendance by age groups (adults, students, children). Reflects the composition of each church
- Average age of congregation. Reveals who each church is serving and reaching
- Baptisms (or similar indicator of conversion growth). A reflection of outreach or lack of it
- Church life stage (growing, stable, stuck, struggling, declining).
- Assets (own or rent). Identifying the physical assets and potential liabilities each church brings to the table
- Travel time between churches. Most successful mergers are within thirty minutes travel time of each other
- Who initiated the merger possibility? Helps in framing the

conversation between the two churches
- What initiated merger conversation? Reveals the possible motivations for merger possibility
- Approval process? Who makes the decision? The denomination, board or congregation? What vote percentage is required for approval?

After working through this and other exploratory issues, if both senior leaders become convinced that a merger possibility is worthwhile to consider, then the two senior leadership teams are brought into the discussion for them to determine, "Is this possible?" For denominational churches, this step may involve permissions or direction from whatever regional body oversees the church.

Negotiation Is Like Courtship (One to Two Months) Where We Ask, "Is This Feasible?"

The best merger possibilities occur when there is at least an eighty percent DNA match between the two congregations in doctrine, philosophy of ministry, and ministry style. Like any good marriage, the more in common, the better the chances of success. But sometimes, as in a good marriage, the right combination of opposites has a strong attraction to each other, such as a suburban church seeking more meaningful engagement with an economically challenged area and a downtown church surrounded by need but lacking in resources to make it happen.

The two leadership teams should keep the discussion confidential if possible until they agree that merging is feasible. In most churches, any public hint of a merger before the leadership can determine feasibility will often undermine the process before it has a chance to be seriously considered.

This is the most strategic stage because all the issues and processes have to be worked out and agreed upon by the leadership before a merger can be recommended. We have identified twenty-five distinct issues that every church merger has to work through. Although only a few issues are potential deal-breakers, all of them have to be addressed. The twenty-five issues are listed and explained in chapter 15.

During this stage both senior leadership teams need to work through the issues, create a premerger due-diligence checklist, a post-merger checklist, and design a timeline for the pre and post-merger journey. This culminates in a decision by the boards *not to merge* or a recommendation to both congregations *to merge*.

Typically, we recommend appointing a feasibility team comprised of five to seven individuals usually from the two boards and chaired by the lead church. The feasibility team should be comprised of church members who are favorably disposed to the idea of a merger and who will address all the issues and make recommendations for the board's approval. The feasibility team makes a good transition team later to monitor the post-merger progress.

The key to experiencing a healthy post-merger outcome is establishing the post-merger leadership team and strategy *before* the merger is approved.

Are you a candidate for a church merger? If your church has a clear mission to reach people and extend its impact locally, then your church is in a strong position to embrace another church through a merger. If your church believes it could become a better church or be turned around by joining another like-minded but more vibrant church, then it is a good candidate for a church merger.

Final God-Check

After all the due diligence has been done to determine feasibility and the leadership of the two congregations conclude that the merger is doable, do one final God-check. Is there a profound sense that God is in this decision to merge? Is there a compelling awareness that this is something the Holy Spirit has orchestrated? Are your motives God-honoring? Has the Bible spoken to you about this merger? Have wise and objective advisors affirmed it? Is there a strong sense that "if we don't do this, we're being disobedient to the promptings of the Holy Spirit"?

Don't move forward with a merger if you don't see God's fingerprints all over it. But if there is an overwhelming sense that God has brought this merger together, then you are ready to go to the next stage.

Don't move forward with a merger if you don't see God's fingerprints all over it.

Declaration Is Like an Engagement (One to Two Months) Where We Ask, "Is This Desirable?"

This phase begins with an announcement recommending a merger to both congregations accompanied with a Frequently Asked Questions document. The FAQ addresses the primary congregational questions and is derived from the answers to the twenty-five issues. We offer a

FAQ template in chapter 15 and actual FAQ examples in appendixes E and F.

Following the announcement are congregational town halls and small group gatherings at both congregations, culminating in a congregational vote or poll by the joining church, if not both congregations. The outcome of the vote or poll will reveal, "Is this desirable?"

Both church leadership teams need to decide what minimum affirmation percentage is acceptable. Should they merge if the vote is less than 90 percent, 75 percent, or 50 percent? Every church has to decide what is their comfort level of acceptance.

Most churches that we've consulted with or surveyed do take votes (both the lead church and the joining church), and the vast majority of those votes are between 80 percent and 100 percent in favor of a merge, as Merger Fact 19 and 20 point out (page 136). Jim reports that every church he consulted that made it to a congregational vote to merge was approved regardless of the percentage required. Indeed, our research affirms that most joining churches require a simple majority to approve a church merger (see Merger Fact 6).

Merger Fact 6

4 in 5 Joining Churches Vote about the Merger, Many Requiring Only a Simple Majority

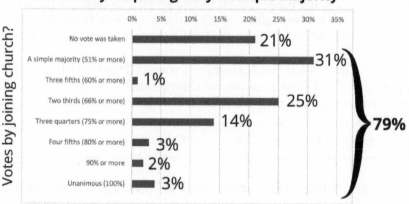

2019 Survey: *At the joining church, what percentage of "yes to merge" votes did your constitution or bylaws require?*

Even if a congregational vote is not required by either congregation, we recommend offering a poll to the congregation to affirm the decision of the ruling body. Though permission may not be needed, taking a poll will reveal congregational buy-in and build ownership for the decision.

This is the most strategic stage in the process because clear, consistent and unified communication is absolutely necessary for the congregation to get on board with the merger. During this time the lead church needs to drive the communication strategy for both churches with a blueprint to overcommunicate the why, the how, and the benefits of the merger.

Overcommunicate, Overcommunicate, Overcommunicate

We've now conducted two major national studies of church mergers. Perhaps the strongest message in the open-ended comments people offered is the need for both the joining and lead churches to communicate better at every stage in the process. As one person explained with great passion, "Communicate, communicate, communicate! With pastors, elders, leaders, and the congregation itself, talk to them all and then talk some more." We will unpack how to overcommunicate in chapter 14, "How to Start the Merger Conversation."

But for here, let us offer a church merger FAQ template. One of the most helpful tools for communicating a church merger to a congregation is a Frequently Asked Questions (FAQ) document, made available to both church's entire constituency, online and in print. Here are some typical questions that a church merger FAQ addresses, especially for a joining church:

- How did this merger idea come about?
- Why are we considering a merger?
- What are the benefits of this proposed merger?
- What is a multisite church? [If relevant to the merger]
- Who will be our pastor?
- Will our church have a new name and what will it be?
- What will happen to the pastor and staff?
- What will happen to the church board and committees?
- What will happen to the church's facilities?
- What will the worship services be like?
- Who will be the main preacher(s) and how will the sermons be delivered?
- How will the budget and finances be managed?
- How will current membership be transferred?

- Will our denomination and affiliations change?
- What will happen to our supported missionaries and organizations?
- What will the merger cost? Can we afford it?
- Who will decide if this merger happens?
- If the merger happens, what will change?
- What is the timeline for this proposed merger?
- What will happen if the merger doesn't go through?
- What are my next steps?

Merger Fact 7

The Average Merger Time Frame Is 8 Months

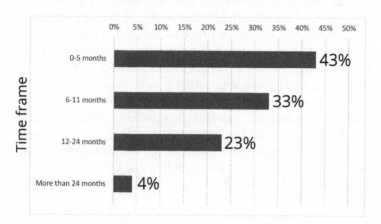

2019 Survey: *How many months passed between the initial discussion to merge and the completion of the merger?*

Consolidation Is Like a Wedding (One to Three Months) Where We Celebrate, "We Did It!"

The phased integration plan of two congregations becoming one church needs to begin immediately after the vote is approved. The two congregations officially become one church in an inaugural joint service. The joining church celebrates its final service and is usually legally dissolved the week prior to the inaugural service. In a multisite merger, there needs to be an emotional and physical separation from the building in order to get full closure before beginning a new chapter. We recommend at least one to three months for upgrading and rebranding the facility, experiencing the life-giving DNA of the lead church, and relaunching its inaugural service as an integrated church. The new chapter for both congregations does not begin with a question, but a statement, "We did it!"

As Merger Fact 7 points out, the entire process usually takes about eight months.

Integration Is Like a Marriage (One to Three Years) Where We Reflect, "How Are We Doing?"

It typically takes one to three years for two congregations to move through the "yours, mine, and ours" phases of a merger marriage. The first few months are the most crucial to long-term success and can be the most traumatic. The new church entity needs to establish quickly who's in charge, a clear reporting structure, and integrated systems. It is helpful initially for the leadership team to have monthly reports from the transition team on post-merger evaluations about staff, ministries, congregation, attendance, and finances—all as a way of answering the question, "How are we doing?"

Adoption mergers tend to move quickly. Reconciliation-based mergers tend to move more slowly because relational healing takes time. Full integration typically takes longer in larger and older joining congregations.

Table 6.2 summarizes the various phases of the church merger process. Then table 6.3 shows a specific, actual example. (Chapter 15 explains more about how to create a timeline.)

Table 6.2

Phase	How It Works	Outcomes
Name: Exploration What you are exploring: Is this a possibility? Marriage analogy: like dating Commitment level: We are interested	Who: Senior pastors and senior boards of both churches Process: Conversations Length: 1 Month	Decision whether or not to proceed to the next level of merger conversation between the two boards (and if necessary the respective denominational leadership)
Name: Negotiation What you are negotiating: Is this feasible? Marriage analogy: like courtship Commitment level: We think we are compatible	Who: Senior pastors, church boards, senior staff (a slightly bigger group than in the previous phase) Process: Appoint a feasibility team to address all 25 distinct issues of a church merger (see chapter 14). Establish a checklist and timeline to determine if a merger is in the best interest of both churches. Length: 1–2 months	Decision to recommend (or not recommend) a merger to both congregations If yes, prepare a public announcement and FAQ to explain the why, how, and benefits of merging to both congregations
Name: Declaration What you are declaring: this is desirable! Marriage analogy: engagement Commitment level: We are doing it!	Who: Senior pastors, boards, all staff, both congregations Process: Announcement recommending to merge and interaction with both congregations, through meetings and other formats, in discussing the why, how, and benefits of merging Length: 1–2 months	A churchwide vote or poll to affirm the decision to merge

Name: Consolidation

What you are consolidating: the union of two becoming one

Marriage analogy: wedding

Commitment level: We are one!

Who: same group as in previous phase

Process: Honor the past in a final service of the joining church and celebrate the future in an inaugural one-church service of the "new" church

Length: 1–2 months

Special services for the joining church

A completed legal merger including the dissolution of the joining church board and commencement of a joint-member transition team

Name: Integration

What you are integrating: the transition of two becoming one

Marriage analogy: marriage

Commitment level: We're secure enough to ask how we are doing.

Who: Senior pastor, board, all staff, lay leadership

Process: Transition Feasibility Team to Transition Team to assess ministry integration and staff fit to determine needed adjustments

Length: 3–12 months

Continue the post-merger plan of updating facilities and integrating staff, ministries, procedures and other assets into one church

Continue monthly evaluations of staff, ministries, congregational morale and financial health

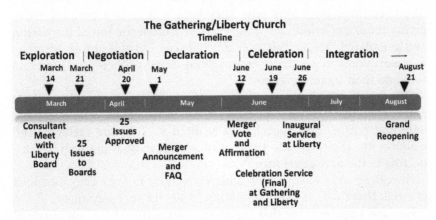

Table 6.3

Not Always Sequential

Not all merger proposals go forward from their first exploration. Sometimes they never go through. Sometimes the initial conversation doesn't go very far but then gets picked up months or even years later.

When the idea of merging with another church was first discussed among the forty or so members of Interbay Covenant Church in downtown Seattle, discussions grew heated. Their longtime pastor, age sixty-one, had announced plans to move on, but few welcomed the idea of the change that inevitably accompanies a merger. Some had been members of the church for a good portion of its sixty-five-year life. Many were predictably wary of giving away their property, losing certain distinctive aspects of their worship style, and closing the book on so many years of vibrant history. The idea was shelved, but it resurfaced months later, again prompted by their pastor's plan to complete his ministry there.

The idea was to join a church named Quest that had been renting space from Interbay for some time. Both were multiethnic and both were part of the same denomination. But Quest was young: founded in 2001, its pastor was young (age thirty-six at the time), the congregation was young (mostly in their twenties and thirties and heavily single), and its music was loud.

Barbara Lundquist, seventy-three, who has served as chairwoman of the Interbay congregation, said people questioned Quest. "They said, 'Who are they? How long have they been a church? Come on, we're giving them our building!'" Two years separated the initial discussion and completed merger, but after much discussion and prayer, Interbay members voted to give their multimillion-dollar property to Quest and fold into their larger neighbor.

"We saw within Quest a freshness, a vibrancy, a vision for the Seattle and beyond that was very appealing to us. It spoke to us," said Interbay's outgoing pastor, Ray Bartel. "We wanted to add our facilities and resources to theirs, to add to what they're already doing well in connecting to the next generation."

"It really is an amazing, incredible story," said Eugene Cho, pastor of Quest at that time. "It's very humbling to me. It's very sacrificial."

Ray and Eugene agree that the merger was driven by a commitment to the larger kingdom of God. What Interbay was doing was "giving ourselves to the next generation," Ray Bartel added.

The brick church building with soaring curved beams, amber windows, beige walls, and a red curtain covering its baptistery did change its appearance. But the church itself will continue to make a difference in its community for yet another generation.[1]

Post-Merger Checklist

Here is a checklist of things to do post-merger, beginning as many as possible the week immediately following merger approval:

- Announce the decision through email, social media, the church's website, and any printed bulletins. In short: overcommunicate across all your platforms.
- Have senior leaders review and discuss chapter 6, "Stages and Speed of a Merger" and chapter 7, "Measuring Church Merger Success" from this book.
- Host a celebratory elder or church board gathering within the first week and review the strategy for the next three months.
- Host a celebratory all-staff meeting within the first week to reaffirm the direction and review the next three months.
- Review and begin acting on all steps indicated in the Merger FAQ document you created, updating it and other documents online, and informing local media.
- Begin executing new systems and procedures immediately, always overcommunicating to preclude misunderstandings.
- Complete planning for the final worship celebration at the joining church and the inaugural worship services of the combined congregation.
- Install new signage the week following the final celebration service at the joining church, and again, overcommunicating to preclude any unnecessary hurt feelings. (Planning for new signage should begin before the merger vote and ordered as soon as the merger decision is official so as to be ready to install at this point.)
- If you intend to keep the joining church facility as a multisite campus, formally install the new campus pastor on the inaugural Sunday.
- Update website, brochures, and email addresses to reflect the new entity within the first month of the completed merger.
- Complete the legal due diligence as soon as possible.
- Complete the reorganization of staff, ministries, and offices within three months of the approved merger.
- Complete any facility improvements within three to six months of the approved merger.

Though we have suggested sequential stages and time frames for the merger process, we affirm again that church mergers are messy. No two church mergers are alike. Each one has a unique set of circumstances and fingerprint—or "church print"—but all will go through similar stages. Some will go back and forth through these stages, some will go faster, and others will take longer. Sometimes when there's a big change, leaders are tempted to slow down to try to bring everyone along. Going too slowly can create more opportunity for resistance to organize and leads to more challenges and pain through the merger process. However, moving too quickly may actually reduce the resistance and the pain and lead to a healthier merger—even if your speed means that some people will choose not to be a part of the newly merged congregation.

The important thing is to prayerfully work through these stages as carefully and thoroughly as possible with the utmost integrity of heart and honoring the heritage of the joining congregation.

Notes

1. John Iwasaki, "Two Very Different Seattle Churches Decide to Unite," *Seattle Post-Intelligencer,* June 3, 2007, https://tinyurl.com/sl3p3lp. See also Pastor Eugene Cho's subsequent blog with updates, https://tinyurl.com/utzzd6c.

7

MEASURING CHURCH MERGER SUCCESS

"Would you do this merger again?" We not only asked that question in our research, but we also asked people to rate the success of the merger (on a scale of one to ten), and then we asked them, "Any comments on *why* you gave it this rating?" To our delight, 476 people told us why. Frankly, reading their responses was one of our favorite parts of analyzing the survey findings. Here's a sampling of why people said they'd do the merger again:

- "The resulting new congregation was stronger and healthier than either of the two original congregations."
- "Our smaller church plant merged into a larger church plant church with the same mission, vision and values."
- "The former congregations are thriving spiritually and numerically."
- "Ninety-five percent of our people stuck through the merger and through the following year. Many became leaders in the new church."
- "From the day we merged, we averaged more in attendance than we did as separate churches added together."
- "We are actually considering multiplication already by sending out a church plant from the merged church."

- "We started with two churches, one with an average attendance of 10–15 and the other 30–35. Since the merger, and since losing about 20 members because they did not want to make the trip to the new location, we have about 40–45 each Sunday—and it's just one year later."
- "The resulting new congregation is stronger and healthier than either of the original congregations."

Bottom line? Some 82 percent of people who took the survey said yes, they'd do the merger again. As Merger Fact 8 indicates, in every type of church, a good number said "yes."

Merger Fact 8

82% of Surveyed Mergers Said They'd Do It Again

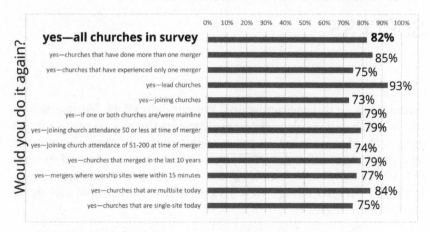

2019 Survey: *Would you do this merger again?*
(Options: yes, no, or unsure.)

Success Clarity Doesn't Come Easily

Like many pastors, Will Marotti enjoys getting to know fellow clergy in his community. Will had initiated a monthly prayer gathering of area ministers, and it met on occasion in the former pharmacy that housed his growing congregation, New Life Church, Meriden, Connecticut. As the pastors prayed for their community and the general needs of their respective churches, Will would ask the others to pray with him for a better location because theirs was overcrowded week after week.

At the conclusion of a December 2005 prayer meeting, a pastor pulled Will aside. "What if our two churches merged?" he asked Will. Seeing Will's puzzled face, he made his case. "You've got no space here and you are bursting at the seams; we have lots of space and we're not growing." The pastor also confided that he'd like to move on to plant a new church, and maybe the merger would make that possible. So they talked further, prayed, and agreed to raise the matter with their respective church boards.

Both boards found the idea appealing. The church with the ample facility was part of a denomination, and its denominational leaders were delighted that Will's nondenominational congregation was willing to affiliate with them, instantly making it their largest church in the area.

Just months beforehand, New Life had already experienced an informal adoption merger. It had gone very well. The lay leader of a large Hispanic cell group had asked to be enfolded into New Life. The process went simply and quickly. There were no assets to transfer. They were the joining congregation and New Life was the lead congregation. The union gave New Life a Spanish language outreach in a city with one of the fastest growing Hispanic populations in Connecticut. New Life brought the pastor of the Hispanic church on its staff part time. The Hispanic church's volunteer worship leader became New Life's worship leader, a role he would stay in for the next several years.

Will trusted that the second merger would go as smoothly, with his church again serving in the lead church role, and so within a few months, plans were finalized for the new, more formal merger. Most of the discussion and excitement surrounded the vision of being able to reach the community for Christ far better together than separately.

The congregations began to get to know each other. The joining church agreed to take on New Life's name and leadership. New Life would move into its 250-seat facility on seven acres. New Life would keep the pharmacy building and open a daycare center there.

All seemed to go well until the third Sunday after the merger. Will wanted to be physically closer to the people as he preached. In the drugstore that had been converted into a house of worship, he had used a small podium and positioned it somewhat close to the first row of the congregation. The church's new location had a high platform with huge furniture that felt like an obstacle to Will.

So just before the morning worship service he snagged a couple of burly men and asked them to move the communion table into a nearby storage room. The table wasn't needed that day because neither church served communion every week. By moving the table, Will would now have room to preach on the floor immediately in front of the first pews—which now had lots of people in them for the first time in years.

That quick decision soon became the rallying point of opposition for certain members of the congregation who had worshipped there for so many years. "Look what those people are doing to our church," one influential elder said as he began to look for others who didn't like the changes that New Life had brought with it.

In the coming months about half of the smaller church left to go to other churches. The former pastor, who remained supportive of the merger and had worked hard to quell the unrest, was commissioned and financially supported by New Life for several years as he moved to another town and planted a new church. (Later the former pastor's new church merged with another church. The planting pastor plays an advisory role and the church is doing well in the new configuration.) Meanwhile New Life weathered the pain of the criticisms, continued to grow, and today has a thriving outreach to the community—even becoming multisite by renting an auditorium for weekly services in the town next door.

Pastor Will regrets the pain he caused by his hasty decision to move the communion table. "I didn't realize the hurt it would cause," he says. "If I could do it again, I'd still replace a lot of the furniture, but I'd prepare the people and walk them through the change."

But Will has no regrets for saying yes to the merger. He continues to believe—as does the joining church's pastor—that the pathway to combine the two congregations is a door that God opened. "We wouldn't be where we are today without help from mergers," Will says. "Our mergers broadened the ministry impact of our church in significant ways."

> Our mergers broadened the ministry impact of our church in significant ways.

Will also wishes he had known a bit more in advance about mergers. His training and early career were in the automotive industry. He and his wife, both longtime followers of Christ, had been active in a church and had learned much about ministry there. When Will sensed God's call into full-time ministry, his pastor invited him to come on staff as associate pastor. Will also served as a volunteer hospital chaplain, northeast director of Evangelism Explosion, and state coordinator for the National Day of Prayer in Connecticut. These were all good experiences, but church mergers were a new idea—how would he know what success looks like beyond the overall vision of reaching more people and making more disciples of Christ?

"My filter is to ask if it expands God's kingdom by bringing more people to Christ," Will says. Beyond that idea, how could he gauge the effectiveness of the churches that had united together?

What Does a Successful Merger Look Like?

As Will Marroti asked, "What does success look like in a merger?"

When some people think about mergers, they assume a model of perfect equality, where each has an equal say and where the core idea of merging is to incorporate the best of both churches into a new entity. We all want to imagine a newspaper article that describes the result of a merger as a greater impact for Jesus on the populations the churches currently serve and that no jobs were lost, or services reduced in the process. Instead the merger reduced operating cost, eliminated potential duplication of services, and created a better efficiency of ministry.

Many, unfortunately, approach merger "success" with the wrong mindset or unrealistic expectations. If you start with faulty expectations, you'll never get to a win. You'll always be disappointed. It's amazing to us how many people approach the idea of a merger assuming that merger success means nothing will change and that everyone will agree, stay, and love it.

What's wrong with this view? It's saying that people want a merger that doesn't change anything, that maintains the status quo—just at an improved level! Let us explain why we view that as faulty thinking. First, let table 7.1 highlight the contrasts:

Table 7.1

How to Think about Merger Success	
Merger Success Is Not . . .	*Instead Focus On . . .*
100% retaining staff, church members and attenders	Retaining people who embrace a shared vision for the future
100% approval of members	100% engagement of those who approve
Saving a facility for emotional or nostalgic reasons	Stewarding a facility for kingdom purposes
Preserving a church name	Leveraging a legacy
Maintaining the status quo	Beginning a new life cycle or starting over with a new vision

We'd like to propose the following measurable standards as a way to define and measure a church merger's success. The milestones or benchmarks we propose in table 7.2, which are based on our research and on experience of merger churches, can apply to the four types of mergers introduced in chapter 5: rebirths, adoptions, marriages, and ICU mergers.

Table 7.2

Setting Milestones Helps You Define Success as a Merger

METRIC	Stabilize	Grow	Multiply
Mission & Vision	Focus is more on the future than the past.	Unified vision & leadership.	Plans are in motion to continue reproducing, whether by another merger, a church plant, a multisite, or another missional entity.
Integration	Majority feels merger was a good thing to do.	"Signature" ministries are fully integrated under a unified vision and leadership. Nonstrategic ministries discontinued. At least a quarter of churches ministries and programs made up of people who joined post-merger.	Attendees no longer see themselves as "us" and "them" but as "we." At least half of the church's committees, ministries, and programs are made up of people who joined post-merger.
Attendance	Attendance is at least equal to the combined attendance of both churches before the merger.	Attendance is greater than the combination of both churches before the merger. Multiple services added.	Facility maximized with multiple worship services and 80 percent capacity at the optimal inviting hour.

	Newcomers since the merger match surrounding community more closely than church demographics prior to the merger.		
Finances	Giving is at least equal to a combination of both churches before the merger.	Giving is greater than the combination of both churches before the merger.	Additional funds are raised for church expansion.
Community Impact	Perception of the church by the community moves from negative to positive, from non-awareness to awareness.	The church proactively engages the community with externally focused ministries.	The church becomes a recognized strategic partner in the community

Stage 1: Stabilize

People need time to process the new missional clarity, new relationships, new patterns, and new life that a merger represents, especially if they're coming from the joining church. In most cases, their membership is automatically transferred (see Merger Fact 9, page 99) and a majority decide to stay after the merger (see Merger Fact 10). Further, the joining church's missionary and community-outreach commitments are usually continued, at least for a season (see Merger Fact 11), but the church "face" with those relationships often changes or is impacted and needs to be restabilized in a new administration.

Ideally, within the first stage of the merger, the church's leadership will have created a new integrated congregational culture that embraces the merger, focuses on the future, provides financial steadiness, and sustains an attendance equal to or greater than that of the combined attendance of the two church bodies prior to the merger. The board and congregation's corporate self-esteem will point to the future, viewing the life of the new congregation as "the best years are yet to come." If a church does this in Stage One, it's on or ahead of the curve. Way to go!

Stage 2: Grow

In the second stage, hopefully solid growth will start to take root, if it hasn't already. This is all part of the joining church taking on the DNA of a healthy, growing lead church. If the first stage of stabilizing went well, then by the second stage the people from the joining church are engaged and excited, not only inviting their friends and neighbors to church, but taking part in their new church's corporate evangelism and outreach.

Our observation is that within the first two stages of a healthy merger, the attendance and the financial base will each have grown by at least 10 percent. Further, new attendees will more closely represent the median age, race, and economic levels of the surrounding community as compared to the church demographics in either congregation prior to the merger.

Stage 3: Multiply

Within the third stage of the merger, more than half the committees, ministries, and programs will be composed of people who joined after the merger and have embodied the church's heart of outreach to the point that they are moving toward reproducing another congregation, whether by another merger, a church plant, a multisite, or another missional entity. As a viable congregation, the church increases its community impact, becoming a valued partner in the community.

As our friend and seasoned church consultant David Schmidt reminded us when he read an early draft of this book, two hundred stuck Christians in one church that merge with one hundred stuck Christians in another church gives you three hundred stuck Christians.

You don't want that! Economies of scale that come from a merger do not necessarily translate into a better church. As Schmidt told us when he reviewed our manuscript, "If the new ministry strategy merely blends two old models that weren't effective in the first place, then you really haven't gained new ground in moving people toward Jesus."

Merger Fact 9

Most Joining Church Members Automatically Become Members at the Lead Church

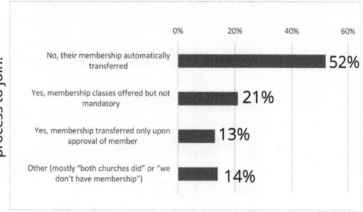

2019 Survey: *Did church members have to go through a membership process to join the lead church?*

Merger Fact 10

Only a Small Percentage of Joining Church Members Depart Post-Merger

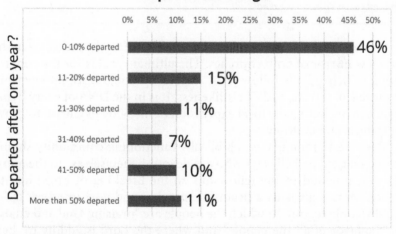

2019 Survey: *One year after the merger, what percent of the people from the joining church had departed because of the merger?*

Merger Fact 11

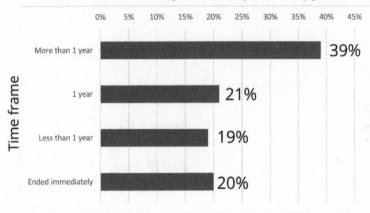

The Majority of Mergers Continue the Joining Church's Missionary and Nonprofit Support

2019 Survey: *How long after the merger were financial commitments of the joining church honored, such as support of its missionaries/nonprofit organizations, etc.?*

> *If the new ministry strategy merely blends two old models that weren't effective in the first place, then you really haven't gained new ground . . .*

The real measure of success of a merger is seen after the merger is in the rearview mirror of both churches. The ultimate goal is for the congregation to help people follow Jesus and for the congregation to grow in its outreach, service, and Christlikeness. It is in the DNA of every living organism, including the local expression of the body of Christ, to grow, reproduce, and multiply.

As Acts 2:42 reminds us, a biblically functioning community should be one marked by believers who are devoting themselves "to the apostles' teaching and to the fellowship, to the breaking of bread and to prayer." Acts 2 gives us a beautiful snapshot and goal to aspire to—a healthy congregation in which the people are "praising God and enjoying the favor of all the people" and where the Lord is adding to their number daily "those who were being saved" (Acts 2:47, see also table 2.2). Ultimately the success of any local church is evaluated by its ability to sustain, grow, and multiply.

Managing Pain and Change

"It will be a new, different church. Might as well acknowledge it and deal with it."

That write-in comment from one of our church merger surveys says it all: Change is coming. Deal with it. Most will agree with the quotation, imagining it through the backdrop of many different emotions—fear, loss, anger, disappointment, disillusionment, grief, uncertainty, and anticipation. The challenge is how to merge in the most God-honoring, compassionate, clear, and missionally focused way. And we hope without any unnecessary pain!

Church mergers are not for the faint of heart. In spite of all the guidelines and best practices presented in this book, church mergers are usually messy, unpredictable, and full of surprises. The positives for successful church mergers are huge, but they do not come without grief and loss. For those dedicated church elders or board members who have the awesome responsibility of overseeing their church, one day you will stand before the real head of the church and give an account of your stewardship as church leaders. On that day God's opinion is the only one that really matters. It won't be about worship preferences, denomination affiliations, skill in defining theological nuances, organizational charting of staff positions, or facility ownership. The most important question will be, "Did we make the best decisions for the sake of God's church and the advancement of his kingdom?"

> God's opinion is the only one that really matters. . . . "Did we make the best decisions for the sake of God's church and the advancement of his kingdom?"

The decisions at stake are not just outward ones but also inward ones about attitude through the painful adjustments. We admire the Phoenix area pastor whose congregation became the joining church. He initiated the merger because he realized that in many ways his church was duplicating efforts of another in the same community. He then shifted to an executive pastor role in the merged congregation. He stayed two and a half years to cement the marriage between his former congregation and the comparable size church they joined. "The merger was an attack on my own security from every angle," he said, referring to his sense of self-image and personal insecurities. "If I didn't deal with it early on, the merger wouldn't work. Even if I said the right things, people would pick up my attitude and try to put a wedge between me and the other pastor." This pastor realized that the way to walk his own congregation through the pain of merging began with himself—his attitude and heart.

Mergers are a viable option for church expansion and kingdom gain. People will leave along the way, and that's understandable. The real test of a successful merger is not that everyone remains but whether pastors and other leaders engaged their congregations at heart levels and provided genuine spiritual leadership through the merger that resulted in deeper faith and a stronger community of believers.

How to Change Church Culture

Mergers are game changers, not status quo keepers. Merger leaders need to understand the dynamics of change.

John Kotter at Harvard Business School has done the best work we're aware of on the science of change, which can help us better understand the process of shifting church culture. His book, *Leading Change,*[1] is the standard on how to drive major change through an organization. Here is his eight-step process, with our comments on how to implement them in a church merger context:

- **Establish a sense of urgency**. Effective church leaders help people see the realities around them and the opportunities before them.
- **Create the guiding coalition**. Successful church mergers gather the right mix of people from both congregations to work together in guiding the congregations to a greater future together.
- **Develop a vision and strategy**. "Without a vision the people perish," according to Solomon's reminder in Proverbs 29:18. Develop a vision that honors the past but looks to the future. When people can see a hopeful picture of the future and how to get there, many will rise to the occasion and help bring it to pass. Present the new strategy as an extension of the past that reflects the values of the joining church.
- **Communicate the change vision**. When there is a lack of communication, people will fill in the vacuum with incorrect and negative conclusions. It is vitally important to overcommunicate the reason, benefits, and process of the church merger to both congregations. Vision "leaks" and therefore needs to be repeated constantly and consistently through all the vehicles of mass communication and social media.
- **Empower broad-based action**. Move forward by involving

progressive thinkers from both congregations to resolve all potential obstacles and give them permission to problem solve outside the box.

- **Generate short-term wins**. Nothing succeeds like success. Go for the early and easy wins to build credibility. Recognize, reward, and celebrate the people who make the wins possible.
- **Consolidate the gains and produce more change**. Build on the early successes to change all systems, structures, and policies that don't fit together and fulfill the vision.
- **Anchor new approaches in the culture**. Create a culture of positive success by demonstrating the impact of greater outreach, transformed lives, community impact, and kingdom gain.

We asked our friend Sam Chand, author of the very insightful book, *Cracking Your Church's Culture Code: Seven Keys to Unleashing Vision and Inspiration*,[2] for his thoughts on bringing culture change to merger situations. He told us:

> Meshing church cultures is a long process. Think of it as a marriage of two full-grown adults—let's say both parties are 45-plus years old. In getting married, they are converging their histories, habits, and cultures into one home. Their new household will go through major adjustments. An outside "counselor" (both pre and post), someone both credible and trusted, can be a big help.
>
> So is honesty in love. This translates into the leaders (boards, elders, trustees, pastors, etc.) spending extended times together having tough conversations in a transparent atmosphere.

Better Together is designed to help you have those tough conversations. No one wants the merger to fail, but one tool for avoiding failure is to examine why it happens. That's what the next chapter is about.

But Not Conflict Free

The biggest finding about mergers from a huge national survey of over ten thousand churches is that merged churches, when compared to their non-merged counterparts, have greater likelihood of conflict that results in people leaving.[3] In many ways that situation seems predictable: any time you merge two distinct cultures, whether under positive or less-pleasant circumstances, there is a chance of conflict, hurt feelings, overlapping power structures, mixed identities, staff and congregational departures, and so on. Most church leaders of the joining church enter the merger conversation with the hope but unrealistic expectations of retaining all the church members and attendees post-merger. Often, they want to minimize potential conflict and departures by preserving as much of the status quo as possible. Yet even in the healthiest church transitions, people leave when a new senior pastor comes to a church. That is inevitable. When it comes to retaining staff and congregants through a merger, the goal isn't to hold on to everyone but to help everyone transition to healthy places of ministry and service, to begin a new chapter together or in another church.

When Will Marotti's younger New Life Church merged with the long-established church, the agreed-on plan was to keep all paid staff from both congregations. Then things turned unexpectedly sour, and many worshippers left from the joining church and from New Life. The exodus also resulted in a loss of more than 20 percent of the income, which led to cuts, first in programs and then staff layoffs. As Will tells in his instructive book, *America's Best Hope*,[4] those were very difficult days. They were draining emotionally and spiritually as well as financially.

If he could go back to that initial "why don't we merge?" discussion, would he do it over again? He would, but he'd approach it with more knowledge. "If we do another merger," he says, "I'll be better prepared for how it works, including any pain and struggle."

He'd also know a bit more about how to define success. "Our standard was that we didn't want to change what's working," he says, "but beyond that, perhaps we didn't map out enough particulars."

Even so, he can now point to many indicators of success. The church has since grown past the merger pains—spiritually, financially, and numerically. New Life helped fund the pastor in the smaller church to launch a new church, and it too is growing. New Life did inherit a beautiful piece of property with great access just off the intersection of two of Connecticut's well-traveled interstate highways. And it retained some great people who love God and want to keep reaching out.

As such, Will wants to keep dreaming big dreams of what God might do. "After all," he explains, "little dreams need no faith. We are to be creative and innovative and to use any legitimate means by all means to transform our community into America's best hope," he says, echoing the title of his book. "We need to continue being open to collaboration and the joining of resources to accomplish God's vision. If God can use me and our ministry to influence many and bring positive transformation to our community, he can use anyone!"

Unfortunately, at the end of the day, merger success is too often defined in the eye of the beholder. But it shouldn't be. It's not a subjective matter of what success is to one person is failure to another. Instead, the standard for success needs to be evaluated by biblical measurements and not by our personal preferences. As mentioned earlier, when each of us stands before God and are asked to account for our merger decisions, we need to remember that God's opinion is the only one that really matters. We want to be able to say, "Lord, we did what we thought was best for your kingdom, not my preferences."

Notes

1. John P. Kotter, *Leading Change* (Boston: Harvard Business Press, 1996). See also a case study of churches: Robert Lewis and Wayne Cordeiro with Warren Bird, *Culture Shift: Transforming Your Church from the Inside Out* (San Francisco: Jossey-Bass, 2005).

2. Sam Chand, *Cracking Your Church's Culture Code: Seven Keys to Unleashing Vision and Inspiration* (San Francisco: Wiley, 2010).

3. Warren Bird and Kristin Walters, "Making Multisite Mergers Work: New Options for Being One Church in Two or More Locations," Leadership Network, 2011.

4. Will Marotti, *America's Best Hope* (Bloomington, IN: Xlibris, 2010), 56–57.

8

WHY MERGERS FAIL

Too many mergers fail. In the business world, the majority do. "Recent studies show the failure rate of mergers is close to seventy-five percent, and the majority don't produce the expected financial returns for years after the merger has taken place," says a management professor at the University of Pennsylvania's Wharton School.[1]

Most church mergers that fail are motivated more by survival concerns than by vision, as we explained in the ICU Merger section of chapter 5. Successful mergers are vehicles of change, not preservers of the status quo. The problem is that the people involved rarely frame the issue as one of survival. Some don't even realize that their sights are no higher than defining success as "staying alive for the foreseeable future."

> Successful mergers are vehicles of change, not preservers of the status quo.

The Good, the Bad, and the Ugly

Typical is the failed merger a Michigan pastor told us about. He framed it as an issue of "squatters' rights" for the joining church, which was the older of the two small congregations that merged. "I was here first," individuals conveyed to him almost as soon as the formal merger took place, "and so I have more to say about how things should work out than the other group does, and our vote counts more."

Yes, both congregations had agreed to merge, signed the necessary documents, and prayed sincerely that God would bless their newly blended church family. But things started going south rather quickly after the lead church, which was a younger congregation that had experienced only leased facilities, moved into the joining congregation's facility, which hadn't been updated in years.

The backfiring of the merger showed up first in the nursery as a team of young mothers set about painting it in brighter colors and tossing older toys and furniture that they deemed unsafe. They assumed—wrongly!—that their energy and enthusiasm would be welcomed by the two grandmothers who had decorated the nursery two decades previously and had served as its unchallenged matrons ever since. The next friction point was in the kitchen when the new group brought in their own three-step coffeemaker system, which a connoisseur in their group had refined over the years, and was certain that the church they were merging with would appreciate over their older, simpler approach to the coffee hour. Soon the troubled merger was being challenged at the church boardroom level in tones of "us" and "them."

No one ever voiced or perhaps even thought about the truth that the older joining church saw the merger as little more than an effort to restore a failed status quo. They loved their church, especially their memory of a more vibrant past, and assumed that the new congregation would be their ticket to preserve the parts of their church that they liked best. Like so many churches, they had lost their ability to discern the times and to biblically engage their culture in a relevant way.

Meanwhile reality for the younger congregation, as the lead congregation, was that they came to the merger primarily to alleviate crushing financial pressures. They were overstaffed (spending 75 percent of their income on personnel), focused largely on themselves, and excited to get a place to call home for little more than the cost of a cosmetic face-lift.

Although both talked about doing great things for God through the merger, each proceeded to continue with its own agenda, one that was largely unchanged from premerger days, one that didn't have much outward-focused or disciple-making vision to begin with.

Both churches were focused on institutional survival with an occasional "yea God!" moment from vacation Bible school, youth-mission trips, or the coming home of a wayward child. No one was desperate to make a dramatic change.

Had this merger centered on a vote for a vision to grow God's mission in the community, it probably wouldn't have settled for merely continuing the past. Lacking true vision, the merger experienced an initial euphoria followed by a slow unraveling until it imploded. Merger Fact 12 shows some of the factors in the unraveling.

Too often, that's what happens, and the merger fails. The good news is that it doesn't need to.

Church consultant Tony Morgan, in reading an early draft of this book, wisely counseled, "This is why it's so important to clarify mission, vision and ministry strategy of the newly merged church before the merger is formalized. The way I say it is like this, 'We have to agree on *why* we do church before we can address the *way* we do church.'"

Merger Fact 12

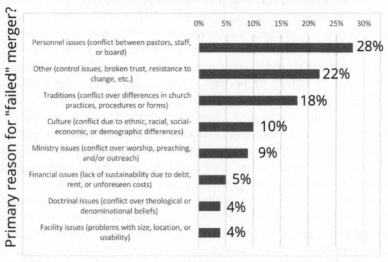

Failed Mergers Most Often Trace Back to Conflict over Personnel or Traditions

2019 Survey: *If your church's experience includes what you would describe as a "failed" merger, what was the primary reason, as you see it?*

Landmines to Avoid

The challenge of institutional survival versus shared mission and vision for the future is central to every merger's success or failure. But even if the missional dream of reaching unchurched people far from God, making disciples of Jesus, training leaders for ministry, and making the community a better place is truly the centerpiece of the merger, there are still several ways it can be derailed. Church mergers can be a fast-track, cost effective, leap-frog way of multiplying church impact. They can also be a huge distraction and a drain of time, energy, and resources. There are landmines to potentially to step on in every stage of a church merger.

> *The challenge of institutional survival versus shared mission and vision for the future is central to every merger's success or failure.*

Landmines in the Pre-exploratory Stage

In chapter 6 we introduced five stages of a merger, which are visually represented in figure 8.1. In the following section, we think through the landmines to avoid at each stage.

5 Stages of a Merger

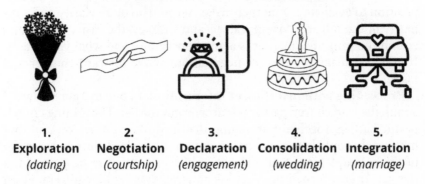

1.	2.	3.	4.	5.
Exploration	**Negotiation**	**Declaration**	**Consolidation**	**Integration**
(dating)	*(courtship)*	*(engagement)*	*(wedding)*	*(marriage)*

Figure 8.1

Waiting too long to consider merging. Unfortunately, the vast number of stuck or struggling churches wait too long to even entertain the possibility of a merger. Many well-meaning church leaders will hang on for years with the vague hope that things will somehow turn around miraculously if we "just have faith," find the "right" pastor or receive a big financial bequest from someone who put the church in their will.

Even worse, many know that change is needed but lack the courage to confront reality. Meanwhile the church declines slowly. The facilities deteriorate through lack of funds and maintenance, becoming more of a liability than an asset. The attendance gets lower as the average attendee age gets higher. The reputation of the church declines as its capacity to do good in the community decreases. Before they realize it, the church has passed a point of no return, in most cases making a merger less appealing to a potential lead church.

As Gary Shockley, executive director of church planting for the United Methodists, told us, "The United Methodist Church has many church facilities that are now worthless and extremely difficult to sell because of deferred maintenance and deferred intervention." Leaders from other denominations have made similar statements.

Landmines in the Exploratory "Dating" Stage

Lack of clarity on the nonnegotiables. Once a church has decided that merging with another church is a possibility, it is important to clearly define what the nonnegotiables are even before a merger opportunity presents itself. Church leaders who know why their church exists (their mission), who know what they are trying to accomplish (their vision), who are guided by well-defined values (the way we do church), and have a clear plan for implementing their vision (their strategy) are in the best position to evaluate if a merger makes sense. The more clarity and similarity of the mission, vision, values, and strategy, the easier it is to discern if the proposed merger is a good possibility and what God wants. It will also make the merger negotiations move forward simpler and faster.

Proceeding with insufficient information. In one merger we heard about, the lead church pastor felt downright misled. The joining church pastor had approached him saying that he'd like to move on and that his church would love to become a campus of the lead church. He spoke of thirty people, but it turned out only four wanted to be part of the merger. It also turned out that his congregation had a bad reputation in the community, so the incoming lead church was initially viewed as guilty by association. It also turned out that they were only leasing the building where they met. The experience affirms the need for churches to check out each other's story beyond the way one person may be presenting it. "Trust but verify" is wise counsel when it comes to exploring a merger.

Confusion about models and roles. Once merger discussions begin in earnest, it is important for both parties to correctly define their relationship to one another. As we have indicated throughout this book, mergers are rarely the joining of two equals, even if they describe themselves that way. One church typically leads and the other follows or joins. Often the joining church sees the merger as a marriage and the lead church sees it as a rebirth or adoption. The lead church mistakenly uses marriage or partnership language that does not correctly convey the relationship out of fear of offending the joining church.

> Mergers are rarely the joining of two equals, even if they describe themselves that way.

This lack of clarity about the model each has agreed on can feel like a bait-and-switch scenario later to the joining church and can lead to resentment and disillusionment post-merger. Or as Merger Fact 13 details, it can lead to the collapse of merger discussions. The sooner both parties understand who is leading and who is following, the smoother the merger deliberations can proceed. Once they can agree to what kind of merger is being proposed, the quicker they can decide if this merger is desirable. Is this a rebirth, adoption, marriage, or ICU merger?

One helpful way of defining the relationship early in the merger conversation is to look at the four different models of how two circles might intersect as illustrated and described in figure 8.1, which shows those options.

Having unclear or different expectations between the two parties leads to aborted, contentious, disappointing, or failed mergers. The diagrams shown in figure 8.1 help clarify the expectations up front and reduce misunderstanding from occurring later in the journey.

Remember the four sets of circles in figure 5.1 (on page 63)? They show four different ways to visualize a church merger. It's very important for both churches to discuss and define together which of these four circle diagrams best describes their understanding of the potential merger. If they don't, they might experience what initially happened when a two-hundred-person congregation joined The Chapel in Akron, Ohio, which had an attendance of several thousand. The joining church wrongly felt this was a marriage of equals (option three) rather than an adoption (option two) or rebirth (option one). As the church's executive pastor at the time, David Fletcher, told us, "The merger was eventually successfully integrated by both congregations, but by using marriage partnership language out of courtesy and good intentions, we probably caused more hard feelings than necessary with inaccurate expectations that we invited."

Merger Fact 13

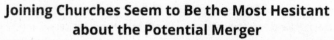

Joining Churches Seem to Be the Most Hesitant about the Potential Merger

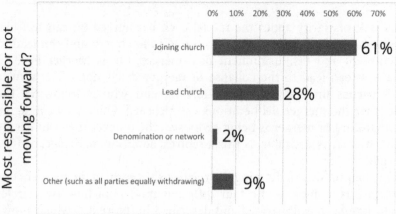

2019 Survey (limited to joining churches): *When the merger didn't go through, who was most responsible for the decision not to move forward?*

Landmines in the Negotiation "Courtship" Stage

Looking back instead of forward. Once two churches have decided that a merger is possible, the merger deliberations can be derailed by focusing on institutional survival or preservation of the past rather than on a shared mission and vision for the future. Even though church leaders may enter into a merger discussion with sincere intentions of a new beginning, often the unconscious but real agenda is to maintain the church without really changing and embracing a new future. They see the infusion of energy and resources as a way to survive rather than to experience a new beginning. Typically, a desire to change will not happen until the pain of not changing is greater than the pain of changing. Successful church mergers occur best when the church knows it needs to change and desires it.

Refusal to release control. The most common landmine occurs when the senior pastor, senior lay leaders, or influential members of the joining church are unable or unwilling to relinquish control of "their" church. Control issues are usually the most difficult issues to overcome in merger deliberations. Sadly, most struggling churches would rather hold onto the steering wheel of their sinking ship than turn the helm over to an effective leader who knows how to sail the ship. They would rather die than change—and many will do just that.

Minimizing the cultural and doctrinal differences. Another mistake churches make is proceeding with the merger even though the early deliberations revealed that their differences were greater than their similarities. Mergers have the best chance of success when there is at least an 80 percent match in doctrine, philosophy of ministry, and ministry style between the two churches. Some of the typical issues that are extremely difficult to overcome are different worship styles, different attitudes toward the role of women in the church, opposite approaches to engaging social isssues, accessibility of leaders, and the transfer of assets. The failure to really understand each other's culture is a major cause for post-merger failure. The better each church understands the other's culture, the fewer landmines each will step on.

> Mergers have the best chance of success when there is at least an 80 percent match in doctrine, philosophy of ministry, and ministry style between the two churches.

Merger Fact 12 identified some of the factors in mergers that happened, but then unraveled and failed. Merger Fact 14 looks into mergers that never happened, and why they didn't.

Landmines in the Declaration "Engagement" Stage

The landmines to avoid during the declaration stage revolve around communication. As we mentioned in chapter 6, this is the most dangerous stage in the process because clear, consistent, and unified communication is absolutely necessary for the congregation to get on board with the merger and setting the right expectations in the post-merger stage.

Undercommunicating. The most important step after recommending a merger to your church is to overcommunicate to both congregations the why, the how, and the benefits of merging. Potential benefits of merging might include greater health and vitality as a congregation, an increased number of people who become followers of Christ through the church, more positive name recognition, more culturally relevant ministries, proven best practices, and financial sustainability. When there is an absence of information about the merger, people will fill in the vacuum with incorrect, incomplete, or negative information.

Communicating to the congregation is done through FAQs (see an FAQ outline in chapter 6 and actual examples in chapter 15), timelines in the church bulletin, on the church website, congregational town hall meetings, and multiple meetings with key counterparts from both congregations. Failing to address all the questions and concerns of the church family can result in a failed church vote or great dissatisfaction post-merger. If people are still asking lots of questions or indicating, "I still don't understand . . . ," then you haven't communicated adequately.

Merger Fact 14

The Main Obstacle to Merging Is Ministry Differences

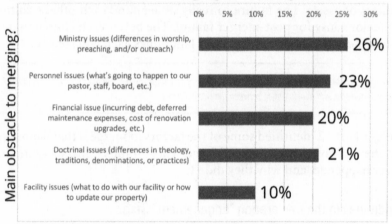

2019 Survey (limited to those that started a merger but didn't complete it): *What is the top concern that, if resolved, would have helped you move forward?*

> If people are still asking lots of questions or indicating, "I still don't understand . . . ," then you haven't communicated adequately.

Inconsistent communication. Our surveys of church mergers affirmed the sentiment that communication is key in any church merger. "Some people thought the first three months of the merger were an 'experiment,'" one survey respondent said. "We merged services at the beginning of summer and the dynamics changed after Labor Day. Some thought things would 'get back to normal.' Clearly, that wasn't going to happen!"

One of the lead churches surveyed said that they wished they had observed and even offered to assist with communication for the joining church. "What we learned is that the leadership of the [joining] church didn't communicate very well—they didn't know how," this lead church board member said. "A lot of information was fuzzy and confusing for the [joining] church."

The pastor of a church in Colorado that experienced a successful merger underscored the importance of communicating in a unified and consistent way. His staff and the joining church staff collaboratively worked hard to give clear and unified communication during the merger process. Doing so "prevented an 'us and them' dynamic from emerging," the pastor said. He looks back at those efforts as one of the biggest positive steps forward during the first three months after the merger.

During the declaration stage the lead church needs to drive the communication strategy for both churches with a strategy to overcommunicate consistently the why, how, and benefits of the merger to both congregations.

Landmines in the Post-Merger "Integration" Stage

Underestimating the pain in the transition. As change management specialist William Bridges states:

> It isn't the changes that do you in, it's the transitions. They aren't the same thing.
>
> **Change** is situational: the move to a new site, the retirement of the founder, the reorganization of the roles on the team, the revisions to the pension plan.
>
> **Transition,** on the other hand, is psychological; it is a three-phase process that people go through as they internalize and come to terms with the details of the new situation that the change brings about.[2]

William Bridges' three-phase process starts with an *ending*, and leaders need to clarify exactly what is ending and what is not. Next comes a disorienting sort of "nowhere" that he calls *the neutral zone*. Jim Tomberlin likes to describe this to his merger clients as the "tunnel of chaos." Expect people to go in and out of the five stages of grief—denial, bargaining, anger, depression, and acceptance. It will begin in the declaration stage but becomes the most acute in the post-merger integration stage. Then comes the new *beginning*. If people don't deal with each of these phases, the change will be "just a rearrangement of the furniture," William Bridges says, with the outcome that "it didn't work."[3]

The grieving stages are very real. Table 8.1 offers examples of what they look like in a merger church setting.

Table 8.1

Merger Grieving Process

Stage	Example (actual quotes)
Denial	"I can't believe this is happening to my church. I did not know that our church was struggling, in trouble, or uncertain about our future."
Bargaining	"Can't we fix our church ourselves? We could buckle down and reorganize, reduce budget, pay our staff less—or even relocate."
Anger	"I feel kicked in the gut. I'm devastated and feel betrayed. I like my church the way it is, and now it will become something I don't know or like. I gave a lot of my time and money here, and now all that effort is down the drain."
Depression	"I am sad. I am losing the church I love. It feels like a death has occurred."
Acceptance	"I will embrace the new reality, accept the new leadership, and trust God for the outcome. I can see some benefits in merging. I am excited about the next chapter of my church."

Change is an event, something that happens. Transition, according to William Bridges, is the emotional and psychological processing of the change. Making the decision to merge is not easy, but it is the transition that determines the ultimate outcome. Transition is about the journey and how to get there. One of the reasons that mergers unravel is that not enough attention is paid to the transition process.

> *Change is an event, something that happens. Transition is the emotional and psychological processing of the change.*

Overpromising and underdelivering. The post-merger integration is the final and most crucial phase in successful church mergers. The biggest mistakes churches make after the merger has been approved are in the integration and follow-through post-merger. Often so much time and energy are focused on getting the merger accomplished that less attention is given to the post-merger integration. In the business world, even experienced merger leaders are often thrown by the integration stage, with unnecessary loss of morale, momentum, and clarity of mission.

There is a tendency to overpromise the benefits of a merger during the negotiation stage and then underdeliver the results during the post-merger integration stage. Many church mergers get off to a bad start because of a failure to integrate operations and systems quickly. The first three months are critical to successful integration. The merged church enters a zone of chaos as people move from the familiar and comfortable way of doing things to an unfamiliar and uncertain way of functioning.

Merger Fact 15

1 in 3 Close the Joining Church During the 4-Month Transition of Becoming a Multisite Campus

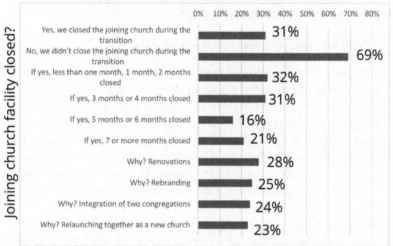

2019 Survey (limited to multisite churches): *Was the facility of the joining church closed for a period of time after the decision to merge? If yes, for how long and why?*

As soon as the merger is approved, the new chapter needs to begin *immediately.* New signs, systems, and procedures must be in place and functioning as soon as possible, preferably the following week. This is especially important in a merger that results in two churches integrating into one location. If a merger results in a multisite outcome, we recommend closing down the joining campus for facility upgrades, rebranding, and integration of the two congregations in one location to prepare for relaunching one to three months later. See Merger Fact 15 for details.

Unclear organizational structure. Parallel to the previous mistake is the landmine of starting the post-merger integration with undefined leadership and unclear reporting structures. On the day after the merger is approved, it has to be clear to everyone in the church—staff, lay leaders, church members, and attendees— who's in charge here and where everyone fits in on the church organizational chart. Confusion here can breed frustration and anger.

Sun Valley Community Church in Phoenix, Arizona, which is pro-filed in several places in this book, was founded in 1990 and by 2000 had grown to an average attendance of over eight thousand people. Two of their five locations came about through mergers. Executive Pastor Paul Alexander, who has been with Sun Valley through both mergers, shares some of his learnings from their merger experience, all dealing with the post-merger integration stage:[4]

- **Programs don't transfer culture, people do.**

After both churches affirmed the merger through a vote, we encour-aged people who attended our original location to go to the new site if they lived in that area. We had a lot of trust built up over time with our people, so they did. But then they came right back. While we were saying that we were one church that met in multiple locations, people came back to the original site and expressed the exact oppo-site. They said that the new location didn't look, act, or feel like Sun Valley. Just because we offered the same ministry "programs" at the new location, it still didn't feel like "us" yet. Much of that trust that we had built up with our people was eroded because we didn't follow through on the promise that we were making that this new location was Sun Valley, when it honestly just wasn't yet.

Just because a joining church votes and technically becomes an expression of your church in a new community, there is still a lot of work to do on that campus to help it become "you."

- **Church leaders are the strongest conduits of culture.**

The fastest way to change the culture of the church is to change the culture of the staff team, which sometimes means changing the actual people on the team. The church staff and volunteer leaders are the culture carriers of the church. In this particular merger we ran into the hard fact that the kind of person who can be on staff at a fast-growing, problem-solving church where new people are meeting Jesus is drastically different than the kind of person who is on staff at a church that has been plateaued or in decline for many years. They're inherently different kinds of people. While we believed the same things about Jesus and the Bible, we were still different kinds of people with different cultures. We initially took the approach to retain and train the staff members of this joining church. This approach unfortunately turned out to be too idealistic.

In the future we would transfer existing staff from established campuses to the new location and allow them to carry our culture with them. These tenured staff intuitively know how we make decisions, how we behave, how we talk, what we value, and how we treat and lead people because they've been living in it for so long.

• **The life-giving culture of the lead church culture needs to wash over the joining church culture.**

New people who "transfer" from the original or sending campus to the new campus (joining church) along with new people attending from the community need to outnumber the people who remained as a part of the joining church. The "original" people from the joining church can no longer be the majority or loudest voice. It's important to remember, however, that even a small minority can create a lot of pain and damage if they have a loud enough voice. These moments will come, and they will require clear and steady, kind but strong, directional leadership.

• **A big impediment to integration is spiritual atrophy.**

There is an often-overlooked spiritual component to a merger between a lead church and joining church. When a joining church has a history of being plateaued or in decline for a long period of time, a protection mindset sets in. This often occurs when a church moves into a "maintenance" phase of the church lifecycle and becomes insider focused. It starts making decisions based on who it is trying to keep rather than who it is trying to reach. On the surface this may come across as merely an issue of strategy, style, or preference. However, insider-focused churches actually experience spiritual atrophy that requires significant work, pain, and spiritual breakthrough to change.

> *When a church moves into a "maintenance" phase . . . it starts making decisions based on who it is try-ing to keep rather than who it is trying to reach.*

Marketplace Merger Landmines

Much business literature is devoted to the topic of mergers and acquisitions. One book cites four reasons for failure,[5] each of which applies to the church world:

- **Cost.** Paying too much. The financial costs may make the merger prohibitive. Be thorough in determining all costs and hidden liabilities.
- **DNA.** Poor strategic fit. Proceeding with a merger when the DNA match is less than 80 percent is a recipe for disaster.
- **Process.** Incomplete or haphazard due diligence. Be sure all issues are addressed before agreeing to a merger. See chapter 15 for a list of all the issues and especially chapter 11 for all the legal matters related to a merger.
- **Integration.** Effective integration is essential. In business parlance, it's much easier to do a deal than to implement it. As authors Galpin and Herndon say, "The key to successful integration is a systematic, thorough, and expedient process."[6] As in the business world, it's less likely to fail if it moves fairly quickly. "Today the businesses must be merged as quickly as possible—often within six to twelve months after the close."[7]

We agree with these cautions. In chapter 15 we'll describe twenty-five crucial issues to work through, any of which could lead to a failed church merger. Our surveys frequently point to culture clash as a common area of failure in church mergers.

Final Words about the Merger Minefield

Recognize and affirm the grieving process, and then love the people and lead the congregation with humility. Overcommunicate, over-meet and over-deliver. The more time together, the more opportunity to bond. Experience early and easy wins. It takes time and intentionality for the two congregations to move from "me and thee" to we.

Tom Bandy, a noted church consultant and author of several titles including *Church Mergers: A Guidebook for Missional Change*,[8] offers a great summary perspective: leaders should never ask the participating congregations to commit to a merger. They should ask faithful Christians to commit to a large, bolder, biblical vision. The merger is only one step in a multiyear plan to expand God's mission through the creation of a new organizational entity.

> *Never ask the participating congregations to commit to a merger. . . . ask faithful Christians to commit to a large, bolder, biblical vision.*

Notes

1. Tim Donelly, "How to Merge Corporate Cultures," *Inc*, May 9, 2011, https://tinyurl.com/vjjma9x.

2. William Bridges, *Managing Transitions: Making the Most of Change*, 2nd ed. (Cambridge, MA: Perseus, 2003), 3.

3. See William Bridges, *Transitions: Making Sense of Life's Changes, Revised 25th Anniversary Edition* (Cambridge, MA: Da Capo Lifelong Books, 2004), 117.

4. Paul Alexander, "5 Lessons I've Learned Leading through Church Mergers," *Paul Alexander Blog*, January 28, 2020, updated by the author for use in *Better Together*, https://tinyurl.com/sbltctc.

5. Timothy J. Galpin and Mark Herndon, *The Complete Guide to Mergers and Acquisitions* (San Francisco: Jossey-Bass, 2007), 2.

6. Galpin and Herndon, *Complete Guide*, 233.

7. Galpin and Herndon, *Complete Guide*, 5.

8. Tom Bandy and Page M. Brooks, *Church Mergers: A Guidebook for Missional Change* (Lanham, MD: Rowman and Littlefield International, 2016).

9

NAVIGATING PERSONNEL CHANGES

When a merger occurs, what happens to the pastor, any staff, the existing board, and the primary committees of the joining church? This is an essential issue—and an emotional one at that—for churches to explore as they talk and pray together about a potential merger.

Almost every church has someone on a payroll, even if only part time. The larger the church, the more paid staff to deal with in most cases. The most common roles to work through are that of pastor, secretary or equivalent, worship leader, youth worker, and custodian. Plus, every church has key lay leaders serving in official roles as well.

Frank Rondon is a good example of a positive transition in which two lead pastors remained together in one church. Rondon, as the joining church pastor, became the associate pastor.

The sequence began when Rondon's denomination assigned him to a church that was once thriving but had gone through some rough times under the previous pastor. Rondon could not reverse the decline or start a new growth momentum. The church even had to sell its building and become portable.

One day Rondon was chatting with a fellow Assemblies of God pastor whose church building was about ten minutes away. That man, who was seventy and thinking about retirement, said to Rondon, who was thirty-five, "I'm looking for a younger leader like you."

This initial conversation led to a merger in which Rondon's congregation of seventy-five to one hundred people, whose ages averaged about forty years old, joined Lowell Assembly of God in Tewksbury, Massachusetts, a congregation with attendance of about 125 and whose people averaged about sixty years old.

As if a divine confirmation occurred, two weeks after the merger, the facility Rondon's congregation had been renting was abruptly closed and demolished!

Even with the merger of two very different generations, Rondon's church didn't lose a single person due to the merger. To him this was another confirmation because of what he had read in business books about mergers. "They all would predict that our merger won't work. The absorbed organization will die." But it didn't. "We relied on the Holy Spirit, not a business book," he says. "Our merger caused everything to increase—attendance, conversions, community impact, and even openness to change among the people of the lead church."

Rondon came in as an associate pastor and remained in that role for two years, serving under the long-standing senior pastor. He preached occasionally, taught the adult Sunday school, and generally helped Lowell Assembly of God to transition to "new wineskins" in worship style and culture.

Rondon considered that the cost required for the merger "tested character and motives, humility, a kingdom mentality, and a long-term view of ministry," as he describes them. Not everything worked the way he thought it would, but overall, he realizes that "the work I put into the congregation before the merger will not go to waste," Rondon commented as he looked back on the merger at the two-year mark. "It takes a humble leader to see everything he has worked for be absorbed by the lead church, but the people I brought still look to me as one of their pastors, and the bottom line is that everything was gained for the kingdom of God." As of 2020, Rondon looked back and said, "I still believe the merger was the best thing that could have happened to us."

Senior Pastor Transitions

The most visible and delicate staff role to discuss in a merger transition is that of lead pastor. "What will happen to our pastor?" is also one of the first questions to address in the merger conversation. We see four possible pathways.

1. No Pastor at the Joining Church

Only 21 percent of churches going into a merger do so without a pastor in the joining church, according to our research (see Merger Fact 16). A good example is Chelsea Community Church, located in a suburb of Birmingham, Alabama. The church of almost three hundred people was growing and looking for larger facilities. One of its members had a friend who attended another church in town—one that no longer had a pastor and was thinking about shutting down after 102 years of ministry. Those two friends made appropriate introductions and soon Greg Davis, the pastor of Chelsea Community Church, was talking with two elders of the other church.

The conversations were very frank. "The community sees your church as a dead or dying duck," Davis told the men. "We need to completely rebirth it." This was painful for them to hear because they realized their congregation would lose its identity. Davis invited them to extend the conversation to the rest of their congregation: "You might not even like what we're doing," he said, observing that his congregation was mostly young and worshipped in a contemporary style, and the other church was mostly older people and worshipped in a more traditional style. "Why don't you shut down for a month, come worship with us, and see what you think?"

The struggling church did just that. At that point, Davis started meeting with their thirty-five people, sharing his heart and vision. "The message about Jesus will be the same, but the methods have to change. I don't want to merge, only two months later for us to be tearing out walls and for you to be upset." He made it clear that if they became part of Chelsea Community Church, they'd change this, remove that and continue to target young couples, not the church's older age group. "Our doctrine may be very similar but we're going to be a completely different church," he said.

The church agreed to everything he laid out. Likewise, the church's denomination, Church of God Anderson, was willing to release the facility to the interdenominational Chelsea Community Church. With a lot of volunteer work, the church facility experienced a complete facelift. "I've been doing church ministry for thirty years and have never seen unity like this," Davis says, "and the transformation has ignited a revival." Even some of the people who used to attend that church have come back. The week we interviewed him Chelsea Community Church had seen five hundred people in worship the previous Sunday.

As Davis had been looked for an additional staff person, who did he find but one of the previous pastors of that church! He was the final pastor at that church, someone who had tried to bring about change and it hadn't been received very well. He had left a year and a half before the merger officially occurred in March 2009. Now people from both congregations have received him well.

In the first year of the merger, four families left. One wanted a smaller church, one felt Chelsea's style was too casual, one didn't like something else about the new style, and one moved away. No one left specifically because of the merger. Indeed, the transition slogan, "putting a new face on history," has turned out to do just that. (In 2015 it was renamed The Connection Church.)

Merger Fact 16

Most Joining Churches Have a Pastor Who Stays

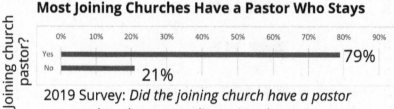

2019 Survey: *Did the joining church have a pastor when the merger discussions began?*

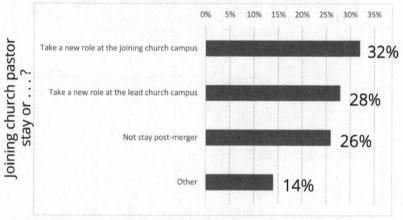

2019 Survey: *Did the pastor of the joining church stay or . . . ?*

2. Pastor Departs after Merger Is Approved

Sometimes no staff position is available with the lead church. Other times the joining pastor is retiring or desires a ministry or career change and is not interested in staying post-merger. Sometimes the joining pastor is financially supported in a new ministry endeavor by the lead church.

Merger Fact 17

For Senior Pastors of the Joining Church Who Don't Stay, the Median Severance Package Is 2–6 Months of Pay (and Likewise for Staff, It's Approximately 1 Month of Pay)

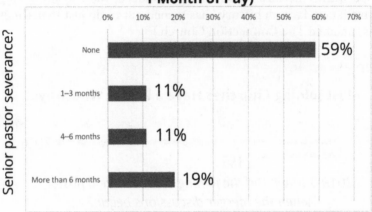

2019 Survey: *If the senior pastor of the joining church did not stay after the merger, what was the severance package for that senior pastor?*

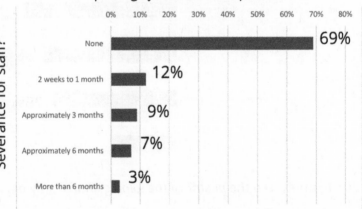

2019 Survey: *Please identify the financial aspects of any joining church staff who did not stay after the merger: What were the typical severance packages for terminated staff of the joining church?*

Regardless of the various reasons for not staying, the pastor's departure is a delicate situation that needs to be handled well. When a pastor decides not to remain, a joining congregation can feel a sense of rejection from its "beloved" pastor, and good will can turn sour toward the lead church. Resentment can also build toward the lead church if it does retain the joining church pastor. Departing pastors hold the key to shepherding their congregations with loving reassurance through this transition.

In all of these situations it is wise to offer a generous severance package and a happy farewell to the departing pastor. Merger Fact 17 offers guidelines. A good departure will help produce a better merger outcome for both congregations. (See the book *Next: Pastoral Succession That Works* for additional tips on smooth pastoral transitions.[1])

3. Pastors Become Co-Pastors

True co-pastoring rarely occurs and for good reason: they rarely succeed because it is hard for two heads to lead together. When a co-pastor merger does occur in a church merger, it is often part of a succession plan for one of the pastors. Most often co-pastorates tend to happen in smaller churches, compounding the financial problems the churches were facing as they went into the merger. Even if the finances were not problematic, we still do not recommend this option for mergers, and have not seen a healthy, growing model of co-pastors from merged churches. (We have seen the rare successful co-pastorate that was unrelated to a merger, however.)

It doesn't work, we suspect, because it's too hard for two different church cultures to come together under the umbrella of sharing the best of both worlds, arbitrated by two people who are trying to be equal with each other. As we've said across this book, merging is like dancing: one person needs to lead, and the other to follow.

4. Pastor Becomes Staff at the Lead Church

This is the most common option, even if it lasts only for a season, in order to allow the joining church's pastor to depart graciously, and it invites a smoother transition (see Merger Fact 16 on page 125). Such arrangements can be spelled out as part of the merger negotiations. For example, the lead church can say, "Both congregations will understand that you'll continue in your current role as the pastor up to the decision to merge, then we will reposition you somewhere else on our team or release you with a generous severance package."

Sometimes the merger arrangements envision more than a transitional role for the pastor from the joining church. In multisite mergers, the pastor of the joining church rarely assumes the campus pastor role; most are redeployed somewhere else on the staff team. The most common roles we hear about are associate pastor, pastoral-care pastor, small-groups pastor, adult ministries pastor, or missions pastor. The most important success factor is that it be a good fit for the person's strengths and ministry passions.

Gary Foran is an excellent example of a transition that proved to be a better fit than senior pastoring. His self-supporting Detroit church of about 130 people, including eight small groups, merged with a church of about three hundred. The lead church pastor had known Foran well enough before the merger to recognize that Foran had a passion for and strength in developing community through small groups—something that had been missing in the larger church.

"It was a match easily made," Foran told us. "I had offered to join their team working with small groups," he says. "I loved building small groups and the other pastor—a friend—was someone I could follow." Foran then stayed on staff of the larger church for the next twelve years, the first nine of which were helping people connect and grow deeper through small-group community. "It was more successful than even we imagined," he says.

It is not easy to give up the authority and privileges of the senior pastor position and submit and adjust to a lesser role in the lead church. It means you are no longer the primary preacher or the one in charge. Failure to navigate this transition well can result in strained relationships and even a premature forced departure.

Here is some advice that Jim Tomberlin often gives to senior pastors who are transitioning into a new role at the lead church, written as an email that he's used:

Dear [NAME OF PASTOR],

You have successfully navigated a very important milestone in your journey and transitioned [NAME OF JOINING CHURCH] into its next chapter. You finished well and are well positioned for the future. Yea God!

Here are a few suggestions on how to navigate the next few months in your new role in the merged church:

- Look forward, not backward.
- Keep a low profile with your former congregation, allowing them to bond with other spiritual leaders in the church.

- Be a peace ambassador. Don't encourage dissention by allowing yourself to be a "dump bucket" for disgruntled individuals from your former congregation
- Be a servant—ask often of your new church, "How can I serve you?"
- Be a team player—make yourself invaluable.
- Live within your budget, don't be late to staff and church meetings, maintain expected office hours, and otherwise work hard to fit into the culture of the church you've joined.
- Don't consistently be the first person to offer an opinion.
- Stay positive and take the high road.
- Lean into your gifts and passions.
- Maintain good friendships both outside and inside the church.
- Call me (or a colleague who has no dog in the fight) when you need to unload or process.

I am proud of you and excited for your new chapter. The adventure continues. God is good. Keep in touch.

Board Member Transitions

Every church has boards and committees or councils of lay leaders. They have various names according to denominational polity and tradition—elders, deacons, trustees, and so on. Often, they are the most influential stakeholders who will make a big difference in the ultimate outcome of a merger.

What happens to them in a merger? Usually the boards and committees of the joining church are dissolved after the merger is approved. Often, post-merger, some of these lay leaders from the dissolved boards and committees are invited to join the board or committees of the lead church. As mentioned in chapter 11 on the legal aspects of a merger, here's our general advice: don't immediately add former board members from the joining church to the lead church board. It is better to let former board members serve on a post-merger transition team that reports monthly to the board. See also Merger Fact 18.

Don't immediately add former board members from the joining church to the lead church board. It is better to let former board members serve on a post-merger transition team that reports monthly to the board.

Their expertise, maturity, and support demonstrated during and after the merger process will reveal their qualifications to serve on the board.

> *Their wisdom, relational connections, . . . and other . . . skills are often some of the most significant benefits that the joining church brings into the merger.*

Their wisdom, relational connections in the community, and other leadership skills are often some of the most significant benefits that the joining church brings into the merger. But take some time before appointing someone to the board you don't know really well. This is the admonition of the apostle Paul to young pastor Timothy: "Don't appoint people to church leadership positions too hastily" (1 Tim 5:22 MSG).

Merger Fact 18

Two-Thirds of Joining Churches Are Represented on the Board After the Merger

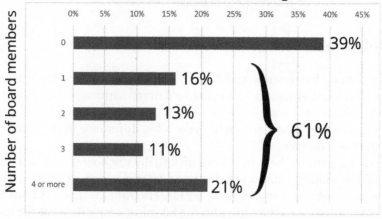

2019 Survey: *As part of the merge, how many of the joining church's board/council/elders integrated into board roles of the lead church?*

Staff Member Transitions

What about the other staff members in the joining church? They are often the ones most fearful of a merger and for good reason—their job security is at risk and their future is the most uncertain. Here's some general advice for staff transitions:

- Avoid promises such as "We'll keep all staff and board members." Numerous people told us that they wish they hadn't made the promise because if staff didn't fit the new culture of the merged church, it was more difficult to help them move to a different place of employment. Promises like that also invite people to take sides: "You didn't keep your promise" or "That's yet another change and loss for us."

A better approach is to put in writing that the merger process offers no guarantees or promises of ongoing employment. Something like, "Staff of the joining church may continue to serve in the same capacity or could be redeployed to another area based on need, compatibility, and skill set. Staff not retained or who desire not to remain will be offered appropriate severance."

- Retain any staff that are genuinely needed and can be afforded.
- Extend an invitation to all staff to apply for any open staff positions.
- Offer generous severance packages relative to how long they've served.
- Be gentle, affirming, and clear.

In addition to the pastor, board, and staff, the other stakeholders in the church also need guidance and coaching through each phase of a merger. They include the lay leaders, volunteers, regular attendees, and those members who participate infrequently or not at all. Each has different needs and issues to be thoughtfully addressed. Each requires a different level of information, communicated in various ways at different times through different channels and formats. Each one will have different access points to the decision-making process, but all will require sensitivity and help in emotionally processing the decision and making the transition.

Notes

1. William Vanderbloemen and Warren Bird, *Next: Pastoral Succession That Works*, expanded and updated edition (Grand Rapids, MI: Baker, 2020).

10

CHURCH MERGERS VS. MARKETPLACE MERGERS

Businesses merge in order to experience a net gain in effectiveness, market share, influence, and financial gain—especially the last. Should any of those values be the motivations for church mergers?

Dollars vs. Souls

One marketplace book on corporate mergers tells the story of two banks in discussion about a merger.[1] One of the bank presidents, who was the point person for the negotiations, was concerned that his employees would be treated fairly should the merger take place, but those overseeing the merger didn't care about the people element. The human side of the merger, he was told, should not be a consideration beyond one person: "The only position you should consider is that of the owner," a member of the board of directors instructed him.

By contrast, Will Marotti's merger story in the previous chapter was all about people development in the two mergers he oversaw! "The whole point of a merger is to develop people as disciples of Christ and to make it possible for more people to experience the love of Christ," Mariotti told us. Although *corporate* takeovers, mergers, and acquisitions are fundamentally motivated by a financial bottom line, the ultimate goal of a *church* merger is lives transformed by Jesus Christ.

> Although corporate takeovers, mergers, and acquisitions are fundamentally motivated by a financial bottom line, the ultimate goal of a church merger is lives transformed by Jesus Christ.

Even with such a stark contrast, it may still be helpful to compare church mergers and business mergers. As table 10.1 demonstrates, church and marketplace mergers must deal with the same issues, though the goals, attitudes, and outcomes may differ.

Table 10.1

Church Mergers Are Different from Marketplace Mergers

Factor	*Marketplace*	*Church*
Prompted by a crisis	Sometimes	Often
Initiated by the smaller organization	Rarely	Usually
Motivated by desire for financial gain	Always	Rarely
Success measured primarily in economic terms	Always	Rarely
Proposed as a win for both organizations	Sometimes	Usually
Involves a vote by the shareholders (business) or membership (church)	Rarely	Usually
Involves a vote by the employees or staff	Rarely	Usually
Involves a vote by the governing board	Always	Always
Involves outside consultant(s)	Usually	Sometimes
Involves asset transfers	Always	Always
Involves personnel changes	Always	Usually
Requires legal and IRS changes	Always	Usually
Involves name change for smaller organization	Usually	Usually
"New normal" requires three or more years to develop completely and achieve full buy-in	Usually	Usually

Note: Response range: never, rarely, sometimes, usually, always

The Urge to Merge

Business mergers tend to be motivated by an opportunity for financial gain and market share. Church mergers tend to be prompted by a crisis more so than are business mergers.

> Church mergers tend to be prompted by a crisis more so than are business mergers.

Perhaps the membership in the prospective joining church has dwindled to the point that the church can no longer pay even the basic bills for upkeep on its building. Maybe a long-term pastor has retired, and the church can't find someone else who can lead it forward. Maybe a flood, aging roof, or new law requiring fire sprinklers has triggered a large-scale rebuilding effort, causing a struggling church to question whether it has the energy, focus, or resources to tackle a challenge that large. In cases like these—and unlike business mergers—the merger is usually initiated by the smaller organization asking to unite with a larger, healthier congregation. It often involves a major financial challenge already existing in the smaller organization, such as serious debt or threats of foreclosure.

Other mergers are prompted by a stable or stuck church that is dissatisfied with the status quo and wants to break out of the comfortable but ineffective state of affairs. The one exception is the marriage merger. This usually involves a strategic partnership between two strong or stable churches. In such cases, the trigger is less of a crisis or dissatisfaction and more of a dream that the two working together can be more effective than each working alone. For marriage mergers, either party initiates the discussion. Financial issues are typically only a minimal factor in such mergers.

In all types of church mergers, the idea is usually proposed as a win for both organizations. It's a win for the kingdom of God, for the witness to the gospel in that particular community, and for the ongoing vision of each local church.

Voting Matters

In most business mergers, voting occurs only in the boardroom. The staff and stockholders rarely participate in the decision to merge with another company. Sometimes they don't even know about it until everything has been decided.

By contrast, churches usually involve many people, and at various levels, in deciding to merge.

When it comes to congregational approval in a church the two most important questions are:

1. Is a congregational vote required for a merger, dissolution, or new senior pastor?
2. If a congregational vote is needed what percentage of the members is required for approval? Is it a simple majority (51 percent), a two-thirds majority (66 percent), a super majority (75 percent) or higher? Success is often evaluated by meeting or exceeding the required percentage. (See Merger Fact 19 and Merger Fact 20 for voting levels reflected by churches in our latest survey.)

Church polity differs in terms of who is allowed to vote on a decision about a merger, but many churches initiate a vote, or at least a poll, even when not legally required by their bylaws. Doing so creates opportunity for people to feel like their voice was heard and therefore will create more ownership for the outcome.

The vote or poll often becomes a point of remembrance when the adjustments feel painful, especially for the smaller church. For example, you might hear, "Two years ago, after much discussion and prayer, ABC Church voted by 84 percent to join us. You have made many adjustments, some perhaps very uncomfortable. Along the way you may have asked if it's worth it, and today we want to again thank and honor all who came from ABC Church."

When it comes to voting on a church merger, consultant Tom Bandy recommends, "Always vote for a vision, never vote for a merger. Merger is just one step toward a larger, bolder, ten-year plan to grow God's mission in the community."[2]

Use of a Consultant

One of Warren's friends, a corporate executive with considerable experience in business mergers, critiqued an early draft of this chapter. He observed that many churches may have business leaders with backgrounds like his. "They could be an asset in the process—or a liability to a potential church merger depending on their previous experiences," he warns. In some cases, they could serve as an in-house consultant, but sometimes that won't help. Another option is to bring in a specialist.

Merger Fact 19

Joining Churches that Vote, Overwhelmingly Approve the Merger

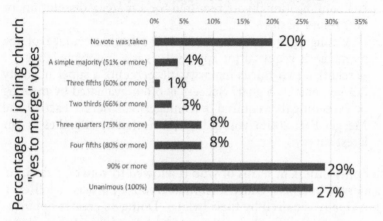

2019 Survey: *At the joining church, what percentage of "yes to merge" votes actually happened?*

Merger Fact 20

Lead Churches that Vote Almost Unanimously Approve the Merger

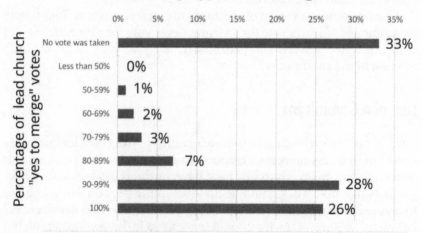

2019 Survey: *At the lead church, what was the percentage of "yes to merge" votes?*

Though contracting the services of an outside consultant is common in the business world, the use of consultants is slowly being embraced in the church world.

There are many potential benefits of a church merger, but there are also many landmines to step on and potholes to fall into on the merger journey. Most church mergers need a facilitator that both congregations can trust and who knows how to facilitate the delicate conversations that need to occur for a successful merger outcome.

A third-party facilitator can be beneficial to the delicate negotiation tensions between two congregations. The facilitator can smooth the way by bringing experienced objective advice that helps guide the merger process. The skillful facilitator helps both congregations to see the realities that the congregations can't or won't see. This person can name the "elephant in the room" that both parties are reluctant to address out of courtesy or fear. The facilitator often becomes the mediator that helps both parties land on resolutions to sticky merger issues. Though mergers have the potential of being a huge win for local churches, there are many potholes to step on along the pathway. It is highly recommended to go down the merger pathway with a skilled guide who knows the terrain.

According to merger specialist David Raymond, "Almost every successful merger has found it essential to use an outside coach or consultant to facilitate the process of merger. An outside party brings both fairness and objectivity to the process, and an experienced consultant can help you avoid mistakes and carry out all of the necessary steps in a timely way."[3] Consultant Tony Morgan told us, "An outside consultant will help the two churches focus on the critical decisions that will determine whether or not the merger will work. Because we don't have any history or relational connections, we can raise the sensitive topics that need to be addressed, particularly around personnel decisions and ministry alignment, and guide both churches through the merger process."

Personnel Changes

Staff transitions are undoubtedly the stickiest issue associated with a merger, in both the church and business worlds. In churches a change in staff is a delicate issue because of the relationship between staff and congregation and also because Christians want to treat outgoing staff with honor, compassion, and when possible, generosity.

If the merger involves a smaller single-staff church folding into a larger church, what will happen to that staff member, who is typically a pastor? Will Marotti's situation of the pastor wanting to go plant another church is happening more and more. But even more often, the pastor is helped to make a transition out of both organizations, such as into retirement or to serve another church in another city. If the smaller church pastor is brought onto the staff with the larger church, it is usually into a new role, not as the senior pastor or co-pastor, as we explained in chapter 9 on navigating personnel changes (which also addresses the issue of paid and volunteer leaders). Rarely does the smaller church pastor stay on in the role of campus pastor if the merger has a multisite outcome.

As Merger Fact 16 observes (page 125), the majority of joining-church pastors continued post-merger in a staff role but very few as the lead pastor, co-pastor, or campus pastor. The one exception is the marriage approach to merger, when the joining church pastor might become the senior associate pastor and eventual successor to the lead pastor. Typically, the options for the joining church staff are to continue in their current role, accept another role, or be released with a severance package.

Name Change

The vast majority of church mergers involve a name change, as Merger Fact 21 points out. The same pattern happens in business mergers. Usually the smaller organization or church takes on the name of the lead company or church. Though the merger itself may occur quickly, the new normal in the merged church usually takes one to three to years to develop and achieve full buy-in by the group that has had to change the most.

Like all business mergers, any formal church merger also requires legal and Internal Revenue Service (IRS) changes. Mergers also involve asset transfers—from equipment to properties and buildings. These steps always require a certain degree of financial cost, even if the labor is donated, such as by an attorney or CPA in one and sometimes both of the congregations. (Church lawyer David Middlebrook explains the legal issues and merger options in Chapter 11.)

Merger Fact 21

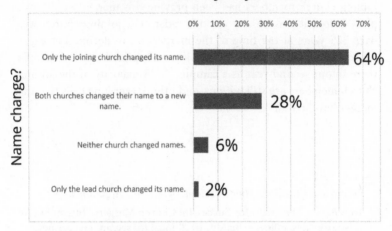

The Joining Church Changes
Its Name in the Majority of Cases

Name change?

- Only the joining church changed its name. — 64%
- Both churches changed their name to a new name. — 28%
- Neither church changed names. — 6%
- Only the lead church changed its name. — 2%

2019 Survey: *Which best describes a name change associated with the merger?*

The Difference Maker

The *attitude* of the lead church makes all the difference in the success of the merger. What you do not want is a report like this, taken from our 2019 survey, of a joining church of 50 people that wanted to start a new chapter and found a church of 250 to merge with:

> Most people in the joining church felt that the lead church should have invested more effort in welcoming, connecting with them, and helping them find meaningful places of service. To most, it felt more like a corporate buyout, where the most valuable assets were welcomed and utilized, while the less valuable were sold off or discarded. The handful of families who have stayed are solidly a part of the lead church, but they represent only about 25% of the total joining church at the time of the merger.

The former pastor quoted above clearly feels that the merger would have been more of a "win" if it felt less like a corporate acquisition and more like a ministry investment. By contrast, here's a survey comment about a church of twenty-five that merged with a megachurch in 2017, becoming its third campus. It reflects the kind of attitude that can lead to greater engagement and fruitfulness by the joining church members:

> In business terms, the merger was an acquisition. . . . Some of the joining church members had been praying this merger would take place before it was on any pastor's radar. The joining church was over 225 years at the time of the merger . . . in decline but eager for revitalization. . . . To everyone's joy, we baptized fifty-two people there in our second year as a campus. . . . A majority of the joining church members are still with us, and I think everyone feels that the merger has thrived.

Notes

1. Buono and Bowditch, *Human Side of Mergers and Acquisitions*, xiv.
2. Tom Bandy, "The Keys for Successful Church Mergers," https://www.ecfvp.org/files/uploads/Bandy_10_things_to_see_in_merger.pdf.
3. David Raymond, "Working with a Collaboration Coach," *Church Collaboration*, www.churchcollaboration.com/Coach.html.

11

WHEN TWO BECOME ONE: LEGAL AND FINANCIAL ASPECTS OF A CHURCH MERGER

Do you need an attorney for a merger, and if so when? The initial material in this chapter (and careful review of the final wording) came from our friend David Middlebrook, a Christian attorney whose firm, The Church Lawyers (thechurchlawyers.com), has helped many churches through mergers. Specifically, their law practice focuses exclusively on religious nonprofit organizations. Cofounder David Middlebrook also coauthored *Nonprofit Law for Religious Organizations: Essential Questions and Answers,*[1] which provides guidance, direction, and clarification of legal and tax laws affecting churches and other religious organizations.

Middlebrook's first response to our request to help with this chapter was, "Put the term *merger* in quotes." Why? "Although the term *merger* is frequently used, it is just one of several legal options available when two churches desire to become one."

In most church mergers, one of the churches will be legally "dissolved." This dissolution is a harsh reality but when a church merges with another church it is not the end of their story. It is the end of this chapter in their story—and the beginning of a new chapter. This continuity is one of the reasons legal counsel is needed for both churches.

Here, according to Middlebrook, are just a few of the legal questions that should be asked:

- Who has the legal authority to approve the merger?
- What constitutes "approval" by the respective church board or congregation?
- Who owns what, and how does the lead church know what it's receiving from the joining church?
- Is there a particular order of events that should be followed?
- What rights do the people have who funded the purchase of the joining church's land, facilities, and other assets, if any?
- What are the obligations of governing boards of the lead church and the joining church? And for how long?
- How should moral (not necessarily legal) obligations be handled? (E.g., the longtime church secretary of the joining church was verbally promised by its senior pastor that the church would "take care" of her after the merger is completed.)
- Does the joining church need title insurance? (E.g., a local business appears after a merger and says, "I wasn't told about the merger, and we've been using the church parking lot for years per our agreement with the senior pastor; I'm finding a lawyer!")

In short, how can a church merger be done legally, morally, and ethically?

> In short, how can a church merger be done legally, morally, and ethically?

Generally, the moral and ethical answers are found in the Bible, while legal direction is found in the governance documents for both churches (i.e., articles of incorporation and bylaws) and applicable state and federal laws.

Legal issues arise in the course of a church "merger." In most church mergers one of the churches will be legally "dissolved." We strongly urge that experienced church legal counsel is hired to walk them through the intricacies of the process. Fees may vary depending on the firm, but generally, it is a small price to pay to ensure that all the legal bases are covered, and the merger is not subject to being criticized or possibly undone.

Three Common Legal Ways to Merge

Although mergers and acquisitions can take many forms, Middlebrook suggests there are three standard options, and most mergers are changes in control rather than an actual statutory merger. "If there's a debt or a mortgage on the property, or if it will be purchased rather than gifted, then the second and third options are the preferred approach," according to Middlebrook.

Option One: Statutory Merger or Consolidation (Least Preferred)

Legally speaking, a statutory *merger* in the United States is a formal and legal procedure done under the relevant state's regulatory requirements for a nonprofit. Generally, articles of merger are filed with the secretary of state and other statutory requirements are fulfilled. The process involves a merging entity (the joining church) and a surviving entity (the lead church). In a true statutory merger, the surviving entity assumes all the assets and both known and unknown liabilities of the merging entity.

In a statutory *consolidation*, two entities come together to form a third new entity. You can imagine a consolidation is even more complex and expensive than a statutory merger due to the extra drafting and transfers of real and personal property.

- *Pro:* Sometimes, it may be the only available method for churches to come together, such as if the joining church has an existing loan that may not otherwise be able to be paid off or assumed, or the decision-makers are simply unable to agree to other approaches. Also, this option can sometimes avoid triggering the existence of a "new" property owner being identified by the municipality and thereby preserve previous code requirements, and it can avoid new code requirements that apply to new property owners (think a large-scale fire sprinkler system).
- *Con:* In this approach, the merger works much like a marriage, and the lead church must assume all liabilities, even those that are unknown. Further, this approach can take more time than the other options to accomplish due to, for example, statutory requirements. Finally, attorney fees can be higher due in part to complications associated with working through third parties.

Option Two: Asset Purchase and Dissolution (Better)

This option is a traditional real estate purchase and sale with the selling entity dissolving after the transfer. One entity (the lead church) purchases all the assets of another entity (the joining church). By purchasing the assets, the goal is for the lead church to provide the joining church with enough funding to pay off its mortgage and other liabilities. After all real and personal property assets have been purchased, the joining church is then formally dissolved by following the relevant state's nonprofit dissolution process.

This option may be appropriate in situations where outstanding debts or liabilities must be addressed at or after closing before the property can be transferred and the joining church can be dissolved.

- *Pro:* Legally speaking, this approach is often a better option than a statutory merger. It allows the joining church to pay off its known liabilities while protecting the lead church from assuming unknown liabilities, such as later discovering a children's minister had an unreported inappropriate relationship with a youth member ten years ago and which the current leaders of the joining church had forgotten or did not know about.
- *Con:* Many churches do not like this idea simply because the process seems "too corporate." Also, the lead church, as the purchasing corporation, must come up with adequate cash to purchase all of the assets of the joining church unless the joining church sells the property for something akin to a symbolic $1 price.

Option Three: Donation and Dissolution (Preferred) in Most Circumstances

In this option, one entity (the joining church) donates all its assets to another entity (the lead church). There is no purchase of assets involved, but rather a gift of real and personal property assets. The lead church accepts all of the assets of the joining church just as it would accept a donation from any other donor. The donating corporation then formally dissolves by filing articles of dissolution with the appropriate secretary of state or a similar document with the correct state office. This process works because the IRS allows a nonprofit organization to make donations to another tax-exempt organization with a generally aligned mission and purpose at any time and mandates such an act on the dissolution of a nonprofit corporation.

As with option two, the joining church is dissolved after all assets have been transferred by gift agreements and by following the relevant state's nonprofit dissolution process.

- *Pro:* This is frequently the cleanest, quickest, most straightforward, and least expensive method of combining two organizations. Little if any liability is involved because only the assets of the joining church are transferred. Liabilities, whether known or unknown, are not automatically transferred. Typically, all that is needed is a vote of the respective churches' memberships (if such voting rights exist) or corporate resolutions to be signed by the individual boards of directors and the appropriate real and personal property gift agreements.
- *Con:* This is not an option if an existing mortgage or other loan is being assumed (unless they are paid off or assumed before closing), it has to be a gift from the joining church to the lead church. Also, there can be a temptation by the lead church to avoid considering requirements a lender would demand to protect their collateral, like a formal inspection, environmental inspection, and title insurance.

Table 11.1

Summary of Legal Options for Merging

Option	Name	Description	Pros	Cons
#1	Statutory Merger or Consolidation (*Least Preferred in Most Circumstances*)	Both churches come together to form a new third legal entity.	Helpful if there is a debt-prohibitor to the merger. Preserves grand-fathered code requirements.	Lead church assumes all known and unknown liabilities. Most legally complicated. Higher legal fees due to complicated legalities.
#2	Asset Purchase and Dissolution (*Better*)	Lead church covers all debt and liabilities	Protects lead church from assuming known and	Could be cost-prohibitive to the lead church.

		through purchase of joining church real estate.	unknown liabilities.	
		Joining church pays off all debts and liabilities with the purchase money from lead church, then transfers all assets to lead church and files for dissolution.		
#3	Donation and Dissolution (*Preferred in Most Circumstances*)	Joining church donates all assets to lead church, then files for dissolution.	Protects lead church from assuming known and unknown liabilities. Least complicated and least expensive.	Temptation by lead church to not complete due diligence or obtain title insurance.

Additional Issues to Consider

Middlebrook also suggests considering the importance of dealing with five other matters, advising that experienced church legal counsel should be involved:

- **Documents:** Prior to any merger option, a study should be made of each church's documents, but particularly the joining church's corporate documents and real property deed(s), to determine how they govern the dissolution process and whether they contain any potentially conflicting statements. Do they identify who has the power to authorize the transfer and dissolution? Are there any reversionary clauses in the real property deed(s) that might prevent the real property or other assets of the joining church from being transferred? Is the consent of a third party, denomination, or other organization required for approval?

Depending on what is found in the documents, the joining church may need to amend its corporate documents and/or remove deed restrictions before it can merge, sell, or donate its assets.

- **Employees:** What will happen to the employees of the joining church? In most cases, all employees who will remain employees of the surviving entity will need to sign employment agreements with the lead church. Any employees who will have access to children may need to have new background checks run and other verifications made. Considerations about healthcare and retirement benefits will also need to be addressed in addition to other human resource matters.
- **Real property:** All land, buildings, and similar physical assets need to be identified and included in the merger. It is amazing how many churches have all but forgotten unused acreage that someone gave the church long ago for the church's youth group to use for camping.

If a church is part of a denomination, it may need to seek denominational approval and determine whether the church property is owned by the denomination before proceeding.

> If a church is part of a denomination, it may need to seek denominational approval and determine whether the church property is owned by the denomination before proceeding.

If the joining church was leasing its space, someone will need to contact the landlord to inquire as to whether or not the landlord would be willing to assign the lease to someone else or renegotiate with the lead church—if indeed the lead church wants to continue to use that space as opposed to strictly purchasing or accepting the donated assets.

If the lead church does not want to continue using the leased space, the remaining term of the lease should be addressed. Commercial landlords are usually upset and sometimes litigious about their tenants skipping lease years before a lease is scheduled to finish. If a pastor or trustee of the joining church signed a personal guarantee on that lease, the landlord could potentially come against them personally for the amounts of any outstanding rent payments owed for the remainder of the contracted lease term.

- **Personal property:** The larger issues regarding personal property must be addressed. Any items that are currently financed or under a lease, such as copy machines, will need to be paid off, returned to the vendor, or assigned (if possible) to the lead church. Personal property that is titled, such as vans or trailers, will need to be collected and transferred over to the lead church. The joining church will need to appoint one or more individuals to go through all of the joining church's major assets to take an inventory. The lead church will need such an inventory of major assets so it can be aware of exactly what it is obtaining and ensure that those valuable items are specifically accounted for and documented as being transferred.
- **Restricted gifts:** Restricted gifts made over the years to the joining church will also have to be analyzed to ensure the restrictions can be fulfilled by the lead church or else procedures for obtaining donor consent to remove the restriction(s) can be followed. For example, what happens to a financial endowment? Generally, these types of funds cannot be assumed by the lead church without written permission from all of the donors who contributed to such a fund. Does the joining church have all of its records? In some cases, gifts made to the joining church may revert back to the donor or another heir if the gift is not treated in accordance with specific requirements that may have been placed on the initial gift by the donor. It is critical to communicate with donors so that gifts to the church can find a new home that is suitable to the donor, and that nothing is lost in the transition.

Dollars Involved in a Merger

Legal fees can vary widely based on the complexity of the matter and the number of legal issues that need to be resolved. Middlebrook says he is aware of recent "uncomplicated" mergers handled by his law firm that have cost as little as $5,000 in legal fees (including drafting gift documents, filing fees to dissolve the joining church, and reviewing title insurance policies). "When there are major factual or legal complications associated with a church merger, then the legal costs can be as much as $50,000," Middlebrook says. Significant complications can include dissension among the members of the joining church, with some of the opposing members feeling so strongly against the merger that they intentionally wreak havoc for those trying to facilitate the transaction. Complications can include situations involving the transfer of significant real estate or large sums of money. Other complicating factors are when the joining church has substantial debt that must be transferred per the requirements of the lender, or when the joining church has a large number of restricted gifts that must be appropriately assigned and possibly returned to the original donors.

Predictably, merger costs vary by church size, as Merger Fact 22 illustrates. Categories for expenses during the merger and subsequent twelve months included debt payment, facility renovations including new technology and equipment, attorney and legal fees, mortgage or rent, honoring existing commitments such as monthly support for a missionary, severance for staff or supported missionaries, publicity and branding (signage, stationery, website, etc.), and ongoing staff salaries. More than one church reported something like, "It cost very little because the merging church had some assets" or "The only costs were for staff because the joining church had sufficient assets to cover their remaining obligations."

Merger Fact 22

A Merger Costs $112,500 (Median) for One-Time Plus First-Year Expenses

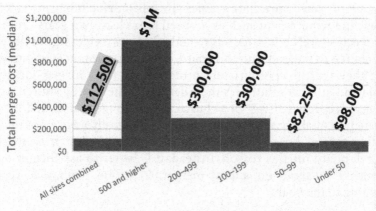

Joining church attendance at time of the merger

2019 Survey: *How much did the merger cost? Please give the grand total for one-time and first-year-only costs.*

If 2 percent of United States Protestant congregations (six thousand–plus) merge annually, as research has indicated, it is easy to understand the economic significance and the spiritual stakes involved in two churches merging well. Many church mergers involve plateaued or declining church congregations who will now be utilized for kingdom growth.

Avoiding a Real Estate Scramble

In chapter 3 we warned against the motive of real estate greed or "steeple-jacking." Mergers involve finances, and sometimes property needs to be sold. However, deception—including the appearance of deception—should never be a part of a merger plan. Although every lead church, post-merger, needs to have the freedom to manage its assets to fulfill its mission and be good stewards of its resources, it needs to be forthright in its intentions concerning inherited facilities. Even when the lead church genuinely intends to keep inherited facilities, the financial realities may dictate otherwise. Remember, the primary work of the church is making disciples of Jesus, not collecting and maintaining buildings.

> The primary work of the church is making disciples of Jesus, not collecting and maintaining buildings.

One simple way to preclude a real estate misunderstanding is to include a timeline requirement such as "not sell for at least two years." Another approach—rarely advisable—is to add one or two elders from the joining church to the lead church's board, for the first year at least, knowing that they will be appropriately protective of their former facility. A problem with this solution is the elders from the joining church would serve as "representatives" of a church that no longer exists, and it could create potential division in the board. We generally advise not initially adding former board members from the joining church to the lead church board for this reason. Instead, it is better to ask former board members to serve on a post-merger transition team that reports monthly to the board.

Escape Clauses and Joint Ventures

In an era of prenuptial agreements, let's-live-together-before-we-marry arrangements and no-fault divorce, should there be a legal escape clause for churches entering into a merger? Should churches do a formal, legal joint venture before actually merging? We sometimes have requests to do premerger joint ventures with an escape clause that allows for the possibility of a merger not occurring. We advise against it in all but a few cases. Also remember that after a church legally dissolves to accomplish a merger, it no longer exists. The joining church no longer exists for the property to revert back to. That's why, as Merger Fact 23 points out, very few mergers have "unmerged."

Merger Fact 23

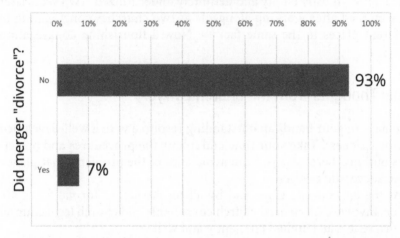

93% of Mergers in Our Study Have Not Been Undone

2019 Survey: *Has your church been part of a merger that "divorced" (that is, "unmerged")?*

Instead of a trial run, go more slowly, give it time, address the hard questions, do the due diligence, and build more trust and unity of vision. Although a formal, legal joint venture is possible, and attorneys will be willing to draft them, it is inviting unnecessary legal fees to memorialize a situation short of an actual merger, which will have legal costs. Instead, develop a plan, maybe including a memo of understanding, but you do not need a new legal entity simply to start talking and cooperating, beginning to worship together, and otherwise following a process that could lead to a merger.

The very day after we started this section on an escape clause, a church leader asked Jim about the wisdom of a joint venture of his church of two hundred with a smaller congregation of 120. They were thinking about merging but both churches had hesitations. As one way to investigate the possibility of merging in the future, they were considering sharing the same facility as two separate congregations. Jim affirmed the wisdom of meeting their immediate needs by sharing an affordable facility that allows them the opportunity to explore their compatibility and the merger possibility. The lead church would have a place to meet and the joining church would have some needed income to continue.

That's exactly what happened elsewhere when North Maine Community Church rented the gym from Northwest Baptist Fellowship in Chicago. North Maine had outgrown its facility in nearby Des Plaines. Northwest Baptist was a historic church, founded in 1858, with beautiful facilities, mostly empty and definitely underutilized. Two years later they merged after working alongside as two churches congregating in different places in the same facility. Now a flourishing congregation exists.

Final Thoughts from the Church Lawyers

You have in your hands an outstanding resource with a well-developed merger process. Take your time and follow the procedures and principles outlined here, and you can avoid a lot of the problems that plague an unsuccessful merger.

At the appropriate time, and by all means before formal votes are taken, involve experienced church consultants and church legal counsel to ensure it is all handled efficiently and well.

Communicate with your local city, town, or municipality, so that you avoid zoning and code-compliance and permitting issues; we have seen situations where a property owner changes, and it triggers some dramatic code-compliance issues.

Resist the temptation to avoid title insurance. Also consider getting an environmental study, especially if there are multiple noncontiguous parcels of land involved. The land donated to the joining church twelve years ago can be a real problem if it has turned into a mechanical-fluids dump over time.

Lastly, church mergers include legal issues, but merging is a fundamentally spiritual endeavor with legal consequences. Cover your plans in prayer and involve experienced church merger consultants and church legal counsel.

P.S. What Documents Should the Joining Church Preserve?

What records might be retained from the joining church after the merger? Here are some suggestions adapted from *Ending with Hope*:[2]

1. Articles of incorporation, constitution, and bylaws
2. Membership records of baptisms, marriages, confirmations, funerals, and other official acts
3. Minutes of governing board meetings and full congregational meetings pertaining to the merger
4. Property papers, titles, and deeds
5. All insurance policies for the twenty-four months preceding the merger
6. The most recent financial audit reports, if any
7. The most recent statistics as reported to the judicatory office
8. Printed histories created for church anniversaries or other significant events
9. Photographs or other visual and audio records of significant points in the church's history, such as its founding and merger
10. Church cemetery records

Notes

1. Bruce R. Hopkins and David Middlebrook, *Nonprofit Law for Religious Organizations: Essential Questions & Answers* (Hoboken, NJ: John Wiley & Sons, 2008).
2. Gaede, ed., *Ending with Hope*, adapted from the chapter by Paul Daniels titled "Congregational Records and Artifacts," 153.

PART III

IS A CHURCH MERGER IN YOUR FUTURE?

12

IS YOUR CHURCH LEADERSHIP MERGER FRIENDLY?

What kind of leader does a merger need? What specific qualities enable a leader to successfully navigate a church merger?

The oft-quoted phrase "everything rises or falls on leadership" is certainly appropriate for church mergers. Successful church mergers do not happen without effective leadership. Even though no two church mergers are alike, we find certain common qualities in the type of leader required to skillfully lead churches down the merger pathway.

All great leaders do three things. They define reality: "Where are we now?" They cast a vision for the future: "This is where we want to go!" And they chart the course: "This is the way to the future; follow me."

> All great leaders do three things. They define reality. They cast a vision for the future. And they chart the course.

Those who successfully lead churches through a merger tend to be winsome individuals who are kingdom minded, mission-driven, strategic-thinking, get-it-done individuals. They are able to rise above their specific circumstances and help others see the bigger picture of possibility. They are strong leaders but not overbearing. They know how to motivate people and build teams. They are bold but gracious. They exude confidence without being arrogant. They are able to keep a calm head in the midst of chaos. They are tough skinned enough to endure the criticisms, but tenderhearted enough to love the people regardless. They not only lead the people but genuinely love them through the process.

Lyle Schaller, a top-selling United Methodist author who was once acclaimed as America's leading church consultant,[1] describes the kind of a leader a church merger needs as a "transformational leader." Writing about church mergers he observes,

> The critical component is a minister who is an effective transformational leader and possesses the skills, including people skills, necessary to create a new worshiping community with a new congregational culture, a strong future orientation, a new set of operational goals, a new sense of unity, and a new approach to winning a new generation of members. . . . The most successful mergers are not a product of a manual on how to unite two or three congregations, but rather are the creation of a transformational leader.[2]

Transformational Leaders Show Humility

A great example of a transformational leader who demonstrates humility is Mark Jobe, pastor of New Life Community Church in downtown Chicago and the president of Moody Bible Institute. In 2008, a Lutheran church that had existed for 114 years was reborn by merging with New Life. The church had been struggling and declining since the 1990s and eventually the congregation and the sponsoring denomination agreed it was time to close the church. The touching story unfolded in this way:

On the day of the dissolution, some two hundred people gathered for the ceremony. It was an emotional time of memories, prayers, and a final Holy Communion for Bethel Evangelical Lutheran Church.

The printed program specified that at the end of the service Ralph Kirchenberg, the seventy-year-old president of the church board, would give the keys to Mark Jobe, as lead pastor of New Life Community Church. Both stood and Kirchenberg began to speak. "It says in the program that we are to hand over the keys to New Life at this point," he said, "but you know this is really not about keys or buildings."

At this point, every eye was on this senior saint whose entire life had been spent in ministry in the closing church. "This is about something a lot more important than buildings and keys." Kirchenberg paused to open a package he had brought with him. From it he pulled out a framed plaque. "It's become popular in recent years for organizations and companies to craft a mission statement, and Bethel has also had its own mission statement. So today we're not really giving you the keys to this building as much as the mission of Bethel Evangelical Lutheran Church."

He took the plaque, held it up, and read it aloud. The mission statement was a very straightforward, powerful expression of sharing the gospel, bringing transformation, and loving the community. It was the type of mission statement that any church which loves Jesus and wants to serve the gospel would be able to endorse. "Mark, we give our mission to New Life, to carry it forward into our community," he concluded.

There wasn't a dry eye in the place. The closing of the church was a reminder to everyone that this wasn't a death, nor was it really even a merger. It was a new means of carrying Christ's mission forward to reach a new generation.[3]

Mark Jobe exemplifies the kind of humble lead pastor that is most conducive to facilitating healthy church mergers. His infectious heart for God, relational skills that communicate both vision and care with well-developed team-building practices has led New Life Community Church to multiply to forty-five hundred people worshipping in twenty-eight multisite congregations across Chicago. As mentioned in chapter 3, fourteen of these congregations come through a merger. May their tribe increase!

Leading from a Posture of Humility

In many of our discussions with church leaders about mergers, especially joining church leaders, we've heard a recurring emphasis on the importance of humility. Churches that are stuck or in decline need humility to acknowledge they are struggling. It takes humility to admit that my church is not doing well and needs a new start. Likewise, lead churches need to also have humility about their role in shepherding new people toward a new vision rather than coming in as though they have every answer to every problem.

Mergers are built on trust and faith. Trust is earned by demonstrating genuine love and concern for the joining congregation, not just for the gain of their facilities, assets, or increased attendance. Faith is extended by the joining church when it believes the lead church is trustworthy.

Mergers have to be approached as two teams humbly uniting around the same vision. This point cannot be emphasized enough. Successful mergers are not primarily about "us" but about extending God's kingdom.

> Successful mergers are not primarily about "us" but about extending God's kingdom.

Humility goes a long way as the posture for leadership. As we overheard one pastor say as he led his congregation and a joining church through a merger, "The largest room in the world is the room for improvement."

Transformational Leaders Care about Other Churches

How approachable are you by the other church leaders in your community? Do you (or others from your church) return phone calls and email messages from local pastors regardless the size of their church? Do you interact with ministerial networks in your area and with other connection points for potential partnership in your community?

Or by contrast, does your church act as if it is the only church in the community? Is your church so self-absorbed and unaware or even uncaring about how other churches are doing? Does it focus primarily on its own needs and programs to the exclusion of similar efforts offered by other churches? Even worse, does your church view other local churches as competition or a threat?

What kind of church leader does a merger need? An approachable one who cares about the local churches in its community. One that genuinely cares about the body of Christ inside and outside its own congregation.

For the 14-campus Woodside Bible Church in greater Detroit, which has done nine mergers to date—all of a rebirth or adoption model—the exploration stage always started with a conversation over coffee. "Our senior pastor until his retirement in 2019, Doug Schmidt, had a burden to encourage and consult with other local churches to help them be as effective as possible. As a result, his phone rang about once a week with an area pastor calling and asking for help in some way," says Beth LaPonsie, the church's campus development director for many years. "His heart was to help other pastors however he could. A lot of pastors have called on him over his twenty years with us, and a few of those have led to mergers. Merging is not so much a strategy for us but a way we're continually helping other congregations."

"Merging is not so much a strategy for us but a way we're continually helping other congregations," says Beth LaPonsie.

Woodside's first merger was in 2006. A pastor located about thirty minutes away said, "We're going to have to sell our building. We're not going to make it." Doug asked why. They talked and prayed. "What if we come in and help rebuild the ministry?" Doug asked.

"We clearly communicated that we will infuse our DNA, and it will become like Woodside Bible Church in a new location," LaPonsie explains. Today almost five hundred people meet at that campus of Woodside Bible.

During the negotiation process for Woodside's mergers, each party affirms what things are musts for them, and they evaluate their compatibility to determine whether they should take the next step toward a merger. Woodside's approach is to replace the senior pastor of each church that merges with them. "They are welcome to reapply for different positions at Woodside but there are no guarantees. While we do our best to honor and help transition staff, they know that our priority is to make the decisions that will best rebuild this ministry," says LaPonsie. "At the end of the day, the joining church is saying 'yes' to new leadership. We're not looking for an arrangement that's a little of them and a little of us."

Woodside's approach is to replace the senior pastor of each church that merges with them.

The joining church brings its nonnegotiables as well. For example, Woodside's second merger, about forty minutes away, was arguably the most influential church in Michigan back in the 1940s. It was one of the country's early megachurches. It started fifteen branch Sunday schools over the years. The church building had aged and was to be torn down, so some of the leaders removed a stained-glass window, intending to install it in their new building. As a way of honoring a ministry that's existed for some 185 years, they asked Woodside to place it in the addition that was planned for this campus. "We said absolutely yes," LaPonsie says.

Woodside has developed a series of internal criteria that also help it discern if it should proceed with the merger opportunity. The questions include the following:

- Are we healthy enough financially to take on this ministry? This requires disclosure by the lead church and joining church about debts, any active litigation, and so on.

- Is it more than twenty minutes from our other campuses? Woodside leadership wants people to commit to one campus. They don't want to create an unintentional competition that invites people to float, depending on what's going on at each campus.
- Is the senior pastor, if still present, willing to relocate? Woodside doesn't leave the senior pastor there. "We believe the people need a new leader, one who knows and has experienced Woodside's DNA," LaPonsie explains. "Merging is difficult enough, so our preference is to move one of our Woodside pastors into leadership. Very early on in the process we'll confirm with the joining church pastor, 'You understand that if we go through with this, it will require you to transition to another ministry.' If the pastor's desire is still to proceed, we will assist him in finding another ministry, invite him to apply for a ministry position at another Woodside campus, or severance him," LaPonsie explains.
- Are the church cultures compatible? This involves asking how difficult it is for the existing body to blend with us, whether both churches' doctrines are the same and sense of mission similar and is the organizational structure workable. "We take a close look at their ministry and see if there are enough similarities to make the 'marriage' work," LaPonsie says.
- As Woodside takes the lead, will the leaders of the struggling ministry agree that the former way of doing ministry will come to an end? The existing board and congregation need to be in agreement with the fact that Woodside will come in and begin to rebuild the ministry and infuse its DNA. Woodside feels that this is critical to a new beginning and the success of the campus. "We treat them with honor and respect, but we also need to be permitted to lead them forward," LaPonsie says.
- Is there enough growth potential at this time? There are always enough unchurched people to reach in any community, but does the combination of the lead church and joining church offer a strong enough base of people and leaders needed for a strong relaunch of the joining church?

Woodside offers numerous opportunities to talk about the merger and to meet with the elders for questions and answers (Q&A). A series of FAQs Woodside developed and circulated are reprinted in appendix E.

Typically, both Woodside and the joining church take a congregational vote. "We want the votes to go through without surprises, and we communicate with the congregation well enough so that the people are prepared," LaPonsie says.

During the implementation stage, Woodside works especially hard to overcommunicate the benefits. In Woodside's approach, each merger represents a new campus, and so mergers are positioned as part of its multisite strategy. "Each time we have posted a merger opportunity or written about it in our newspaper, we tend to include a list of advantages for people to read," says LaPonsie.

Why Merge with a Large Multisite Church?

Woodside wants to convey to prospective joining churches, "We care about you, and any merger is a mutual win." Woodside's strategy represents advantages we see at many multisite churches that add some of their campuses via merger. Here are five of the positive outcomes Woodside has voiced to prospective joining churches:

Increased outreach: When churches expand to multiple locations, they dramatically increase their outreach. The research on multisite expansion affirms that the number one reason churches added new sites was for evangelistic purposes.[4] This strategy enables a church to expand the reach of its evangelistic vision. Doing so also sets the stage for multiplication, as new campuses can and will birth other campuses in neighboring communities.

Increased resources: Campuses can come together to share ideas and encourage one another. Multiple campuses provide a broad base of leaders to strategize with and learn from. They can share ministry resources while still developing local leadership and ownership.

Engaged followers: When you reproduce (i.e., add more campuses), you involve more people in ministry and many people actually reengage because church is now closer to their neighborhood. Research has concluded that the ideal launch distance for a multisite campus is within fifteen to thirty minutes' driving time from the sending campus.[5]

Improved quality: Each time Woodside launches a new site, we rethink how we do ministry, which in turn improves quality. Because certain overhead and personnel expenses are shared, costs also tend to drop. Also, centers of excellence emerge. For example, one campus may develop an effective neighborhood group strategy that we decide to share and implement at other campuses.

Improved leadership development: Multi-campus ministry increases leadership development. The most successful multisite leaders are typically home grown. Developing staff from within the congregation works well and certainly fits the biblical model (Eph 4:12, Rom 12:4–8, 1 Cor 12:1–11, etc.).

Finally, the integration takes time with bumps expected. "We advise, 'Don't expect everyone to be supportive until about eighteen months.' It's an emotional time. People are both glad and are hurting."

But over time the integration happens. For example, in Woodside's eight mergers, a majority of the people have stayed. At first, it's "You guys" or "Woodside says." Then it's "Our ministry is alive again." At the end of the day, people begin talking like they're at the same church and in the same blended family—which they are.

Why Merge with a Small Single-Site Church?

Your church doesn't have to be large to extend care to other churches, which can sometimes lead to a merger. It doesn't have to be multisite either.

Consider the example of what happened to three churches—two Lutheran, one United Methodist—all in nearby South Dakota towns, and each drawing ten to twenty weekly. "We had three small churches that were all looking toward closing their doors," explains Rhonda Wellsandt-Zell, who was pastoring all three churches at the time. "When I suggested we come together as one, everyone thought I was crazy. But the Holy Spirit stirred the souls of the people to capture the vision of becoming one church. Through the power of the Holy Spirit, we became one—and the church is thriving!" The merged church took on a new name, a most appropriate one for their story: Spirit of Faith Lutheran-Methodist Church (of Woonsocket, South Dakota—whose total population is about seven hundred people).

As Wellsandt-Zell led the vision to merge, she constantly emphasized prayer and a dependence on the Holy Spirit. "We took the attitude, 'If we're going to die, we're going to die healthy, but if we're going to live, we're going to live boldly,'" she says. But the congregations chose to live boldly. "Our joy after the merger was far more than any of the pain," she says, looking back over the eighteen months she stayed after the merger. Even through the sadness of closing two of the churches, "There was great joy, delight, hope, and promise in the merger," she adds.

In working toward the merger, she formed a Leadership Team (the Church Council, a blend of members from each of the three congregations) and a Vision Team (mid-age and younger leaders). "I saw a group of young leaders evolving in the church. They were hungry for finding a new way forward. They had hopes and dreams," she observed, "but I kept anchoring them with the message that we needed to deepen our relationship with God and with other people." Through many creative and intentional outreach efforts, the church served its community in the name of Jesus and became a group marked by contagious faith, excited to invite friends and family to join them. In fact, the momentum grew so strong that "people didn't want to miss church because they were excited to see what would happen next!" she reports.

The merger happened in 2018, with the outcome of building a new church building (where the United Methodist church once stood) and the selling of a parsonage. It also involved partnership with the redevelopment program of the ELCA (Evangelical Lutheran Church in America)—"Their help was priceless and gave us a solid foundation to stand on for the work we did," Wellsandt-Zell says. Indeed, the church's story has been widely cited in the denomination as a model for other churches to find a new future.[6]

The seventy-five worshippers today continue to have an optimism about their church and their future.

As in the Woodside Bible story above, the benefits of the Spirit of Faith merger are many: increased outreach, increased momentum, engaged followers, increased hope, and improved leadership development.

Transformational Leaders Understand the Grieving Process

All church mergers involve pain and sacrifice from both congregations. For the lead church the sacrifice and pain mostly revolve around time and money. This includes paying off debt or managing facility improvements or sale of the joining church, and spending time in countless meetings, in relocating people, in updating equipment, and in hiring new staff. It's lots of work but it usually includes a sense of exciting anticipation.

The pain and sacrifice for the joining church is more emotional. The joining church is giving up core aspects of its identity—its name, facility, staff, and control. Even when the joining church fully embraces the merger, there is still sadness and a sense of loss. It feels like a death to them because it is the end of the church as they know it—where they have poured their blood, sweat, and tears. This is the church where they were baptized, got married, dedicated their children, donated their tithes and offerings, and buried their loved ones. Though their story continues by merging with another church, this chapter of their story is coming to an end, and they're afraid that many memories will be forever lost.

Lead churches need to understand that everyone in the joining congregation will experience the five stages of grief (which we summarized in table 8.1). Also, as we've told various stories across this book, we've made a point of acknowledging the pain people experience. Bottom line: don't make the mistake of underestimating the pain in transition. It deserves your attention and respect.

Insider's Look at What Mutual Respect Looks Like

At one of the gatherings of the elders and senior staff of Sun Valley Community Church (introduced in chapter 8) and Bethany Community Church, the group did a table exercise that captured the benefits and also the challenges of their church merger. They set four tables, each with six people. Each table was an even mix of people from both churches. Each individual was asked to anonymously identify one positive that most excited them about this merger on a 3×5 card. On a separate card, they were asked to identify their biggest concern about this merger. Then each table group summarized and shared their list. Here is a summary of what they captured:

The positives

- The greater kingdom impact of joining together
- The synergy of a united vision and strategy that propels forward momentum
- The outreach potential of reaching both younger and older generations in our city
- Maximizing our facilities

The concerns

- Dealing with change of culture, identity, and control
- Dealing with potential loss of staff, ministries, members, and friends
- Communicating vision and implementing transition in a unified, honoring, caring, and healthy way

Then each table brainstormed and presented to the whole group how they would address their concerns. They voiced a lot of helpful suggestions. They boiled them down into one single summary statement to guide the merger process forward in a healthy way: "Cast a compelling vision clearly, consistently, and repetitively with grace, mercy, and humility to both the mind and the heart." As one of the Sun Valley elders put it, "I believe it is far more important that [our leaders] Chad and Scott cast a compelling vision that helps begin to form that bond of trust between pastors and congregants. They must strike a tone of empathy for their grieving, a sense of urgency for the lost, God's unstoppable vision for their future, and lastly a compelling vision for that particular campus. I believe it's in those last few weeks of vision casting that trust is gained and faith is required."

This is great advice for every merger! But even while going forward, be prepared for the church family of the joining church to respond to a merger announcement with a whole range of emotions, from joy and excitement to uncertainty and grief.

Lead churches show respect to joining churches by acknowledging the grieving process and allowing its expression. Some people will get through it quickly; others will take some time. Most will land in a good place, give the merger a try, and a few will move on. In a typical merger that's handled well with mutual respect, expect to lose up to 20 percent of the joining church family in the twelve months after the merger. Seasoned church consultant Tom Bandy, introduced in chapter 8, told us, "It's my experience that missional mergers depend on awakening the experience of Christ in the hearts of at least 20 percent of the members of each church. That 20 percent will have the credibility to lead another 60 percent into the merger. The remaining 20 percent can and should be left behind if necessary, regardless of how much they give."

> Expect to lose up to 20 percent of the joining church family in the twelve months after the merger.

Learning from the Pain

We introduced Justin Anderson in chapter 3 as experiencing a merger of three congregations into a church named Redemption.[7] A year after his merger experience, he wrote a poignant blog, identifying five critical lessons he learned. We excerpt it below to demonstrate some of the pain he and his church experienced and to show how he managed it.

"Pain" Lessons from the Merger

The mergers were easily the biggest thing we'd ever done, and we struggled to find people to guide us through the process. All three churches were healthy, growing, vibrant congregations. None of us "needed" each other, and none of our churches were in a position of strength or weakness as we attempted to navigate the process.

Here is what I learned:

How much and how well are you really leading your church?

Theoretically, I've believed in the plurality of eldership. Prior to the merger, Praxis Church [the church Justin was leading at the time of the merger] had seven elders, and I, as lead pastor, was first among equals. When we merged the churches, I became one member of a five-man leadership team charged with leading the vision and future of Redemption Church. I went from having more pastoral experience than my entire eldership combined to having the second least amount of experience.

Immediately, I realized that I hadn't really led my elders. Instead, I'd been a (mostly) benevolent dictator who was rarely questioned. I've grown more as a leader in the last five months than perhaps the previous six years combined. I'm learning more about leadership every day and see this merger as a great opportunity to gain invaluable leadership lessons.

1. Patience actually is a virtue.

At Praxis, because of our structure, youth, and culture, we made decisions very quickly and implemented them just as fast. Because of this, we often made missteps that had to be corrected, and we missed opportunities because we didn't wait to make sure our direction was the right one.

In a larger structure like Redemption Church, we've lost our ability to act as quickly as before and the wisdom of our new leadership team has served to slow our decision-making process significantly. It frustrated me at first, but I quickly saw the benefit as we reversed course on several ideas that I initially thought were best but turned out not to be. This saved us a lot of work and hardship.

2. Don't underestimate your congregation's capacity for change and vision.

Big changes, like a merger, aren't always popular. People simply don't like change, and I knew some people wouldn't like this change in particular. After finalizing plans for the merger, I expected a five percent rate of attrition in leadership, attendance, and money. I couldn't have been more wrong.

In the five months following our announcement, we've lost virtually nothing. No leaders left, nearly every member is still around, attendance is at record highs, and people are giving sacrificially. I significantly underestimated our people's appetite for vision, but I won't do it again.

3. Together is better—and it's the future.

Throughout the merger planning, we continually asked this core question: "Are we better together than we are apart?" Our churches were closely aligned doctrinally and philosophically, and we had already partnered together on two significant endeavors. We often returned to the questions: Did we really need to merge? Couldn't we just continue to work closely together?

Five months into the merger and looking forward to the exciting plans and vision on our near horizon, I firmly believe what I suspected all along—we are better together than we were apart. When it comes to vision, ideas, leadership, resources, and prayer, 1 + 1 + 1 = 10.

4. Relational connectivity is key.

In Larry Osborne's book *Unity Factor*,[8] he talks about having a three-fold unity on your leadership team: doctrinal, philosophical, and relational. I've learned a ton from Larry over the last couple years, but nothing has served us as well as his lesson on three-fold unity. We knew going into our merger discussions that we had doctrinal and philosophical unity, but the relational unity was something of a question mark.

I can't overstate how important relational unity is when you are considering a merger. Things will get tough, some conversations will be hard, and if you don't have the kind of relationships that allow honest, frank dialogue without your feelings getting hurt, it won't work.[9]

In my (Jim's) merger consulting with these churches, I found that Justin had the right balance of being a strong leader and a teacher with genuine humility. He had been in a long mentoring relationship under the lead church pastor for years before the idea of merging even surfaced between them. Their respectful relationship laid a solid foundation for their successful mission-driven merger.

Justin Anderson beautifully embodied the kind of leadership that is merger friendly, especially in his ability to appreciate the pain and grieving of the people involved in a merger. His approach laid the groundwork for what has become a flourishing church that has multiplied into ten congregations across Arizona, even as Anderson has followed God's ongoing call to San Francisco to plant a new church and his executive pastor, Tyler Johnson, has become the lead pastor.

Notes

1. Warren Bird, *Lyle E. Schaller: The Elder Statesman of Church Leadership* (Nashville: Abington, 2012), 4.

2. Schaller, *Reflections of a Contrarian*, 148.

3. Story adapted from Geoff Surratt, Greg Ligon, and Warren Bird, *A Multi-Site Church Roadtrip: Exploring the New Normal.* (Grand Rapids, MI: Zondervan, 2009), 171–172.

4. Surratt, Geoff, Greg Ligon, and Warren Bird, *The Multi-Site Church Revolution: Being One Church in Many Locations* (Grand Rapids, MI: Zondervan, 2006), 18, 24.

5. See http://leadnet.org/multisite, scroll to the "downloads" section and see relevant research such as "2019 Multisite Survey Report" and "Multisite Church Scorecard: Faster Growth, More Believers, and Greater Lay Participation."

6. For example, see this video by the ELCA South Dakota Lutheran Synod, https://vimeo.com/340215561.

7. See the church's account of the mergers at https://tinyurl.com/usjnhfq.

8. Larry Osborne, *The Unity Factor: Developing a Healthy Church Leadership Team*, 4th ed. (Vista, CA: Owl's Nest, 2006).

9. Justin, Anderson, "5 Critical Lessons from a Church Merger," May 22, 2011, https://tinyurl.com/w4vvvnm.

13

IS YOUR CHURCH A GOOD MERGER CANDIDATE?

It's hard to find a church that couldn't be considered as a candidate for a merger, either as a lead or joining church. We especially believe that the merger option may be the best option for many of the 80 percent of churches in the United States that are stuck or struggling. Thus, there are thousands of potential merger partners out there at any given point in the life cycle of a church that we depicted in figure 0.1. If so, which of those might want to merge with you?

In chapter 12, we looked at the leadership attitudes necessary for a merger-friendly posture. This chapter will explore some specific guidelines for determining if your church is a viable candidate for merging.

- As you explore the options, here are the four exploratory questions we introduced in chapters 3 and 6 that frame the merger conversation. They will help you determine if your church should even entertain a merger possibility: Would our congregation *be better* by merging rather than remaining separate?
- Could we *accomplish more* together than we could separately?
- Would our community be *better served* if we joined together?
- Could the kingdom of God be *further enlarged* by joining together?

Remember that like all living things, churches have a life cycle. In their early years, they grow a lot, just like a human being. As the decades go by, they often face a growing number of challenges, just as people do with their own health. But unlike human beings, whose physical bodies have a limit, churches can begin a new life cycle. The opportunity to change life cycles begins with every new pastor. Unfortunately, many old, dying churches think hiring a younger pastor is the solution. But once they hire the younger pastor, the church doesn't accept the necessary changes to reach the next generations. In too many cases, regrettably, the new pastor wasn't allowed or didn't know how to start a new life cycle. Sometimes that new cycle of life may best be accomplished through a merger.

> *The opportunity to change life cycles begins with every new pastor.*

Choosing to merge for what we describe as missional motives is always better than having to merge as a last-ditch survival effort. Many come through the merger affirming that indeed the pain was well worth the change.

Lead Church Opportunities

If you're a potential lead church, then the candidates could include many types of joining churches:

Strong, Stable, or Stuck Churches That Want to Multiply Outreach and Impact

Back in our "Why Merge?" discussion of chapter 3, our opening poster-child example was the marriage merger account of Arizona pastor Justin Anderson, which we also further described in chapter 12. His approach, one that seems to have potential for huge fruitfulness, is akin to the hundredfold crop that comes from seed planted in good soil as Jesus described in Matthew 13:8.

Justin was founding pastor of the dynamic and growing Praxis Church near the campus of Arizona State University. It had grown in attendance to twelve hundred, meeting in two locations. Then it merged with the older and more stable East Valley Bible Church in the suburbs of Phoenix, a church that was even larger in attendance. Both congregations were healthy, though at different life stages. Their pastors had a long personal relationship with each other. The merged church took the name Redemption Church.

Why then did they merge? The primary reason was to maximize their strengths in order to multiply congregations across Arizona. They combined the resources, talents, and gifts of each church with a vision, as their website describes, to saturate the state of Arizona "with the spread of the Gospel, the establishment of healthy local churches, and the multiplication of disciples." [1]

Struggling Church Plants

One pastor told us, "I heard recently about a two-year old church plant that just couldn't make it and dissolved. Before they shut everything down, I wish we could have heard their story, and they our story. We might have found a way to work together to continue what they had started."

For other churches, that wish is becoming reality. In one instance, a Tennessee church of 250 had planted a church five years previously that just wasn't making it financially. It was fifteen to thirty minutes away and had potential as a second campus for the church of 250. That's just what happened as this lead church took back in the church plant of forty. The merger process went smoothly. As the lead pastor explained, "Our two churches were already very familiar with one another, having worked together on many ministry projects."

In another instance, a Pennsylvania church of 170 had gone multisite. A church in the area had closed and merged with it, becoming the church's second campus. The wife of the senior pastor explained that the merger was not without setbacks. "The merger happened with much prayer," she said. "At first, an elder at the joining church was so opposed to the merger proposal that he held it over his head in front of the congregation and dramatically threw it onto the floor saying, 'We will never accept this!' But then he left the church. We tried the proposal again, and this time the people were ready. God removed every obstacle. I remember attending a worship service during a time of uncertainty and singing 'Savior He Can Move the Mountains' and understanding the song like never before!" Then two years later the multisite campus was released to become an independent church once again. "They are thriving in making disciples today," the wife of the senior pastor told us.

Struggling Established Churches

Dan Kimball, author of *How (Not) to Read the Bible*,[2] is pastor of Vintage Faith Church, a nondenominational congregation in Santa Cruz, California. The church had started with a 7 p.m. Sunday night worship gathering but Kimball quickly realized that it needed an additional Sunday morning service, mainly because of young families with children. He and others began searching locally for a place to meet, approached a Presbyterian church whose attendance was small and declining, and asked if the church had available space to rent. The Presbyterian church, mostly elderly people, could worship at 9 a.m. and Vintage Faith could start at 11 a.m. "Their leaders knew who we were, as we are in a fairly small town," Kimball says, "and out of their mission-oriented heart—they were founded in 1889 with very mission-minded focus that continued as part of their DNA—they offered to allow us to meet there at no cost."

Vintage Faith moved its 7 p.m. gathering to the building and also launched an 11 a.m. service. Over time, the Presbyterian church asked Kimball to teach at its 9 a.m. service, keeping the organist and Presbyterian format. "We got along so well and shared the same vision to reach our town, that after a year we discussed becoming one church which we eventually did," Kimball explains. "We took time to get to know each other, build trust, ask a lot of questions, and meet with the Presbytery leaders before we formally became one church." After two years of serving together, including months and months of prayer, discussion, and many meetings, the churches decided to partner together longer term. When that happened in 2008, First Presbyterian Church simply changed its name to Vintage Faith Church. The staff members from both churches joined together as one staff.

Vintage Faith also took on the Presbyterian church's financial responsibilities. The Presbyterian church was overspending $35,000 more than its offerings and living off its fast-dwindling savings. After the merger, Vintage Faith also spent money on building improvements and opening a seven-day-a-week coffeehouse and music venue for local college students in the church building. (Even today the seven-day-a-week coffeehouse is thriving and has become a major local university hangout. This provides a lot of connection to university students.)

Some fallout is always predictable in a merger and about half the Presbyterian church ended up leaving because of the changes Vintage Faith brought to the teaching, worship, and other programs. "We all did our absolute best to communicate and explain, but some couldn't accept the changes and went to another traditional church in our town,"

Kimball says. But those who stayed became extremely active and served in ministries. By the ten-year mark after the merger, roughly 40 percent of the original joining church congregation were still part of Vintage Faith.

One woman who was part of the Presbyterian church for over fifty years comes every Sunday to the 7 p.m. service and sits in the front row. "She beams and is thrilled seeing her church now filled with young people," Kimball reports. Indeed, there have been many discussions that imagine aloud how Jesus is pleased with the stewardship of the building, which previously was barely used during the week and is now completely active. "We even gutted the fellowship hall to turn it into the coffee house, art gallery, and music venue that is filled with local university students through the week," Kimball adds.

Kimball is very enthusiastic about this model for others because about 60 from the Presbyterian church joined about 300 from Vintage Faith in 2008; by 2020 today weekly attendance was about 350. "Our story has been a very Kingdom-minded adventure, and I think there is a lot of potential with this type of partnership," he says. "Older churches dying out that are in these wonderful, no-mortgage buildings and young church plants needing a building. And then there's the bonus of intergenerational relationships. We're breaking down barriers and embracing different viewpoints, while living out the mission of Jesus."

Pastor-Less Churches

For 29% of joining churches, succession issues played a major role in the decision to merge, as we mentioned in chapter 4. Probably the greatest opportunity for a church merger is with churches that currently lack a pastor or will be losing their pastor in the near future. It is estimated that 30 percent of America's 320,000 Protestant churches will change senior pastors in any given year. In addition, it is estimated that 40 percent of Protestant churches have senior pastors who are approaching retirement or a change of vocation.[3]

In reality, a merger is a vehicle for choosing a pastor. A congregation may be voting to approve or dis-approve a legal merger, but they are ultimately deciding who will be their next pastor. As succession planning is becoming more accepted, senior pastor succession through merging will become more common.

> In reality, a church merger is a vehicle for choosing a pastor. A congregation may be voting to approve or dis-approve a legal merger, but they are ultimately deciding who will be their next pastor.

When Pastor Brian Tome of Crossroads Church in Cincinnati heard that his good friend Pastor Glen Schneiders of Crossroads Church ninety miles away, across the state line in Lexington, Kentucky, was thinking about succession planning, he called Glen.

"Do you think there's any consideration of Crossroads Cincinnati and Crossroads Lexington becoming one church?" he asked.[4]

Though both churches were independent churches in two different states, they shared the same church name and a fifteen-year friendship. Schneiders, sixty-three at the time, had started Crossroads Lexington in 1987. It had grown to twenty-five hundred people attending weekend services on four campuses. Tome started Crossroads Cincinnati in 1996 which had grown to more than twenty thousand people attending weekend services on five campuses. Both churches were healthy, financially strong, and shared similar styles of worship and ministry.

Schneiders responded, "It's not so much about me retiring as what's best for our church."[5] He told Tome he would pray about it and take the idea to the elders. After giving it some consideration and consultation, the elders felt drawn to the idea and to Crossroads in Cincinnati.

In September 2016, the elders unanimously recommended merging Crossroads Lexington with Crossroads Cincinnati. That November the church overwhelmingly approved the merger, believing they would be better together. And they were right! Today Crossroads is a church of thirty-four thousand attendees meeting in ten locations across Ohio and Kentucky.

Joining Church Opportunities

Regardless of whether your church is strong, stable, stuck, or struggling, it may be a great candidate to join with another church locally or nationally (and a review of table 5.2's "Four Merger Profiles" might help you identify which type of merger to seek out). If your church becomes the joining church in the merger, then how would you find a suitable lead church? Look around your community. Is there a church that God is blessing and that is having a significant impact that you might consider joining? Is there a healthy church that you have affinity with or a denominational tie that would allow you to do better ministry together? Nationally, is there a church outside of your community that you align with philosophically as well as theologically?

Merger Fact 24

Almost All Mergers Come from the Same or Similar Church Tradition and Ethnicity

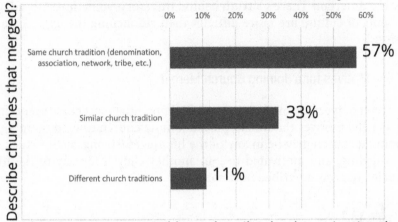

2019 Survey: *How would you describe the denominational or network background of the churches that merged?*

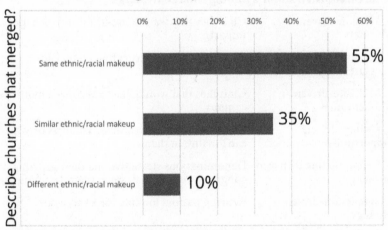

2019 Survey: *How would you describe the ethnic/racial difference between the congregations that merged?*

We laughed a few times as we saw the way people answered our 2019 survey. As Merger Fact 24 shows, we asked if the two merging churches were from the same, similar, or different ethnicities and/or theological traditions. One church said "different" and then explained: "Both were ELCA at the time and from previous LCA tradition, but previously from different traditions—United Lutheran (German) for lead church and Augustana Lutheran (Swedish) for joining church." We can imagine that the merger did require adjustments, especially on potluck food Sundays, but they did have a lot more in common in believing that they were different! There's a truth behind this story: sometimes the adjustments of culture are more difficult than reconciling theological traditions!

Nine Motives for a Joining Church Merger

As you prayerfully explore ways to find potential merger partners, consider the motives that might push a joining church toward merging. A joining church may be in any of the life stages (strong, stable, stuck, or struggling) and motivated to join another church for any of the nine major reasons described in chapter 4:

Table 13.1

Nine Circumstances for a Joining Church to Merge	
1. Mission-driven Mindsets	Churches that want to multiply outreach and impact
2. Economic-driven Pressures	Churches that are struggling financially
3. Multisite-driven Momentum	Churches that would like to become a multisite campus
4. Facility-driven Opportunity	Churches with underutilized facilities or who can't maintain them
5. Denominational-driven Strategy	Denominations strengthening their growing congregations and salvaging their declining ones
6. Succession-driven Strategy	Retiring pastors looking for a successor
7. Reconciliation-driven Hope	Church divisions and splits being reunited
8. Multiethnic-driven Strategy	Churches desiring more diversity
9. Pastor-search Option	Churches looking for a pastor

Willing to Change?

Joining churches must be willing to change. This is the most important first step toward a merger. The unwillingness to change is the primary issue that prevents mergers from happening. Unfortunately, the majority of *struggling* churches would rather die than change. Or, more specifically, they've often misdiagnosed—and severely so—the root causes of the trouble they're in, and they need to allow someone else to establish the pathway forward. But sadly, many will die because they don't want to change or give up control of steering even though the church is in a death spiral.

Meanwhile, *stable* or *stuck* churches can be even more resistant to needed change because there is no sense of urgency. Often stable or stuck churches are financially strong, which creates an artificial sense of well-being making it more difficult to see the need for change. Yet, when the pain of *not* changing exceeds the pain of changing, a merger conversation can occur.

We love the question that our friend Stephen Gray asks churches that are on a declining slope in their life cycle, as he helps them think through their options. He calls it his million-dollar question: "What if we were able to help you live out the vision that you were founded for in the first place, leading to an exponential impact in your community?" No church wants to close, nor does it want to live in ongoing "maintenance mode"; every church has a purpose that it wants to fill.

As a joining church the first and most important step is recognizing the need to change. Your answer to this kind of question could be a sign that you should explore a merger from the perspective of a joining church. Our church merger research revealed that the majority of mergers are initiated by the joining church (see Merger Fact 25 on page 191). If you believe the purpose of your church could be best fulfilled by joining another like-minded church, then don't wait to be asked; initiate the conversation. We explain how to initiate a merger conversation in chapter 14.

How to Discern If This Is God at Work

How do you discern if a merger is right for your church? Most importantly, do you sense that God is at work? Here is a story of how one church struggled with whether the merger opportunity represented God's leading. Then after the story, we close the chapter with a self-assessment form exercise.

God May Already Be at Work

When Capstone Church of Anderson, South Carolina, was offered a five-hundred-seat sanctuary on eight acres of land in historic downtown Anderson by Central Baptist Church, it wasn't sure if it wanted to accept this gift. The offer caught Capstone Church completely by surprise.

"We had met each other just a few months before," Capstone's pastor David Barfield explained to us. "Our church had wanted to do a giveaway day to bless the community on the west side of downtown. We needed a local place to make it happen, and we had noticed Central Baptist's facility there." Each time Barfield or his church staff drove by the Central Baptist church facility, they prayed about it. One day they noticed a car there, so they knocked on the church door.

Capstone was a nontraditional church of 150 people meeting in a movie theater in the suburbs. Central Baptist, founded in 1952, and for many years a bustling congregation of four hundred with a sanctuary that seated five hundred, now found itself located in an economically depressed, high-crime neighborhood. It had a tall steeple, 1970s green carpet, and twelve people attending, all over age sixty. They no longer had a pastor. Though both churches were Southern Baptist, they were very different from each other in worship style and method of ministry.

The initial door-knock conversation in 2008 led to permission for a one-time Saturday use of the Central Baptist parking lot and facility. "They had a heart to touch their community but not the resources to do it," Barfield explains. "They were hesitant at first about working with us, but this initial project allowed Central to begin making a difference again."

> They had a heart to touch their community but not the resources to do it.

After the successful event known as Give Away Day, the two churches went their separate ways. A few months later Capstone decided to do another community day. The people of Central Baptist not only said yes but also asked, "Can you help us line up a preacher for our Sunday services?"

A few months later, they asked again to meet with David Barfield. "I thought they were planning to ask me for more help with pulpit supply," he said. "But there at McDonalds, over a Dr. Pepper and two coffees, two members of Central Baptist asked, "What would it be like if we gave you our church?""

Capstone was an unconventional growing church with few resources, and Central was a dying conventional church with a huge facility asset. Could Capstone even afford to upgrade and maintain such a gift?

Sometimes It's Hard Work to Discern God's Leading

"We had no intention of asking for their facility," Barfield says. "All we wanted was to love the people of the community. We were delighted that Central Baptist loaned us a base from which to do so. But now we had to wrestle with this significant invitation of them giving us their building."

And wrestle they did—both in heartfelt prayer and in much conversation—because neither option seemed to be an obvious or clear choice. According to Barfield, "We had a lot of costs to count; if that church failed there, we might too."

In seeking wisdom within the Capstone community, some said, "I don't think this is a good idea." Others were unsure, feeling it was just "an" idea. Others were certain it was a "God" idea.

From the launch of Capstone Church in 2002, people were praying and planting seeds financially for a location from which to operate. Not a church but a mission-operation center. Always the idea was to reclaim a "dark" storefront or warehouse. The church understood that God had already prepared both a place and a people. "Where?" was still a question. And then seven years into the mission, a major possibility drops into its hands. What to do?

There were lots of potential negatives such as whether Capstone would lose people in the relocation (they did), whether it would take too much money to refit the facility (it took less than expected), whether those who made the move would be willing to invite friends (they did), whether Central Baptist would dislike the changes and go back on their promises (they didn't on either count), or how to shift from occasional serve days to living in a place where need was constant (Capstone's decision was to give until they give out, whether food or clothes or light bulbs). In fact, Barfield showed us a fourteen-item list of concerns that Capstone members had voiced, and a nine-item list that Central Baptist developed.

The church and its leaders determined to keep listening and praying. "The decision had to come from God, because no one was manipulating it," he affirms. "We knew that every location we've used as a church—a school, hotel, and movie theater—has given us an opportunity to reach a different type of people. We wanted to reach out to people on the fringes in the downtown community; was this building the kind of structure and location that would help us connect with folks that have been bypassed and left behind?"

Barfield remembers his emotions going back and forth like a pendulum. "Selfishly, I remember thinking, I do not want to pastor there," he says. "But God wants a brightly burning light right there in that area. And this is not about our opinion, but what God wants us to do."

This going back and forth went on for weeks for Barfield, his staff, his elders, and the congregation. "We walked the streets, counted the cost financially, talked about whether people would drive there, and queried the church's college group and ministry groups," he says. And was it coincidence or divine leading that Barfield had been doing a sermon series on Moses, Joshua, and the promised land when the merger opportunity arose?

Ultimately, they decided that this is where God wants us. "It wasn't a lightning-bolt moment, and it seemed to take forever, but it actually took only several months."

After deciding, they next had to go back to the members of the joining church and help them through the process of releasing their forty-five-thousand-square-foot facility, $8,500 bank account, and eight acres to Capstone. Total cost to Capstone was about $200,000, mostly for renovations and also for legal fees, much of which the Capstone congregation raised in a special offering over three weeks.

A Bittersweet Farewell

The joining church clearly felt good about passing on the legacy and mission to another congregation carrying their Southern Baptist banner but, as Barfield confides, "I know Capstone didn't do things the way Central did on many fronts and I'm sure that was a little scary to them, but all agreed the results of touching the neighborhood for Christ were more important than traditions." After the merger, most of the joining church members soon moved on to a more traditional church. "That was a little bittersweet, but we understood," Barfield says. "We blessed the legacy they left us, and they stayed long enough to see what God was up to. They saw that we're putting a dent in the darkness of the area we serve every week, that genuine love was being shown, and to them that was the confirmation they needed to know that the hand of God was in the merger."

After Capstone Church took formal possession of the Central Baptist facility, Capstone closed it for three months for renovations before reopening it with a new name, style, and structure. Within two years of the merger, Capstone Church had grown in a healthy way, with the average age decreasing by ten years. The last five of the original remaining attendees stayed with Capstone for nearly two years and then departed on a positive note for a more traditional-style church.

Barfield is thrilled about the new facility and location because of what they represent. "Buildings are not sacred; it's what happens inside the building that is sacred," he says. "Church is not about where you meet; it's who you meet and who you meet with." To Capstone Church, its new location is not the promised land of comfort but a promised land as a launching point for mission. Plus, he recently told us, "We have been able to encourage other churches through our story of connection and merger. We have felt a strong calling to assist others in bringing life and light to 'dark church buildings.'"

Always Watch for Who Might Be Knocking

The story is not finished. Capstone continues to partner with and serve other churches to provide leadership with worship and teaching as well as volunteers for kids and community programs. They have stated goals to reclaim kingdom property for kingdom purposes. They are working diligently to replant, reorganize, or reignite churches to become vital to the communities in which they are located.

The best merger outcomes are preceded with prayer, integrity, and healthy communication. There must also be a sense of discernment that this game-changing decision is consistent with God's leading.

How did Capstone determine if this merger was right for them? Pastor David Barfield was preaching through the book of Joshua when the offer came to Capstone. Through a series of confirming Scriptures, the members of the congregation believed they heard God's voice, that this was their "promised land to possess." They saw God's hand through circumstances that they did not orchestrate or particularly desire. It knocked on their door. They sought God's wisdom as they counted the cost. Though the merger cost Capstone about $200,000 in legal fees and building upgrades, God provided all the money without borrowing.

> The best merger outcomes are preceded with prayer, integrity, and healthy communication.

Barfield's advice to other church leaders concerning church mergers is that "if it's a God-thing, it will happen. Don't try to manipulate it or make it happen. It needs to be a natural, organic, indigenous process. Then keep your eyes peeled for potholes to step into."

Merger Candidate Self-Assessment

Alternatives to Merging

One way to determine your church's readiness to merge is to explore alternatives. Maybe merging is not your best pathway? For example, instead of merging, you might consider the following:

- Change your worship style.
- Change the pastor.
- Change other leadership.
- Change the mission.
- Change location (relocate).
- Close or dissolve.
- Continue in the current location with the same programming.
- Continue in the current location and tap into building equity to fund new programs.
- Share your campus with two or more congregations that jointly own and use one facility. (This is not a landlord-tenant–shared building situation, but janitorial, maintenance, and office staff are shared, the facility is owned by a nonprofit corporation that is controlled by the congregations, and a joint board coordinates the shared use of the building and allocates expenses.)[6]
- Rent your church facility to other groups.
- Close the church and tap into the church's property equity to provide funds for a restart and to give the building a face-lift.
- Sell the current property and relocate the congregation.
- Sell the church's property and give funds to a church-planting organization to start one or several new churches, or place funds in an endowment to build new churches perpetually.
- Sell the church's property and give funds to several nonprofit organizations.

If Merging Makes Sense, Ask Yourself These Key Questions

Your self-assessment process will depend on whether you are the lead church or the joining church in the merger. If your situation is the rarer merger of two equals, then still review all of the following questions.

Keep in mind that the average time for a merger will be around seven to ten months between the initial discussion and the merger actually happening (see Merger Fact 7 on page 94). So, when you're ready, things might move very quickly.

For each of these questions, the framing decision is whether merging is likely to lead to a better answer.

All churches, both lead and joining:

- To what extent are the hopes, dreams, and potentials of your church being fulfilled at present?
- Would you categorize your church as strong, stuck, struggling, or declining? How satisfied or dissatisfied are you with that status?
- Could your church mission be accomplished better in a merger relationship with another church rather than alone?
- Is there a specific church you would consider merging with?
- Has your church been approached by another church to consider merging?
- How willing is your church to take risks and be open to change?
- How strongly does your church really want to grow numerically?
- How convinced are you that a merger is likely to increase the spiritual health and growth of your membership?

If you're likely to be the *lead* church:

- Does your church have a clear mission, vision, values, discipleship pathway, and ministry strategy?
- How does a merger help fulfill your church's mission?
- Does your church have a multisite strategy?
- How open and prepared are you for the opportunity to become multisite through a merger?
- Has your church outgrown its facility?
- Is your church healthy and growing at least by 5 percent a year?
- Does your church have people living in the area of the merged church?
- Can your church release and send 10 percent of its people to a church merger and still be healthy?
- Is the dream for your church bigger than its current capacity to fulfill it?
- Has your church set aside money to fund merger costs?
- Does your denomination or network have funds or assistance available for a merger?

If you're likely to be the *joining* church:

- Has your church been declining for more than three years? If so, how capable are you, given your present resources, to make the major changes necessary to turn your church around?
- How closely does your church reflect the composition of the surrounding community? Is the profile of your church moving toward or away from the average age, ethnicity, and education level of your church's immediate community?
- How likely is it that your church will exist ten years from now if things continue at their present rate?
- Is your church without a pastor, having difficulty finding one, or not likely to find one when your present pastor leaves?
- How strong is the financial viability of your church without outside help? Is it moving toward being financially stronger or weaker?
- Do you want your church to flourish even if it means giving its leadership and assets to another church?
- Does your congregation and leadership sense an urgency to make the major changes that a merger will represent?

Take the Merger-Readiness Assessment Test

Do your answers lead you to conclude that your church may be a good merger candidate? If your church believes it could become a better church or be turned around by joining another like-minded but more vibrant church, then it is a good candidate for a church merger.

One next step is to actually score your church's readiness for a merger, using a scale of 1 to 5. Estimate your score on each of the questions below, add up the tally, and then look at the interpretation. This assessment is not the voice of the Lord, but it will give you an indication of how God might be leading. Statements 1-7 are for all churches. Then for statements 8-10, answer only one set, the set that seems to most closely match your circumstances.

Table 13.1

Merger Readiness Self-Assessment

Statement (All Churches)	*Self-Rating (1=no, not at all, 5=yes, strongly so)*

1. Could the kingdom of God *be further enlarged* by merging with another church? _____

2. Would your community *be better served* if your church and another church merged together? _____

3. Could your church and another church *accomplish more* together than we could separately? _____

4. Would your congregation *be better* by merging rather than remaining separate? _____

5. Is your church anticipating *succession*, without a pastor, or having difficulty finding a pastor? _____

6. Has your church been *approached* by another church or denominational leader to consider merging? _____

7. Are you aware of a *church planter* in your area who has lots of people but no facility (whom your church could potentially help by sharing its facility)? _____

ONLY for Potential *Joining* Churches

8. Is your church having trouble reaching the next generation with the gospel? _____

9. Is your church facing financial pressures, unable to meet its financial obligations or maintain its facilities? _____

10. Are there one or more healthy, vibrant, growing churches in your area that you could imagine merging with? _____

ONLY for Potential *Lead* Churches

8. Is your church currently multisite or open to becoming a multisite church? _____

9. Is your church growing and in need of more space? _____

10. Does your church's leadership have a big heart toward revitalizing area churches? _____

Total _____

The higher your total, the stronger you are as a merger candidate. If you score at least 20, do explore further the idea of merging. If you're above 30, merging seems to be a very good fit. If you're about 40, merging seems to hold huge promise for your church.

Now you're ready to begin conversations with potential merger candidates—and that's the focus of the next chapter.

Notes

1. See http://www.redemptionaz.com/ in the "Outward Focus" section.

2. Dan Kimball, *How (Not) to Read the Bible* (Grand Rapids, MI: Zondervan, 2020). See also Dan Kimball, *They Like Jesus but Not the Church.* (Grand Rapids, MI: Zondervan, 2007).

3. See William Vanderbloemen and Warren Bird, *Next: Pastoral Succession That Works*, expanded and updated edition (Grand Rapids, MI: Baker, 2020), 34.

4. Kevin Eigelbach, "Cincinnati's Crossroads Megachurch to Merge with Lexington's Crossroads Christian: 'We're Better Together,'" October 16, 2016, WCPO CIncinnati, https://tinyurl.com/wfglepj.

5. Eigelbach, "Cincinnati's Crossroads Megachurch to Merge."

6. See David Raymond's more detailed explanation at his website www.churchcollaboration.com.

14

HOW TO START THE MERGER CONVERSATION

The day after the first edition of this book came out, I (Warren) was speaking to the pastors and staff of Liquid Church, a New Jersey congregation that was exploding with new life, outreach, and baptisms. As I finished my talk about managing growth, I pulled out the book and said to Pastor Tim Lucas, in everyone's hearing, "Has any church approached you about merging?"

"No one," he quickly responded.

"Someone will," I countered. "And you'll need this book."

Tim later said that the idea of merging with another church had never even crossed his mind. He thanked me politely, and after I left, he put the book on the stack of read-this-someday books piled high on his desk.

But God was up to something. At 6:30 the very next morning, one of Liquid's pastors received a phone call from an elder he knew at an area church. The caller said his church would love to talk with Liquid Church about becoming a campus of Liquid Church. The pastor almost dropped the phone. A whirlwind of activity began, starting with "where's that book Warren gave us?" After much prayer, many meetings, and quite a few additional "God moments," the merger happened. As Tim recounts in *Liquid Church: Six Powerful Currents to Saturate Your*

City for Christ, the merger was a success on every level, and it even led to a second equally successful merger.[1]

Wow! Although this chapter is about what you can do to initiate conversations about a merger, stay on alert. As happened with Tim Lucas, don't be surprised if God has gone ahead of you!

Stay on alert. . . . Don't be surprised if God has gone ahead of you!

Any Church Can Initiate

Healthy mergers usually are the result of a relationship built on mutual respect and trust. As you build relationships with local pastors and other ministry partners to serve your community together, merger possibilities emerge.

How to approach another church about a merger seems like the million-dollar question that everyone wants to know. More often, the potential joining church initiates the conversation, but not always, as Merger Fact 25 indicates.

The clearer you are on your church's mission, vision, values, and strategy, the more effectively you can prayerfully entertain whether a merger makes sense. Driving distance is also a factor. Most mergers in our survey occurred within a thirty-minute drive between the two congregations, as Merger Fact 26 indicates. The farther away from each other, the greater the community and cultural differences to overcome. Yet long-distance mergers can be successful when there is a strong identification with the mission, vision, values, and strategy of the lead church.

Further, if you are a multisite church, merger opportunities will most likely present themselves to you. Often a local church in your community or beyond will initiate a conversation with you about a possible merger.

Our surveys of church mergers asked people how they framed the conversation and invitation to merge. Their responses fell into several categories, all under the banner of relationships marked by trust. Here are some examples we have seen that have the broadest replicability.

Merger Fact 25

Both Joining Churches AND Lead Churches Initiate Mergers

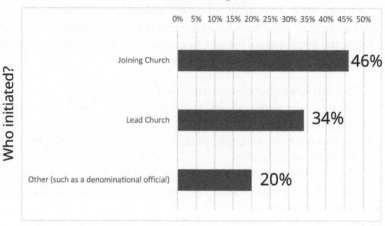

2019 Survey: *Who initiated the merger?*

Merger Fact 26

The Vast Majority of Mergers Are within 30 Minutes of Each Other

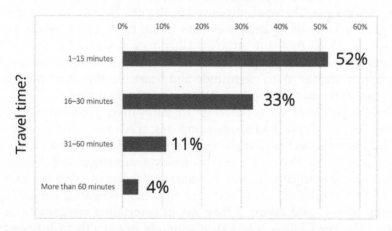

2019 Survey: *What was the travel time between the meeting locations of the churches prior to the merger?*

Conversations Based on Relationships

Several stories in this book describe a relational connection between two churches. In some the pastors knew each other, some were introduced through their denominational or network leaders, while in other examples people in one church knew someone in the other church and introduced the appropriate leaders to each other. Most of the conversations begin with a sense of tentativeness:

- "Would your church ever consider . . . ?"
- "Would your church be willing to adopt (or join) another church in our denomination?"
- "Is there a way we could partner together that might be a win for both churches?"
- "I wanted to tell you that we are looking toward launching a multisite campus in your community. Would you be interested in joining with us?"

One pastor told us, "There are perhaps dozens of churches within twenty minutes of our church building. If I initiate a discussion, they might misunderstand us and think that all we want are their assets. The truth is that I want to help them turn the corner by joining with us and at the same time fulfill the mission of both of our churches. So I'm beginning to reach out to them."

We're very impressed with Scott Chapman, senior pastor at The Chapel in greater Chicago (introduced in chapter 3). His church is multisite and several of its campuses have come by mergers. When The Chapel began its multisite strategy, Chapman instructed each of his campus pastors, "Find ten pastors in your zip code whom you can bless and help to thrive." With an attitude and heart like that, it's little surprise that more merger opportunities have come their way.

The Chapel went on to develop an innovative, proactive merger strategy to launch more multisite campuses, reach more communities, and help more churches all at the same time. The church's New Campus Developer, Kristy Rutter, became an innovative merger matchmaker. As a merger investigator, Rutter developed a process of using the internet to find struggling churches, studying their websites, contacting them in person, and asking if they would entertain a merger conversation with The Chapel. It was such a unique strategy that *Christianity Today* profiled her.[2] The core of her strategy, she told *Christianity Today*, is to develop relationships:

The key to all mergers is relationship. The more relationships you have with other churches and their pastors, the more opportunities will arise. The best proactive merger strategy comes out of a heart to help other churches. We have helped far more churches with resources that have not merged with us than churches that have.

Rutter's vivacious personality and genuine concern for each church opened the door to many merger conversations. She not only spearheaded several mergers for The Chapel, but also helped several Chapel candidates merge with other churches that were a better fit. She went on to develop this process, helping churches nationwide as a consultant with my (Jim's) previous consulting company, MultiSite Solutions. She guaranteed every client a list within three months of at least ten vetted merger candidates followed by help for them with the merger process. Sadly, her untimely death ended the momentum of her series of contacts but not The Chapel's commitment to local pastoral relationships and multiplication through mergers strategy.

Merger Fact 27

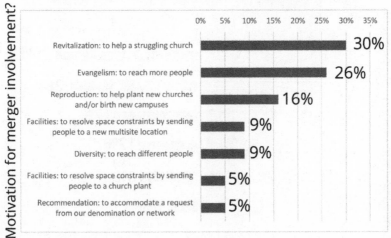

For *Lead* Churches, the Greatest Reason to Merge Is to Help Revitalize a Struggling Church

Motivation for merger involvement?

Revitalization: to help a struggling church	30%
Evangelism: to reach more people	26%
Reproduction: to help plant new churches and/or birth new campuses	16%
Facilities: to resolve space constraints by sending people to a new multisite location	9%
Diversity: to reach different people	9%
Facilities: to resolve space constraints by sending people to a church plant	5%
Recommendation: to accommodate a request from our denomination or network	5%

2019 Survey (asked only of lead churches): *What motivated your church to get involved with a merger?*

Riverside Church, in a northwest suburb of Minneapolis, added a second campus through a mission-advancement merger. "Reaching lost people was the most important thing for all of us," says Tom Lundeen, lead pastor of the lead church. His executive pastor, Skipp Machmer, adds this advice about the best way they found to build relationships with the church that joined them, "Eat together, ideally in homes, so that you move from sitting in rows to circles. We started getting to know one another around a table eating versus in meetings all the time. Creating space to develop community together was critical for relationships. When someone comes into someone else's home, it communicates that you are welcome, and you are a friend. I have heard over and over again how helpful and impactful that was for the group that joined us.

We've seen the idea of genuine, caring relationships between church leaders build positive connections in churches across the country. After all, as Merger Fact 27 points out, many potential lead churches have a heart to help revitalize a struggling church, and sometimes that results in a merger. As Merger Fact 28 points out, the greatest motive to merge is survival.

Merger Fact 28

For *Joining* Churches, the Greatest Reason to Merge Is Survival

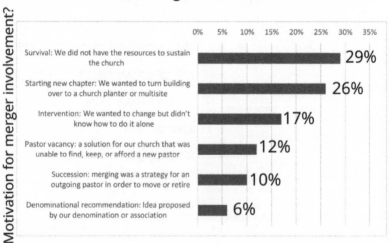

2019 Survey (asked only of joining churches): *What motivated your church to get involved with a merger?*

Church Hires a Pastor—And the Congregation Comes Along

We mentioned earlier that 40 percent of multisite campuses come by way of merger. These mergers happen in many different ways—sometimes with a struggling congregation, while other times with a stuck, stable, or even strong congregation.

One of the nation's fastest-growing churches gained several campuses in 2019 when it invited an area pastor to oversee its campus pastors at their eleven multisite locations, as well as help them start new campuses. Not only did he say yes, but his entire congregation came with him—all three campuses! Thus, Northview Church, led by Steve Poe, through the merger added three more campuses at once (bringing their total to fourteen at the time). As the joining church pastor, Mark Malin explained in a letter to the congregation:

> Our churches have so much in common. We are both multisite churches. We both have a strong desire to reach people who are far from God. We both have a strong desire to multiply our influence by planting more churches throughout Indiana in towns of all sizes. And we are both deeply committed to reaching the next generation for Christ.
>
> We have begun asking ourselves the question, "Could our churches be better together?" Could this be a way to plant more churches in more towns to reach more people who are far from God?

Church Helps a Struggling Church—And Later Invites It to Merge

Another example of a rebirth merger comes from Brian Walton, lead pastor at Calvary Christian Church in Winchester, Kentucky, from 2005 to 2014.

Walton knew of a church that for all practical purposes was closed. Sunday services hadn't been held in its facility in almost a year. A handful of people were still loosely affiliated with the building and would gather for a handful of functions each year. An eighty-four-year-old woman maintained the building—making sure the lawn was mowed, utilities paid, and so on. She said she just felt like God had told her to wait. "We spent a number of months learning her story, asking questions, and building relationships," Walton reports.

After about six months, Walton began a weekly Bible study on Thursday nights. "We didn't do the meetings in order to bring an agenda or to discuss plans; it was just Bible study and relationships," Walton says. After ten weeks he asked the Bible study group, "Would you like to explore some ways that we could go further with this?" A few months later this dying church was reborn when they launched weekend services as it merged with Calvary Christian.

The merger experience went so well that Calvary Christian began a prayerful process toward a second merger. "I've begun meeting weekly with the pastor there," he reports. "If the Lord moves and blesses, we will eventually bring up the subject. If he doesn't, we won't."

Church Asks for Help—And the Responding Church Suggests a Merger

Silver Creek Fellowship (who became the lead church) and Northside Fellowship (who became the joining church), about fifteen miles away from each other in Silverton, Oregon, have had a long-standing friendship and have jointly sponsored several events in the past.

Silver Creek Fellowship had been experiencing growth and blessing, but Northside had been through some serious leadership difficulties. As a result, Northside had experienced rapid decline, going from a Sunday attendance of over 150 to about 50 in six months.

"It seemed like the church might die, so I was invited by the Northside elders to come and meet with them to give them counsel and advice," Pastor Rob Barnes told us. Barnes felt that God wanted him to share a Scripture with them that included the lines "come with us and we will do you good" and "if you go with us, it will come about that whatever good the Lord does for us, we will do for you" (Num 10:29, 32).

Barnes used it to encourage them to see that they could become a part of the blessing that God was giving Silver Creek Fellowship. They did, and Northside Fellowship was rebirthed by merging with Silver Creek Fellowship.

Church Sends Exploratory Letters to Area Churches

What happens if you exhaust or lack a network of church relationships for exploring merger possibilities? We've seen both would-be lead churches and would-be joining churches canvass their area with personalized form letters, written on church letterhead.

Below are two actual examples that are among the best we've seen, with slight edits, including the addition of boldface. (If the second letter seems familiar, we first introduce it in chapter 4.)

Lead Church Inquiry

Dear Pastor [Name],

As co-laborers in our city together, it is our desire to be good neighbors with you, and let you know our intentions as a church.

Christ Fellowship is exploring opportunities with other local churches across Miami-Dade to see if there is any interest in engaging in a strategic partnership or merger conversation with our church.

It is estimated that more than **90 percent of people in Miami-Dade County do not attend church.** In our desire to help people follow Jesus, we are compelled to establish Christ Fellowship congregations in the surrounding communities where we are drawing significant numbers of people. In pursuit of our vision, Christ Fellowship has begun a **search for commercial facilities, schools, closed buildings, or property in your area. We are also open to strategic partnerships, rental agreements, or mergers with existing churches.**

Christ Fellowship began in 1917 as a church plant in Perrine, from the downtown Central Baptist Church. Under the twenty-three-year tenure of Dr. Rick Blackwood, Christ Fellowship became a multisite church in 2005. In 2019, Omar Giritli became the Lead Pastor having served the previous ten years on the staff of Christ Fellowship.

Christ Fellowship is a multi-generational, multicultural church with an average weekend attendance of nearly 10,000 people from 87 different nationalities, meeting in multiple locations across Miami-Dade County. We have a diverse staff of over 150 employees. Christ Fellowship also has a strong focus in reaching people for Christ internationally with global campuses in the Caribbean and Latin America. You can visit our website at cfmiami.org or find us on social media @cfmiami.

We deeply respect your congregation's history as well as its current ministry and understand if this invitation is not of any interest to you. However, we are following a process outlined in the book *Better Together: Making Church Mergers Work* by Jim Tomberlin and Warren Bird. We also believe that it is our Lord's desire and prayer expressed in John 17 that the world knows us by our love for one another and our unity in the shared mission to make disciples of all nations.

If you are interested in exploring any of these possibilities with us, or know of another church in your area that might be, please feel free to contact me at . **We will keep any correspondence with you confidential as we explore this conversation graciously together.**

I am grateful for your prayerful consideration. I look forward to connecting with you.

Kindest regards from your co-laborer in the Gospel,
[name and role, in this case Director of Campuses]

Joining Church Inquiry

Dear Pastor [Name],

Torrey Pines Christian Church is exploring several strategic growth opportunities, including merger with another church. We are writing to you and to several other area churches to ask if there is interest in **merging with our congregation**—and either **relocating** to or operating a **separate site** on our **ten-acre campus.**

If you are interested in discussing this possibility, please contact [name, email, cell phone]. He leads a team created by our board of directors to assess the feasibility of a merger or of other possibilities, including the hiring of a new minister to fill our open senior pastor position.

Torrey Pines Christian Church was founded in 1958 as a Disciples of Christ congregation on North La Jolla Scenic Drive, just a half mile from the University of California at San Diego. Annual attendance has fallen from its peak 15 years ago of 500 per Sunday to 200-250. Our campus has a **400-seat sanctuary**, a 100-seat chapel, and buildings for childcare, administration, and multi-use. **We have no debt, and believe these buildings are not being used to the full potential of God's glory**. Thus, we have embarked on assessing new ways to serve our community.

We are following a process outlined in a book, *Better Together: Making Church Mergers Work*, by Tomberlin and Bird. We will keep correspondence with you confidential within our 7-person team, and request that you keep it confidential to as small a group as possible. If you are interested in investigating possibilities, here are our next steps:

o By [date], please let us know if you are interested in exploring a potential merger.

o By [date], complete and return our enclosed questionnaire and submit any questions you have of us.

o By [date], if we both seem interested, let's set up a face-to-face meeting.

We appreciate your prayerful thoughts and consideration.

Yours in Christ,
[name and role]

Church Pursues Reconciliation

Is your church the cause or the result of a church split that occurred years ago? If so, most likely there is a need for healing and reconciliation. Even if a merger isn't the outcome, reconciliation is the right thing to pursue; it is honoring God and bringing a powerful testimony to the larger community. As Jesus prayed, "May they be brought to complete unity to let the world know that you sent me" (John 17:23). The apostle Paul challenged the church at Philippi:

> If you have any encouragement from being united with Christ, if any comfort from his love, if any fellowship with the Spirit, if any tenderness and compassion, then make my joy complete by *being like-minded*, having the same love, *being one in spirit and purpose*. Do nothing out of selfish ambition or vain conceit, but in humility consider others better than yourselves. Each of you should look out not only to your own interests, but also to the interests of others (Phil 2:1–4, emphasis added).

Someone has to take the first step toward a reconciliation. Could it be you? It could result in a reunion merger like the Louisiana churches we mentioned in chapter 4.

Church Pursues Diversity

Do you desire to be a more inclusive multiethnic church? Reach out to the local minority church and partner together in serving your community. Visit the services, take the pastor to lunch, exchange pulpits, develop a friendship, and see how God leads. Finding or becoming a good merger candidate starts with being a good neighbor to other churches in your community. As you serve together the community that you share in common, you may discover a comradeship that introduces the possibility of merging together. This approach is not for the faint of heart, but it can reap exponential kingdom gains as you demonstrate the power of the gospel to bring diverse groups together under the banner of Jesus.

> Finding or becoming a good merger candidate starts with being a good neighbor to other churches in your community.

We were intrigued by a pastor who added this comment to one of our surveys of church mergers: "You didn't ask why we merged." He went on to explain that he was pastoring an established church that was in transition from a traditional model of ministry to a more contemporary one. His church was also trying to transition to become a neighborhood church once again. "As the community began to change and members moved to the suburbs, we found we were losing a grip on the community the church was in," he said. Part of the change was a growing Hispanic community that "we desired to reach but weren't able to do." He developed a relationship with a Hispanic pastor in the community, and they partnered to reach the community.

That effort led to a formal merger of the two churches.

"Now we are a multigenerational, multiethnic, and multicultural church that not only reflects the community but is also finally poised to reach the whole community," the pastor concluded.

> Now we are a multigenerational, multiethnic, and multicultural church that not only reflects the community but is also finally poised to reach the whole community.

Do You See a Common Theme of Missional Advancement?

The church landscape across the United States is being transformed by realignments of churches around a compelling mission, often sharing a common theological orientation. We are convinced that we will see more of these kinds of mergers occur that revolve around mission advancement.

These new alignments or "tribes" are coming out of a mutual desire for greater impact. They are motivated by the strength of synergistic possibilities that a merger offers, "Two are better than one . . . and a cord of three strands is not quickly broken" (Eccl 4:9, 12). They are the new mini-denominations that are exponentially growing as a result of mergers of mutually healthy and like-minded churches. If your church has a compelling mission and strategy to reach more people and extend its impact, then invite other churches to join you who share your cause.

However, if you are drawn to a church out of a shared sense of mission, a common denomination, or network affiliation, initiate the conversation and get the discussion going.

> If you are drawn to a church out of a shared sense of mission, a common denomination, or network affiliation, initiate the conversation and get the discussion going.

Keep Looking beyond the Walls of Your Church

At least 1 percent of the Protestant churches in your community are going to close this year.[3] Could those churches instead be redeemed or revitalized through a merger with your church? Approach those churches with humility and a kingdom-of-God mindset about their situation and propose the possibility.

Meanwhile, serve your community together with other churches. Build bridges of trust with other local church leaders, always using the following ideas:

- **Connect**: Take the initiative to get acquainted. You share a common geography, why not share friendship over a cup of coffee?
- **Resource**: Share information, materials, and training freely. Make your expertise available. Develop coaching or mentoring opportunities.
- **Partner**: Collaborate together in areas of common interest and for the common good of the community.
- **Ask:** Could our two churches be better together by merging?

The community will be better served, local churches will be strengthened, and the kingdom of God will be extended. Mergers are more likely to grow out of that soil.

Notes

1. Tim Lucas and Warren Bird, *Liquid Church: Six Powerful Currents to Saturate Your City for Christ* (Grand Rapids, MI: Zondervan, 2019), 157–171.

2. Ed Stetzer, "Strategies for Church Mergers by Kristy Rutter," *Christianity Today*, May 29, 2014, https://tinyurl.com/qwyuteq.

3. Researchers have not determined a number of annual closures for US Protestant churches. Complicating factors are how to count mergers, transfers to other denominations, multisite campuses that close, nondenominational churches that close, etc. Estimates range from 4,000 to 10,000 that close annually. A conservative estimate of 4,000 would be approximately 1 percent of the nation's roughly 320,000 Protestant churches.

15

TOOLS FOR THE MERGER JOURNEY: TEMPLATES, EXAMPLES, AND A CHECKLIST

A growing number of churches have not only experienced success with multiple mergers, but they've also developed tools to use with future mergers.

For example, Ginghamsburg Church, a United Methodist congregation just north of Dayton, Ohio, has created a detailed feasibility study template to guide Ginghamsburg's leadership as they prayerfully consider whether a particular merger makes sense for their situation. The idea, according to Karen Smith, operations director, is not to replace the role of prayer but to provide helpful guidelines. "A feasibility study won't make the decision for you," she says, "but it can reveal if there are significant barriers that could prevent a merger from being successful since these evaluations are both an art and a science."

One of Ginghamsburg's mergers was with the hundred-plus-year-old Fort McKinley United Methodist Church, which in 2008 was a fading congregation of only forty weekly attendees, in an economically challenged neighborhood about fifteen miles from Ginghamsburg's original campus. Today it's a vibrant church of over 250 weekly worship attendees and it's bringing new life and hope to its at-risk community and changing the world one life at a time—locally, nationally, and globally. A weekly Sunday breakfast serves about 150, including many homeless men and women from area shelters. A Tuesday night dinner and Bible study draws in neighbors, and the Fort McKinley community has access to the nearby Ginghamsburg-supported food pantry. Fort McKinley also served as the neighborhood anchor partner for a community development project that built twenty-five new lease-to-own homes in the fifteen blocks behind the church for families struggling to afford housing. In the summer of 2019, the Fort served as the base of operations for disaster relief after an F4 tornado ripped through a nearby neighborhood, part of a cluster of eighteen tornados striking the Dayton area on Memorial Day. The Fort congregation provided financial resources and hours of labor to restore homes and relocate uninsured families left homeless. This merged church has skin in the game!

Most people at the church describe the process as a restart. Marilyn Hess, a member there for more than sixty years, grew up in the church and still serves in the church's food pantry and on its board. "Tears come to my eyes many Sundays," she says. "I never thought I'd see another era of great activity, enthusiasm, and service in this church."

Marilyn and her husband, Hugh, were part of the prayer meetings and vote to join with Ginghamsburg. They had to process some tough questions such as whether they'd be willing to give up their traditional choir and singing from hymnals. "I remember asking, 'How many of our traditions do we have to get rid of?' " says Marilyn, only to hear, "Any that keep people from coming to Jesus." When the issue was put that way, she was willing. "This was a dying church and we felt this neighborhood needed a church here." She voted yes.

Her husband Hugh, likewise, saw God's hand in the merger idea. "I didn't think the changes would be quite like this," he said shortly after the decision time. "But I voted 'yes' and stayed because it's not about me." He too saw the mission as more important than his own comfort.

Prayer, Changed Lives—And a Feasibility Study

Although it's important for the people of the joining church to sense God's leading, there is also merit in the research necessary to compile a thorough feasibility study. The intent, according to Karen Smith, "is to evaluate opportunities and barriers in four different areas before making a decision."

The market and culture summary compile a side-by-side comparison of the lead church (Ginghamsburg) and the joining church (in this case Fort McKinley). "It asks who we have the potential for reaching in the target community, what is the current culture or missional DNA of the church to be acquired as well as the makeup of its congregation, and how well do the makeup and opportunities of the target community and church match up with Ginghamsburg's missional calling," says Smith. It starts with each church's mission statement and related branding and suggests the cultural impact of the merger. Areas examined include ministry organizational structure, worship style, attendance and growth patterns, and target audience. It also looks at the demographics of each church, such as using census data from a combination of ZIP codes for population, median age, race, median household income, and percentage of individuals below the poverty level.

The operational and technical summary takes a hard look at the joining church's facilities and existing ministries. It itemizes the worship, media, and sound equipment and the condition of each major item. Same with office equipment. The physical plant profile looks at square footage room by room, seating, parking size and condition, plus HVAC (heating, ventilation, and air conditioning). Detailed notes describe disadvantages, such as the condition of the bathrooms and adequacy of sewage lines, issues with handicap access, roof condition, and adequacy of existing lighting. Ginghamsburg funded an environmental study that examined for asbestos, mold, water intrusion, and lead paint.

Another table summarized personnel and ministries. It covered budget issues related to finding and installing a campus pastor, makeup and function of the board, and an overview of all church ministry—both current status and current options in a merger. This section amounted to several pages covering everything from children's ministry to the church's community food pantry. Its details described, for example, the existing GED-completion program and outlined how it could be merged with the appropriate department at Ginghamsburg. It also detailed who is paid, how much, and what they do, in this case, a pastor, janitor, secretary, choir director, organist, bell choir director, senior citizen's director, and childcare providers—most on a very part-time basis.

The section on financial due diligence covers a wide range of issues. The ideal, according to Smith, is "a church with no debt and that still has funds available to address immediate issues identified by the study should a merger move forward." Areas include current giving patterns, current operational costs, review of any indebtedness and financial assets, insurances, tax status documentation, and claims and litigation records, if any.

The point of the financial study is to outline existing issues and a potential process for moving forward. For example, bank accounts would be opened and managed by the Ginghamsburg CFO. All current

Fort McKinley monies and investments would be moved into these new accounts. All Fort McKinley ministries post-merger would be subject to the same financial controls that exist currently at Ginghamsburg. Future projects are also itemized, from installation of a monitored fire detection system to wireless microphones, with timing tiers also noted (one, two, or three, depending on immediacy).

The final section of the feasibility study includes study recommendations and next steps. It advises whether the merger should move forward and if so, what the next steps might be. Once the decision to merge was made, a more detailed document with about fifty action steps was created, each line noting a projected start and finish date and who would be responsible for making it happen.

Even with all this due diligence, Ginghamsburg leaders always return to the issue of changed lives. As Smith says, "The greatest confirmation was the signs of transformation in the surrounding community—new neighborliness and hope, new community partnerships achieving results together, and people within the neighborhood who started calling 'the Fort' their church even though they may never have set foot in the door."

> Even with all this due diligence, Ginghamsburg leaders always return to the issue of changed lives.

The feasibility study took many hours, the talents of many people, and a few dollars, such as the environmental test. Ginghamsburg uses the feasibility study document in evaluating other potential mergers, recommending one church for an ongoing mentoring relationship with Ginghamsburg and rejecting another. "The match with our calling is of first importance," says Smith. "For instance, we didn't move forward with one church because the community was at a higher socioeconomic level than we felt called to reach. Second, Ginghamsburg had a great opportunity with college students at a university literally across the street. We do college ministry, but it is not an area in which we have a strong, proven track record of success. Once again, not a match."

But yet they keep looking. As Dave Hood, Fort McKinley's campus pastor during the transition, told us, "How many near-empty buildings are awaiting a mighty work to be done in them?"

Your Church Merger Toolbox

You may want to take Ginghamsburg's feasibility study, described above, and convert it into your own checklist for evaluating a potential merger. Or use the 25 Issues to Determine Merger Feasibility document later in this chapter to create an even broader feasibility study.

Here's a few more tools that I (Jim) have developed and found to be very helpful for churches on the merger journey. Taken together, you might call them a church merger toolbox:

1. Church Comparison Profile

We encourage senior church leaders to assess the merger possibility in the Exploration stage (of chapter 6) by making a side-by-side comparison profile of their two churches. Often when the two church teams see the comparisons, the similarities and differences stand out. This initial exercise also helps the leaders to clarify who is the lead church and who is the joining church.

Table 15.1 shows not only the profile, but examples from two actual churches.

Table 15.1

Church Merger Profile	Date completed: _____	
Topics	**Lead Church**	**Joining Church**
Church Information – Church Name – Address – City, State, Zip	The Gathering Church 7107 S. Yale Ave. Tulsa, OK 74136	Liberty Church 7777 S. Garnett Rd. Broken Arrow, OK 74012
Church History – Year Founded – Denomination – Lead Pastor – Year Became Lead Pastor	2006 Southern Baptist Brad Jenkins 2006 (founder)	1982 Southern Baptist Paul Taylor 1986

Statements		
– Mission	Our mission is to help people follow Jesus and share his story	Our mission is to intentionally help people become biblical disciples of Jesus in a relational environment
– Vision	n/a	n/a
– Values	Community. Mission. Worship.	on website
Staff (Number of FTEs)	4	7
Current Budget, Last Year's Income, and Current Debt	[provided but omitted from this book]	[provided but omitted from this book]
Worship Seating Capacity	300	400
Worship Service Time	9 a.m., 11:00 a.m.	9 a.m., 11:00 a.m.
Average Weekend Attendance		
– Adults	95–140	193
– Students	8–10	23
– Children	45–60	50
– TOTAL	170	250
Average Age of Congregation	20s and 30s	45
Baptisms (YTD)	10	0
Church Life Stage (strong, stable, or struggling)	Strong	Declining
Physical Assets		
– Property/ Land/Acreage	n/a	28 acres, insured for $5.5M

– Worship Center	n/a	Seats 400
– Education Center	n/a	
– Office Building	n/a	
– Other	Equipment trailer $50K–$75K	
Drive Time between Churches	5 minutes	same
Who Initiated Merger Possibility	Tulsa Metro Baptist Network Director of Missions	same
What Initiated the Conversation		
– Partnership	X (Praying for a permanent facility)	X (Succession)
– Crisis		
– Financial Challenges		
– Pastor Search		
– Mission		
– Other		
Approval Process (Who and % Required)	Elder plus congregation by simple majority	Elders, with church affirming the decision
Contact Person		
– Name	Brad Jenkins	Paul Taylor
– Title	Lead Pastor	Senior Pastor
– Email		
– Office Phone		
– Cell Phone		
Abbreviations: FTE=full-time equivalent, YTD=year to date, K=thousand, M=million		

2. Feasibility Template: 25 Issues Every Merger Must Address

As churches move into the Negotiation stage of the merger conversation (of chapter 6), we have identified twenty-five distinct issues that every church merger has to address to determine feasibility. Though every church merger is different and has a unique "church print," all will have to work through these twenty-five issues to assess their compatibility. Which issues are the most important and how they will be addressed will vary from church to church, but all the issues have to be addressed.

We recommend that the leadership teams of each church review these twenty-five issues separately and identify the problematic ones. Then review each other's list together. Most of the items will be non-issues, but usually three to five issues surface that could be potential deal breakers. If the two leadership teams can find a resolution to these problematic issues, then a merger is feasible and can be recommended to their churches for approval or affirmation.

This process will also give both churches the information needed to create a set of public FAQs (Frequently Asked Questions) as they present the merger to their respective congregations in the Declaration stage.

As you read through the list below, give a rating in the left-hand column for each. In comparing the difference between the lead church and joining church, give a rating of one to indicate minimal concern, two to indicate moderate concern, and three to indicate major concern. Table 15.2's list of 25 Issues to Determine Feasibility that have to be addressed in every church merger is then followed by an example of how specific churches worked through the list.

Table 15.2

25 Issues to Determine Feasibility (for Each Board to Complete Separately)		
Rating	**Doctrinal**	
_____	1. Theological beliefs	Is our church theologically conservative, moderate, or liberal? Is our church charismatic, reformed, or dispensational? Do we share similar or divergent views on the Bible, baptism, spiritual gifts, divorce, the role of women, response to LGBT issues, social justice issues, etc.?
_____	2. Governance	How similar or different are the two churches when it comes to local church government? Are

we more congregational or episcopal? Is our church board governed, staff led, or overseen denominationally?

_____ 3. Affiliations   Are the two congregations affiliated with the same denomination, network, or association? If not, is there compatibility? Are the affiliations mandatory? Will they remain or change?

Philosophy of Ministry

_____ 4. Mission   How does each church answer the question: "Why do we exist?" An honest answer will reveal how close or far apart we are on the primary purpose of the church. The strongest mergers are those that are primarily mission-driven, and with strong similarity of mission.

_____ 5. Vision   Vision is the picture of the preferred future. It describes where each church is going. How does each church answer the question, "If we succeed in fulfilling our mission as a church, what would our church look like ten years from now?" How similar are the two visions? Are the two congregations creating a new vision together? If not, can we embrace the vision of the other church?

_____ 6. Values   Values are the principles that guide a church on how it does ministry. They reflect what really matters to a church. How similar or divergent are our values?

_____ 7. Discipleship   Effective churches are intentional about making
Strategy   disciples of Jesus. How similar or divergent is our discipleship pathway?

_____ 8. Worship Style   Often worship style is the primary basis for choosing a church. How similar or different are the worship styles of our churches? Are we contemporary, traditional, or blended? Is our worship style more participatory or performance-oriented? Does our church have choirs or worship bands, drums or organs, pews or theater-seats, stained-glass or video screens? If we are not similar, are we willing to accept a different worship style?

_____ 9. Preaching   Who will be bringing the weekend messages to the congregation? Will the sermons be delivered in-person or by video?

_____ 10. Membership   What are the requirements for church membership at our church? Will those requirements transfer to the other church? If a merger does occur, will the membership transfer automatically or will a membership class be required?

_____ 11. Programs   What church programs and ministries are nonnegotiable and therefore untouchable? What programs could be integrated into the new entity and which ones would need to be recalibrated or eliminated?

_____ 12. Budget   Budgets reflect the priorities of a church. What do we learn about each other by reviewing the budgets? What percentage of budget goes to staff, debt reduction, ministries and missions?

Personnel

_____ 13. Expectations   How does our congregation understand the merger relationship? Is this merger a marriage, an adoption, a rebirth, or an ICU merger? (See table 5.2.) How each party sees the merger determines their expectations of the relationship. The sooner both churches can define the relationship and get on the same page concerning expectations, the smoother the merger process will go.

_____ 14. Lead Pastors   The first question that has to be addressed if there are two lead pastors involved is the status of the lead pastor of the joining church post-merger. Will the joining church pastor be redeployed in another staff position within the church, or be given a severance package? (See chapter 9.)

_____ 15. Boards and Committees   Will the existing boards and committees be integrated, recalibrated, or eliminated? Will the board members stay the same? Will all, some, or none remain?

_____ 16. Staff   Are the job descriptions, pay levels, contracts, and benefits comparable or dramatically different? What will be the staff needs in the new church entity? What staff will remain in their current position, be redeployed to another area in the church, downsized, or released? What are the severance policies?

_____ 17. Missionaries   Will funding support for the missionaries, para-church ministries, and organizations supported by the church be continued, phased out over time, or ended upon completion of the merger?

Legal

_____	18. Lawyer	Do we have legal counsel to guide us through the legal steps of a church merger?
_____	19. Church name	Will there be a name change of one or both congregations? How will that be decided?
_____	20. Voting	How will the decision to merge be decided and by whom—the denomination, the board or the congregation? What do our church bylaws require? Will a congregational vote be required? If so, what will be the process and what percentage is required for approval? What is the lowest approval percentage the two churches are willing to accept?
_____	21. Dissolution	What will be the dissolution process of the joining church? Will this be a strict merger, asset purchase by the lead church, or a donation by the joining church? What do the laws of the state dictate? (See chapter 11.)
_____	22. Property or Facility	What will the new church entity do with any property and/or facilities gained in the merger? Will the property and/or facilities be kept or sold? Is there a reversionary clause in the joining church bylaws dictating the outcome of church property in the event of dissolution? What are the legal requirements and state laws for transfer of church property?
_____	23. Assets and Liabilities	What tangible assets do the two churches bring to the table in terms of property, facilities and equipment? Is there an inventory of all property and equipment? Due diligence is a must to determine what repairs, maintenance costs, and hidden liabilities come with these items.
_____	24. Debt Management	What debt does either church bring to the merger? How manageable is it? How will it be addressed?
_____	25. Timeline	When is the earliest possible date a merger could occur between the two churches? What are the things that need to happen and by when for a merger to occur?

Working through the 25 Issues to Determine Feasibility is the hard and prayerful work of merger deliberations. It is an essential step in helping both churches learn each other's culture, identity, and other relevant issues. Every church, like every human being, has a story. The better you know each other going into the merger, the better the chances of the merger being approved and the better the integration will be post-merger. We hope this process will surface all the hidden liabilities and potential landmines that could derail the merger. It is a proactive step that not only helps to determine feasibility but will also help preempt surprises and generate congregational confidence as you demonstrate that you have done your due diligence.

In fall 2010, co-lead pastors Scott Ridout (now the president of the Baptist denomination named Converge) and Chad Moore of Sun Valley Community Church in Gilbert, Arizona, initiated a conversation with the senior pastor of the Bethany Community Church in neighboring Tempe to let him know of their plans to start a multisite campus in his area. These pastors had all served their congregations side by side in the same greater community together for two decades although their churches were at two different stages in their life cycles. Sun Valley had been growing steadily since the church started in 1990 and was bursting at the seams with nearly four thousand attendees during weekend services. Bethany Community Church was in a seventeen-year decline. It was down to one service with eight hundred people attending there. Meanwhile, Sun Valley had hundreds of families attending from Tempe, where Bethany was located.

In that initial conversation, Scott and Chad proposed the possibility of joining forces with Bethany to become one church with Sun Valley, instead of starting a new campus. After many conversations between these leaders, a dialogue began with the elders of Bethany and the Sun Valley leadership.

Initially, Bethany's elders made the decision not to pursue the idea of a merger. This culminated in the senior pastor, courageously and humbly, resigning. He stated his reasons for resigning was his love for the church, his inability to turn the church around, and the belief that he was not the right pastor to lead them into the future. He graciously tendered his resignation with the hope his departure would be a catalyst for the change that was needed for a better future.

Two months later the elders restarted the conversation with Sun Valley, resolved some earlier misunderstanding, and, with the prayer support of Sun Valley's leaders, began to wrestle through the best scenario for the future of Bethany. After numerous meetings, discussions, and lots of prayer seeking God's will, both leadership teams agreed to contract Jim Tomberlin to assist them in exploring the feasibility and desirability of the two churches becoming one through what can best be described as an adoption process.

Both churches moved through the various merger stages and within ten months of the initial conversation with the senior pastor, the Bethany elders recommended to their congregation "to join forces with

Sun Valley Community Church," posting the explanation on the Bethany church website.

The recommendation required a 75 percent approval by the membership. It passed by 80 percent and became Sun Valley Community Church–Bethany Campus three months later.

Two examples of how churches have addressed the twenty-five issues are in appendixes C and D. The first example reflects how Sun Valley Community Church, mentioned above, resolved the issues with Bethany Community Church. The second document by Christ Fellowship Miami reflects a lead church being proactive with the issues even before there is a merger possibility.

3. Timeline Template

In chapter 6, we outlined the stages of a merger and showed an actual timeline example (table 6.2). How do you create a timeline? Start with a discussion of these two questions: When is the earliest possible date a merger could occur between the two churches? What are the things that need to happen, and by when, for a merger to occur? In short, you start with the completion date and work backwards.

Though every merger is different, the key components of the merger conversation fit into the five stages described in chapter 6 and illustrated in the timeline below (Figure 15.3):

- Exploration (1–2 months): Governing Bodies Determine Possibility
- Negotiation (1–2 months): Governing Bodies Address 25 Issues to Determine Feasibility
- Declaration (1–2 months): Merger Announcement & Vote/ Poll to Determine Desirability
- Consolidation (1–3 months): Final Service Celebrates the Past & Inaugural Service Begins New Chapter
- Integration (1–36 months): Facility Upgrades, Grand Opening and/or Relaunching, Governing Body Monitors Merger Implementation

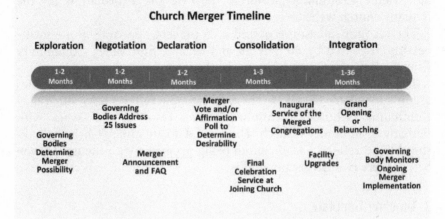

Figure 15.3

4. Merger Recommendation Example

The Declaration stage (of chapter 6) begins with a recommendation to merge if congregational approval is required, or with a merger announcement if the decision is decided by the board or denominational leadership. Typically, this is announced verbally, simultaneously at both churches, and then posted on their respective websites with a corresponding FAQ. Here is how Prospect Christian Church in the Chicago suburbs made their announcement—short and clear, presented in a unified voice, and pointing people to options for more information:

> It is with great excitement that the leadership team and trustees of Prospect Christian Church unanimously recommend that Prospect Christian merge with The Bridge Community Church of Des Plaines. The details of this merge are included in the Merge FAQ that is being handed out and available at the church and on the web site.

5. Frequently Asked Questions for Church Members

One of the most helpful tools for communication in the Declaration stage is a Frequently Asked Question (FAQ) document, as mentioned previously in chapter 6, that is made available to a church's entire constituency, both online and in print. Below are the typical questions that a church merger FAQ seeks to address. Then in appendixes E and F you can see examples of FAQs from specific churches.

- How did this merger idea come about?
- Why are we considering a merger?
- What are the benefits of this proposed merger?
- What is a multisite church? [If applicable]
- Will our church have a new name and what will it be?
- Who will be our pastor?
- What will happen to the existing pastor and staff?
- What will happen to the church board and committees?
- What will happen to the church's facilities?
- What will the worship services be like?
- How will the sermons be delivered?
- How will the budget and finances be managed?
- How will current membership be transferred?
- Will our denomination and affiliations change?
- What will happen to our supported missionaries and organizations?
- What will the merger cost? Can we afford it?
- Who will decide if this merger happens?
- If the merger happens, what will change?
- What is the timeline for this proposed merger?
- What will happen if the merger doesn't go through?
- What are my next steps?

6. Vote and Poll Ballots Template

The Declaration stage begins with a merger recommendation or announcement to both congregations accompanied with an FAQ document. This is followed by congregational town halls and small group gatherings at both congregations, culminating in a congregational vote or poll by the joining church, if not both congregations. The outcome of the vote or poll will reveal, "Is this desirable?"

Even if a congregational vote is not required by either congregation, we recommend offering a poll to the congregation to affirm the decision of the ruling body. Though permission may not be needed, offering a poll will reveal congregational buy-in and build ownership for the decision.

The following examples are well-thought-through, clear, concise, positive, spiritually focused invitations for congregational approval or affirmation. The first example is a poll from Southbridge Fellowship church in Raleigh, North Carolina, to the church that was looking to join them:

> For the past several months God has been stirring the hearts of the Elders of Covenant Church to the possibilities offered by joining Southbridge Fellowship. Living under the awareness of the responsibility of spiritual leadership, we believe this uniting of the two churches is God's preferable future for our congregations. We believe this unanimously and with deep conviction.
>
> We now bring it to the people of Covenant Church for affirmation.
>
> We dare not make a decision of this magnitude based on a popular vote of our own preferences—for or against. Your responsibility as a regular attendee is to examine your own heart and affirm or reject the Elder Board's recommendation to join Southbridge Fellowship based on your own sense of God's leading.
>
> So to the regular and faithful attendees of Covenant Church, the question before you is this: based on what you have seen and heard, as well as your own prayerful search for understanding, **can you affirm with us that this union is led by God?**
>
> __ **YES** I affirm and support the conviction of the Elders of Covenant Church that God is leading us to join Southbridge Fellowship.
>
> __ **NO** I cannot affirm and support the conviction of the Elders of Covenant Church that God is leading us to join Southbridge Fellowship.
>
> **Please answer the question below only if you are a member of Covenant Church.**
>
> __ **YES** After prayerful consideration, I have determined it is God's will for me to transfer my membership to Southbridge Fellowship. I understand that my membership transfer will be complete upon the signing of the Southbridge Fellowship Membership Covenant.
>
> __ **NO** After prayerful consideration, I am not ready to transfer my membership to Southbridge Fellowship.

Comments:

_____

_____

_____

Name (please print very legibly):

_____

Here is another ballot example. Notice also how even the nonmembers were invited to express their opinion on the proposed merger:

Vote on Proposed Merger

Please indicate with an (X) your responses below, marking all relevant lines:

_____I AGREE with the recommendation of ABC Church's senior pastor and elders and vote in favor of our church merging with XYZ Church.

_____I DO NOT AGREE with the recommendation of ABC Church's senior pastor and elders and vote against our church merging with XYZ Church.

_____ I am a member of ABC Church.

_____ If the merger is approved, I would like my membership automatically transferred to XYZ Church as of today.

_____ I am not a member but am a regular attender of ABC Church.

Please sign and provide your information below (note: anonymous votes will not be counted).

_____

Signature   Name (please print)

_____

Phone   Email

7. Merger Process Checklist

Here is a brief to-do list to review as you go through the merger process. We assume that you're starting with an education about mergers by reading this book with your board and staff. The chapters referenced below, from *Better Together*, provide further explanation of each item.

- Clarify the mission, vision, and discipleship pathway of your church. Why does your church exist—its mission? What is it trying to accomplish—its vision? How is it making disciples—the discipleship pathway? (Chapter 2)
- Assess the health of your church. Is it growing, plateaued, or declining? Are you strong, stable, stuck, or struggling? (Chapter 2)
- Clarify the motive behind merging. Is it economic, facility, mission, multisite, reconciliation, denomination, succession, pastor search, or multiethnic driven? (Chapter 4)
- Check with your denomination, association, or network for guidelines, resources, and opportunities around church mergers. (Chapters 4 and 16)
- Find a mentor, coach, or consultant to assist you through the merger process. (Chapter 16)
- Determine if your church is the lead or joining church. (Preface and chapter 1)
- Identify churches with merger potential. (Chapter 13)
- After finding one or more churches to potentially merge with, begin the merger conversation around the three questions that frame the merger process. Is this merger possible? Feasible? Desirable? (Chapter 6)
- Determine which merger model best represents your merger opportunity. Is it a rebirth, adoption, marriage, or an ICU merger? (Chapter 5)
- Do a demographic survey of your community, perhaps using US Census Bureau data, Wikipedia, or survey information from one of several providers. (Chapter 16)
- Assess the redemptive potential of your community. How many churches? How unchurched is the population? (Chapters 13 and 14)
- Complete a church merger comparison profile. (Chapter 15)
- Create a timeline of the five stages of the merger process: dating, courtship, engagement, wedding, marriage. (Chapters 6

and 15)
- Address all merger issues and identify the potential deal breakers. (Chapter 15)
- Identify the potential landmines. (Chapter 8)
- Determine financial costs of the merger. (Chapter 11)
- Define what a successful merger would look like one, three, and five years later. (Chapter 7)
- Prepare a legal document for church dissolution and transfer of property and assets on approval of the merger. (Chapter 11)
- Determine the vote or poll process and what percentage is required for acceptance. (Chapters 6, 10, and 15)
- Evaluate all ministries to determine integration, recalibration, or elimination. (Chapters 6 and 15)
- Create a communication strategy and FAQ for both churches. (Chapters 6 and 15)
- Develop the integration and implementation plan to commence on merger approval. (Chapters 6, 8, and 15)
- Plan the final celebration worship service and initial inaugural worship service. (Chapters 6 and 15)
- At each major decision point, confirm God's leading through prayer, Holy Spirit promptings, scriptural confirmations, wise counselors, and unmistakable divinely orchestrated circumstances. (Chapter 13)

Pastoral Perspective on Merging

Our final tool is a pastoral letter written by Scott Ridout to the board and staff of both churches just before the vote. It reads like a letter from the apostle Paul! Here's the condensed summary of what he wrote:

My prayers for Bethany/Sun Valley Staff and Leadership
This morning I was thinking about this opportunity we have . . . an opportunity I believe has been given by God and leadership that has been led by God in the process, and I want to begin by saying "thanks."

Here are my prayers for you as you will lead the change . . . Not things I want *from* you, but things I desire for you . . .

My first prayer is that you would be as convinced as I am that we are better together than we would ever be apart.

My second prayer is that as a result of coming together, we would experience a level of community that we've never had with any other group of people before.

Third, I pray that our collaboration and cross-training would be unmatched by any other ministry and a model for other churches.

Connected to that, my fourth prayer is that the celebrations we have for each other would be genuine and life giving.

My fifth prayer is that you personally would be fulfilled in ministry, reach the full potential of your gifts and experience a fruitfulness in your life that you have never seen before.

Sixth, and this is the hardest one, my prayer for you is that you will embrace the pain of change for a more impactful future together.

Finally, my greatest hope for you is that, in our time together, you will experience personal transformation in Christ.

We will do our best to make sure we are leading toward His purpose, in His power, for His glory.

Wow! With leadership like this, no wonder this church continues to flourish. May every merger reflect this attitude and heart for a kingdom-advancement, outreach-minded, life-giving partnership.

16

WHERE DO YOU GO FROM HERE?

Living Word Church in Pelham, Alabama, probably represents a lot of churches. A good man started it, reached people through it, ministered sacrificially, and along the way led them to acquire land and build facilities including a 280-seat auditorium. He served as the church's only pastor for twenty-five years and abruptly died of a heart attack—without a succession plan. That left his widow and about forty members with some tough decisions.

The story shifts from common to uncommon at this point. Before his death, the pastor—who had envisioned a growing church—had talked with his wife about forming a partnership with Church of the Highlands, a fast-growing Birmingham church based about twenty miles away that had begun expanding into campuses around Birmingham. The widow called Highlands on behalf of her church, saying to pastor Chris Hodges, "You can have everything if you don't sell it."

After the merger, Church of the Highlands took six weeks to renovate the building, expand parking, and add technology for its heavy emphasis on video teaching feeds. Highlands then sent a worship team to lead weekly services. Members who lived in the area were encouraged to attend that campus. Four years later, "it's our most successful campus," Hodges says, "and we're in the process of enlarging the facility. One of the joining church's members told us that what has happened has been a fulfillment of their prayers for many years. That kind of story needs to happen more often!"

And the story doesn't end there. The campus also hosts a Hispanic service, which now draws more than three hundred people weekly. It had been a small church meeting in a Pelham basement and was invited to join the new Highlands campus there. "We have the same vision, the same theology," Layne Schranz, associate pastor at Highlands, said. "We realized we could do more together."[1]

Kingdom Advancement through Church Mergers

At the end of the day, we need more churches not fewer—but those churches need to be prevailing, life-giving, high-impact, reproducing churches, churches that are making a difference, not just taking up space or holding on. Healthy churches, like all living things, reproduce. But if a church cannot turn itself around, then is it more of a liability than an asset? Is it really wise to keep it going if it's unhealthy and irrelevant? Could not two strong churches have an even greater impact by joining forces, and ultimately through their synergy, create even more reproducing churches? Our hope is that this book will stimulate further movement on revitalizing and synergizing existing churches through mergers that will result in propagating healthier, reproducing churches.

> Our hope is that this book will stimulate further movement on revitalizing and synergizing existing churches through mergers that will result in propagating healthier, reproducing, and multiplying churches.

Church mergers have moved for many to the front burner—and for some it is *the* next big thing. But in some ways, this is not a surprise. Any place where churches have been established for two or more generations will have a need for mergers. The research documents ongoing growth in this rising phenomenon, and we've tried to offer helpful language and categories to facilitate this conversation. We have drawn from surveys of hundreds of churches and personally interviewed dozens of them over a decade to bring to the surface the important trends and proven best practices. But most important, we wanted to write a book that would help church leaders discern if a merger is a possibility in their future, and if so, how to do it healthily and successfully.

Are you sensing the "urge to merge"? If you have become convinced that a merger could be a viable option for your church, what is your next step? Where do you go from here? Here are some suggested next steps to get you started down the road toward a church merger:

- *Define reality.* The first task of leaders is to define reality. Where is your church in its life cycle? Is it growing, plateaued, or declining? Courageous church leaders do not live in denial but embrace reality and help others to see it. For help see figure 5.1 and table 5.2.
- *Clarify the purpose of your church.* What is the mission, vision, and discipleship pathway of your church? The more clarity you have around what God is calling your church to *be* and then *do*, the better you will be able to determine whether a merger is in the best interest of your church. If you need further help in this area, here are four must-read books: *The Unstuck Church,*[2] *Church Unique,*[3] *Simple Church,*[4] and *The Multi-Site Church Revolution.*[5]
- *Assess the health of your church.* Is your church a candidate to be a lead church or joining church in a merger? Is your church strong, stable, stuck, or struggling? Take the self-assessment test in chapter 13 to determine merger readiness and identify the merger model in chapter 5 that best describes your merger potential. Also take the free online Unstuck Church Assessment to see where your church is in its life cycle at https://assess.theunstuckchurch.com/.
- *Do a demographic survey of your region.* What is the socioeconomic and racial makeup of the larger community you serve? Does your church attendance reflect the demographics of the larger community? What is the best way to reach and serve those beyond the walls of your church? Check out the US Census Bureau online,[6] Wikipedia[7] (for your city/town and county), and the Chamber of Commerce[8] info for your city to better understand the community you are called to reach and serve. For a thorough, scientific demographic analysis of your community, commission a Kingdom Analytics study[9], Church Analytics study[10], or a Joshua Survey[11] for your region.
- *Assess the redemptive potential of your community.* How many people are unchurched, dechurched, or anti-churched in your community? There is a simple way to get a rough estimate of the outreach potential within your church's reach by simply identifying the total number of churches in your community where people can hear the gospel and multiplying it by seventy-five people (the average church attendance in the United States). Then compare it against the total local population figure. That will give you a rough estimate of the redemptive potential and underserved people in your community.

National studies indicate that 60 to 80 percent of Americans do not attend church on a weekly or near-weekly basis.

- *Assess the church landscape in your community.* One out of one hundred churches in your community is likely to close in the next twelve months. Are any of those good candidates to merge with you? On the other hand, are there any vibrant churches you may want to merge with? Are there any churches in your denomination, network, or region with whom you could initiate a merger possibility conversation? Are you engaged with any local churches in strategic ministry partnerships that could develop into a merger conversation?
- *Study this book.* Go through *Better Together: Making Church Mergers Work* (this expanded and updated edition) with your staff and lay leaders. Engage your staff and lay leaders in the merger conversation. Discuss the pros and cons of merging with another church. Is this something your church should consider?
- *Find help.* Seek out a mentor, coach, or consultant to assist in facilitating the merger process. There is no need to pay the "stupid tax" that others have already paid. There are many landmines you can step on and potholes to fall into on the merger journey. It is good stewardship and wise to have an experienced guide to assist you along the way. Also seek advice from your denominational or network office. Talk to others who have experienced a church merger. Bring in a consultant. Or invite Jim Tomberlin's team at The Unstuck Group to walk with you through this process.

Seek advice from your denominational or network office. Talk to others who have experienced a church merger. Bring in a consultant.

As wise King Solomon says, "Plans fail for lack of counsel, but with many advisers they succeed" (Prov 15:22). Every church merger needs a facilitator that both congregations can trust who knows how to navigate the delicate conversations that have to occur for a successful merger.

- *Keep praying.* Intercede with an open heart that God will direct your steps and reveal merger possibilities if that will best serve the kingdom purpose for your church and your community. God spoke through his prophet Jeremiah telling his people in Babylonian captivity to "seek the peace and prosperity of the city to which I have carried you into exile. Pray to the LORD for it, because if it prospers, you too will prosper" (Jer 29:7). God said to Jonah, "Should I not have concern for the great city Nineveh, in which there are more than a hundred and twenty thousand people who cannot tell their right hand from their left?" (Jonah 4:11).

- God cares about the people in your region. Walk and pray around your community. Pray for God's burden for the lost and the least where he has planted your church. Ask God to show you where he is working in your community and then join him there with others who share your concern.

More Mergers on the Horizon

Healthy, mission-driven mergers are happening in an unprecedented way today. We believe that even more church mergers are occurring at a faster pace than when we published the first edition of this book in 2012. Church mergers, which were on the rise before the COVID-19 pandemic, will be an increasing part of the "new reality" going forward. We've entered a new era in which the more historically practiced ICU model of mergers have been eclipsed by a new era of mission-driven mergers, from multisite campuses to new homes for church planters to revitalizations in mainline contexts. The big difference in these new kinds of mergers is that they don't reduce church impact from two local churches down to one. Instead of diminishing kingdom presence and witness, they can gain greater influence, sometimes even multiplying it exponentially!

The idea of leveraging local church strengths to create ministry synergy and mission advancement is the core message of this book. Rebirth, adoption, marriage, and even occasionally ICU mergers can and are succeeding and are worth considering because they offer another option besides holding on or dying. This approach to a healthy merger offers great hope and possibilities to the 80 percent of churches across the United States that are stuck, struggling, or declining.

> The idea of leveraging local church strengths to create ministry synergy and mission advancement is the core message of this book.

Certainly, your church can flourish through merging with another. If you're already a vibrant church with solid growth, merging offers a way to extend your reach and impact. This book is a guide on how to navigate successfully the merger journey for the strong and the struggling church.

Parker Hill Community Church in Scranton, Pennsylvania, was started in 1853 and Mark Stuenzi has been its lead pastor since 1989. During his many years there, he and his wife have built a number of relationships in the community, including relationships with believers in other churches. When a nearby church was struggling to find direction for its future, two key leaders from that church came to Stuenzi and asked for some advice. Over a breakfast meeting, Stuenzi encouraged them to consider a merger with another like-minded church. "I left the door open for the possibility that the 'adopting' church might be someone other than us, but also encouraged them to consider a relationship with us," he explains. A long process of what Stuenzi calls "dating" followed that initial breakfast conversation. "Eventually, a merger was completed that totally changed our future as a church," Stuenzi says.

Later Parker Hill welcomed another adoption, again with very positive results. "Both were real 'God-things,'" he reports. "Both of the declining churches that we adopted have provided us with facilities and resources at just the right time. Our first adoption led us to adopt a multisite strategy and opened the door for much growth. Our second adoption provided us with a building for our student ministries at a time when they had outgrown their space. We were given a beautiful 150-year-old building—with only four parking spaces!" However, it was near enough to the main campus that parents could drop off and pick up their students conveniently.

The adoptions have given birth to much spiritual fruit already. For some, the Parker Hill adoptions have brought reconciliation through the healing of old wounds. Parker Hill's first merger was once a growing evangelical church. During a messy church split in the 1980s, many people who left that church ended up attending Parker Hill. The adoption process brought some of those people back together and brought a sense of closure to many who had left that church. "I know very personally how much that meant to at least one person," Stuenzi says. "My wife had grown up in that church, came to Christ through a Vacation Bible School there, and was baptized in that sanctuary. There was a sense of closure for her."

For others the mergers have given them hope. Harry was eighty years old when the first merger happened. He eventually became a sound technician in the children's ministry area. "It was great to see him serving every week—in his suit and tie—in a room that had previously been used only for the occasional potluck dinner," says Stuenzi. "During his first week in this new role, he was in tears because, as he told us, 'I never thought there would be so many children in this building again.'"

Parker Hill Community Church is all about helping people find their way back to God through Jesus Christ. The church's passion, according to Stuenzi, "is to provide a spiritual home for people throughout northeast Pennsylvania." Church mergers have helped Parker Hill achieve that mission. "We will actively pursue this as a future strategy for outreach," Stuenzi says. Such is the promise and fruit of a Holy Spirit–guided, mission-focused merger. And today as never before, courageous, faith-directed leaders are exploring the possibility that a merger may be the vehicle that God uses to be *better together* in reaching more people, serving their communities better, and further extending the kingdom of God.

Two churches can be *better together* through a healthy merger! As we affirmed earlier, "Two are better than one because they have a good return for their labor" (Eccl 4:9).

Is there a church merger on *your* horizon?

Notes

1. Greg Garrison, "Dwindling Pelham Congregation Rebounds after Merger with Megachurch," *The Birmingham News*, September 3, 2011, https://tinyurl.com/uslhyqj.

2. Tony Morgan, *The Unstuck Church: Equipping Churches to Experience Sustained Health* (Nashville: Thomas Nelson, 2017).

3. Will Mancini, *Church Unique: How Missional Leaders Cast Vision, Capture Culture, and Create Movement* (San Francisco: Jossey-Bass, 2008). See also Will Mancini and Warren Bird, *God Dreams: 12 Vision Templates for Finding and Focusing Your Church's Future* (Nashville: LifeWay, 2016).

4. Thom S. Rainer and Eric Geiger, *Simple Church: Returning to God's Process for Making Disciples* (Nashville: B&H Publishing, 2011).

5. Surratt, Ligon, and Bird, *The Multi-Site Church Revolution.*

6. See www.census.gov/ and navigate to American Community Survey.

7. http://en.wikipedia.org

8. www.uschamber.com

9. www.kingdomanalytics.com/

10. www.churchanalytics.com

11. https://joshuasurvey.com/

APPENDIX A: MERGER RESEARCH

Several layers of research have gone into the creation of this book:

1. **2019 National Survey**. We received 962 usable responses from a 74-question survey fielded 9/4/19–12/31/19. We report the findings in the 28 "Merger Facts" graphics found across the pages of this book. The survey was promoted with major sponsorship by the authors, The Unstuck Group, Leadership Network, ECFA (the Evangelical Council for Financial Accountability) and our publisher. We received additional publicity from 4Sight, Aspen Group, Converge, ECFA, Exponential, Ministry Solutions, Mosaix Global Network, MultiSite Solutions, NewThing Network, Portable Church, Samford University Ministry Training Institute, TheChurchLawyers.com, Vanderbloemen, unSeminary, and XPastor.[1]

2. **2011 National Survey**. We received 424 usable responses from a 51-question survey fielded 3/3/11–5/10/11 by Leadership Network with support by many other individuals and organizations. We report the findings in this book, most updated by the 2019 survey. The findings were also published by Leadership Network as "Making Multisite Mergers Work: New Options for Being One Church in Two or More Locations" by Warren Bird and Kristin Walters.[2]

3. **Leadership Network Phone Survey**. The research trigger for the first edition of *Better Together* was a phone survey Leadership Network sponsored through Barna Research in December 2007. Primary findings included that 2 percent had merged in the last three years, 5 percent had, during the last year, discussed merging in the "next two years" (and an additional 2 percent had discussed sharing their facility with another congregation as a possible step toward a merger). Among the 5 percent that had discussed merging, one-fourth (24 percent) said they'll continue to move toward a merger ("definitely" or "probably), and the rest said they're not likely to merger (71

percent) or they didn't know (5 percent).

4. **Academic Research**. Many doctoral dissertations exist that analyze specific merger issues or specific churches impacted by a merger. We have obtained and reviewed as many of them as possible.

5. **Field Consultations**. Many stories in this book come from first-hand experiences of the authors. Across many years (2003-2020) Jim Tomberlin has conducted consultations with over one hundred churches that are exploring or working through the merger process. Likewise, Warren Bird has conducted several dozen merger interviews, ranging from in-person to phone and email.

All named stories in this book are told with the permission and verification of those described in the stories.

Notes

1. Researcher note: for the 28 Merger Fact graphics, the number (N) of participants represented in each is as follows: 1 N=279, 2 N=269, 3 N=684, 4 N=629, 5 N=82, 6 N=430, 7 N=605, 8 N=772, 9 N=495, 10 N=536, 11 N=490, 12 N=147, 13 N=90, 14 N=92, 15 N=606, 16 N=493, 17 N=195, 18 N=526, 19 N=438, 20 N=536, 21 N=529, 22 N=232, 23 N=537, 24 N=609 and N=510, 25 N=651, 26 N=658, 27 N=935, 28 N=186.

2. See earlier footnote with bibliographic reference on this report.

APPENDIX B: MERGER FACTS

The following material summarizes the 28 Merger Facts found across the book. All of the research comes from our national survey of 962 participants described in Appendix A.

1. 20% of Mergers Become a Location for a New or Replanted Church. (See page 7.)

2. Multisite Momentum Shows No Sign of Slowing. (See page 40.)

3. Almost 6 in 10 (59%) of the Joining-Church Facilities Continue to Be Used. (See page 42.)

4. Not All Declining Churches Are Financially Struggling. (See page 64.)

5. For Most, the Merger Strategy to Become a New Church Developed over Time. (See page 70.)

6. 4 in 5 Joining Churches Vote about the Merger, Many Requiring Only a Simple Majority. (See page 82.)

7. The Average Merger Time Frame Is 8 Months. (See page 84.)

8. 82% of Surveyed Mergers Said They'd Do It Again. (See page 92.)

9. Most Joining Church Members Automatically Become Members at the Lead Church. (See page 99.)

10. Only a Small Percentage of Joining Church Members Depart Post-Merger. (See page 99.)

11. The Majority of Mergers Continue the Joining Church's Missionary and Nonprofit Support. (See page 100.)

12. Failed Mergers Most Often Trace Back to Conflict over Personnel or Traditions. (See page 108.)

13. Joining Churches Seem to Be the Most Hesitant about the Potential Merger. (See page 112.)

14. The Main Obstacle to Merging Is Ministry Differences. (See page 114.)

15. 1 in 3 Close the Joining Church during the Transition to Becoming a Multisite Campus, on Average for 4 Months. (See page 117.)

16. Most Joining Churches Have a Pastor—Who Stays. (See page 125.)

17. For Senior Pastors of the Joining Church Who Don't Stay, the Median Severance Package Is 2-6 Months of Pay (and Likewise for Staff, It's Approximately 1 Month of Pay). (See page 126.)

18. Two-Thirds of Joining Churches Are Represented on the Board after the Merger. (See page 130.)

19. Joining Churches that Vote Overwhelmingly Approve the Merger. (See page 136.)

20. Lead Churches that Vote Almost Unanimously Approve the Merger. (See page 136.)

21. The Joining Church Changes Its Name in the Majority of Cases. (See page 139.)

22. A Merger Costs $112,500 (Median) for One-Time Plus First-Year Expenses. (See page 149.)

23. 93% of Mergers in Our Study Have Not Been Undone. (See page 151.)

24. Almost All Mergers Come from the Same or Similar Church Tradition and Ethnicity. (See page 177.)

25. Both Joining Churches AND Lead Churches Initiate Mergers. (See page 191.)

26. The Vast Majority of Mergers Are within 30 Minutes of Each Other. (See page 191.)

27. For Lead Churches, the Greatest Reason to Merge Is to Help Revitalize a Struggling Church. (See page 193.)

28. For Joining Churches, the Greatest Reason to Merge Is Survival. (See page 194.)

APPENDIX C: 25 ISSUES TO DETERMINE FEASIBILITY: SUN VALLEY AND BETHANY COMMUNITY CHURCH

We have identified twenty-five distinct issues that every church merger has to address to determine feasibility, as introduced in chapter 6 and described in chapter 15. The following document comes from Sun Valley Community Church, mentioned throughout the book and the lead church in this case, describing how it resolved the twenty-five issues with Bethany Community Church, the joining church in this case.

Doctrinal

1. Theological beliefs

Sun Valley and Bethany have very compatible historic orthodox, evangelical, theological beliefs. The one distinction is in Sun Valley's view of pastors being a type of elder, therefore the title of pastor being reserved for men.

2. Governance

The structure of leadership in the constitution and bylaws of both churches are similar in this respect. However, Sun Valley's practice/interpretation has been "staff-led, board-protected," whereas Bethany's present practice is "elder-led." Sun Valley Community Church is led by the executive team, which consists of the lead pastors, campus pastors and select executive level staff members. The board of servant leaders is constituted by up to nine leaders, the majority of which are lay leaders selected from all campuses in addition to the lead pastors. Lay servant

12. Budget

We are one church: one vision, one leadership team, one budget, one staff, and one bank account. Giving, budgets, and current account balances from Sun Valley and Bethany will be combined and managed by the Sun Valley church administrator, executive team, and board of servant leaders to address the needs and mission of all campuses.

Personnel

13. Expectations

This merger is an "adoption," which is defined as "a stable or stuck church that is integrated under the vision of a stronger, vibrant, and typically larger church." In this scenario, Sun Valley is the leading church and Bethany is the joining church.

14. Senior Pastor

Scott Ridout and Chad Moore share the lead pastor role at Sun Valley and will assume that role for the Bethany campus as well.

15. Boards and Committees

The Elder Board will be replaced by one central board of servant leaders (all of whom must still qualify according to 1 Timothy 3 and Titus 1, like our elders). This board consists of the lead pastors and a large majority of lay members selected as representatives from all campuses. Local campus leadership will be led primarily by the executive staff team of that campus under the leadership of a central executive team, which consists of the campus pastors, lead pastors and selected executive team members from different campuses.

Sun Valley does not use committees but does have task forces. Committees that serve in an area of ministry focus (such as missions) will come under the supervision of the staff over that area. The staff and board of Sun Valley have the power to assign task forces to tackle issues they deem important but not necessarily the primary focus of the staff and board (i.e. the building task force on the Gilbert Campus). All other committees at Bethany that are not converted to staff or Board-assigned task forces will be phased out.

16. Staff

We are committed to "retain and train" the existing Bethany staff, provided that giving on the Bethany campus can support this commitment. Pay/benefit packages will be examined and will come into alignment within the standard ranges of Sun Valley in/prior to [DATE].

17. Missionaries

The same commitment that has been given to the staff is given for Bethany's missionaries. Missionaries will not be penalized for duplication on both campuses. Like all staff and ministries, all missions/missionary emphases are subject to evaluation.

Legal

18. Lawyer

(Not addressed in this document.)

19. Church Name

Sun Valley Community Church—Bethany Campus. We will adopt the name Sun Valley Community Church but will be known as the "Bethany Campus" to honor our heritage. Sun Valley has great and growing name recognition in our valley, and it makes sense to keep that name. In written form, we will identify that campus as "Bethany/Tempe" so that people not familiar with Bethany can know the location of the campus.

20. Voting

While the Gilbert campus needs no congregational vote, we will do a confirmation vote. Our understanding is that the Bethany campus needs to have a congregational approval by three fourths of members present. This vote will not only make Scott Ridout and Chad Moore lead pastors at Bethany, it will replace the constitution and bylaws of Bethany Community Church with the constitution and bylaws of Sun Valley Community Church.

21. Dissolution

(Not addressed in this document.)

22. Property/Facility

Sun Valley's expressed plan is not only to keep the campus, but to maximize its use for Kingdom impact. The Bethany campus is one of the most strategically located campuses in Phoenix. Our vision for Tempe/Chandler/Ahwatukee is unwavering. Most likely we will have a campaign for campus renovation and deferred maintenance within the first year of the adoption. Sun Valley will assume ownership of all property of Bethany Community Church.

23. Assets and Liabilities

We have sent our information to the leadership of Bethany Community Church. We would like to see the information on the Bethany Community Church property, the Bethany Learning Center, the deferred maintenance needs, the missionary house in Mesa and any other property that Bethany may own. Sun Valley will work with the leadership of the Bethany elders to work out the best possible scenario for handling the assets and liabilities of Bethany Community Church with integrity.

24. Debt Management

We have sent our information to the leadership of Bethany Community Church. We have handled our debt with integrity. We have $[NUMBER] million in debt: $[NUMBER] million on Building A, $[NUMBER] on Building B. We will not take on any more debt on Gilbert Campus and, in fact, have completed the downstairs children's area (about 20,000 square feet) debt free.

25. Timeline

We suggest the following timeline, which was suggested by [NAME] from Bethany:

- August 7 – Make the adoption announcement.
- Next six weeks – Host a number of town halls and discussions to answer questions and dream the possibilities of our future.

(We suggest having Chad Moore and Scott Ridout speak on several weekend services during that time.)

- September 25 – Take a congregational vote.
- October 9 – Host a Celebration Service commemorating the years of great ministry God has given us as a church.
- October 16 – Have the first service as Sun Valley Community Church—Bethany Campus.

APPENDIX D: 25 ISSUES TO DETERMINE FEASIBILITY: CHRIST FELLOWSHIP MIAMI

Like Appendix C, the following is an actual document prepared by a church to prepare for a potential merger with another church. We recommend that churches who see mergers in their future think through these issues before a merger opportunity presents itself or in preparation of a proactive invitation for churches to consider joining them.

Introduction

After the leadership teams of two churches conclude that a merger is possible, the next question is to determine if a merger is feasible. Are we compatible? Are we similar enough to merge? What are the issues that need to be addressed for a merger to happen? What are the issues that would prevent a merger from occurring?

Below is a list of 25 issues that have to be addressed in every church merger. Most of them will be non-issues. Usually there will be 3–5 problematic issues that could be "deal-breakers." If the two leadership teams can find a resolution on these problematic issues, then a merger is feasible and can be recommended to their churches for a vote. The time between the recommendation to merge and the vote is the time the two congregations are determining if this merger is desirable.

Doctrinal

1. Theological beliefs. Is our church theologically more conservative or more moderate/progressive/liberal? Is our church charismatic, reformed, or dispensational? Do we share similar or divergent views on the Bible, baptism, spiritual gifts, divorce, the role of women, etc?

> *Christ Fellowship is a theologically conservative, biblically-centered church affiliated with the Southern Baptist Convention. We are respectfully complementarian in our functioning as a local church and affirm women in leadership at all levels except for the office of pastor.*

2. Governance. How similar or different are the two churches when it comes to local church government? Are they congregational or episcopal? Is our church elder-governed, staff-led or overseen denominationally?

> *Christ Fellowship in a congregational church with a policy governance model that is pastor-led and board-protected.*

3. Affiliations. Are the two congregation's members of the same denomination, network or association? If not, is there compatibility? Are the affiliations mandatory? Will they remain or change?

> *Christ Fellowship is part of the Southern Baptist Convention and adheres to the SBC beliefs as reflected in the Baptist Faith & Message document.*

Philosophy of Ministry

4. Mission. How does each church answer the question: "Why do we exist?" An honest answer will reveal how close or far we are on the primary purpose of the church. The strongest mergers are those that are primarily mission-driven.

> *Christ Fellowship exists to help you follow Jesus.*

5. Vision. Vision is the picture of your preferred future. How does each church answer the question, "If we succeed in fulfilling our mission as a church, what would our church look like ten years from now?" How similar are the two visions? Are the two congregations creating a new vision together? If not, can you embrace the vision of the other church?

> *Christ Fellowship's vision is to establish Christ Fellowship churches across Miami, the Caribbean and Latin America.*

6. Values. Values are the principles that guide how a church does its ministry. They reflect what really matters to a church. How similar or divergent are our values?

> *Christ Fellowship values are...*
> 1. ***Excellence*** *is what we strive for*
> 2. ***Serving*** *is how we lead*
> 3. ***Generosity*** *is our privilege*
> 4. ***Humility*** *is our posture*
> 5. ***Passion*** *is what drives us*
> 6. ***Fun*** *is our style*

7. Discipleship Strategy. Effective churches are intentional about making disciples of Jesus. How similar or divergent is our discipleship pathway?

> *Christ Fellowship's next-step discipleship pathway is:*
> *Attend a weekend service*
> *Join a small group*
> *Serve on a team*
> *Tell others about Jesus*

8. Worship Style. How similar or different are the worship styles of our church from the other church? Are we contemporary, traditional or blended? Is our worship style more participatory or performance-oriented? Does our church have choirs or worship bands, drums or organs, pews or theater-seats, stained-glass or video screens? Often worship style is the primary basis people like or dislike a church. If not similar, are we willing to embrace a different worship style?

> *Christ Fellowship worship style is contemporary and participatory with performance exceptions. Our worship bands use drums, acoustic and electric guitars, piano, and bass. Seating varies per campus. Some have chairs and some have pews with stained glass windows. We utilize video screens at all of our locations.*

9. Preaching. Who will be bringing the weekend messages to the congregation? Will the sermons be delivered in-person or by video?

> *Lead Pastor Omar Giritli is the primary teacher at Christ Fellowship who is broadcasted live to all campuses. In addition, there are two other teaching pastors who are also broadcasted to the campuses at times. Local Campus*

Pastors teach live, in-person at their campuses several times throughout the year.

10. Membership. What are the requirements for church membership at our church? Will those requirements transfer to the other church? If a merger does occur, will the membership transfer automatically, or will a membership class be required?

Members from the joining church will be given the opportunity to take Christ Fellowship 101 and will be invited to transfer their membership if desired.

11. Programs. What church programs and ministries are non-negotiable and therefore un-touchable? What programs could be integrated into the new entity and which ones would need to be re-calibrated or eliminated?

Christ Fellowship has intentional and well-defined programs to implement our vision but is open to incorporating new programs that improve our strategy or accommodating programs to facilitate the needs of a joining church.

12. Budget. Budgets reflect the priorities of a church. What do you learn about each other by reviewing the budgets? What percentage goes to staff, debt reduction, ministries and missions?

Christ Fellowship operates debt-free under the supervision of a CFO and the board of trustees. Our budget break downs into these categories:

- *Personnel: 48%*
- *Missions: 20%*
- *Facilities: 19%*
- *Ministry: 13%*
- *Debt Reduction: 0%*

Personnel

13. Expectations. How does each congregation understand the merger relationship? Is this merger a marriage, an adoption, a rebirth or an ICU merger? How each party sees the merger determines their expectations of the relationship. The sooner both parties can define the relationship and get on the same page concerning expectations, the smoother the merger process will go.

As the lead church, Christ Fellowship will keep its lead pastor, staff, name, vision, strategy, values, assets, and locations. The kind of merger will be determined on an individual church basis.

14. Lead Pastors. The first question that has to be addressed if there are two lead pastors involved is the status of the lead pastor of the joining church post-merger. Will he or she remain as pastor of that location (if it becomes a multisite campus), be re-deployed in another staff position within the church or be given a severance package? This is usually already decided between the two lead pastors in the Exploration stage.

Depending on the needs of the joining pastor he/she would either be re-deployed to another staff position or given a severance package. Lead pastors who have joined Christ Fellowship in the past have successfully re-deployed to other positions and are still part of Christ Fellowship years later.

15. Boards and Committees. Will the existing boards and committees be integrated, re-calibrated or eliminated? Will the board members stay the same? Will all, some, or none remain?

Christ Fellowship's board will stay the same, but the board and committees of the joining church will be dissolved with the legal dissolution of the church.

16. Staff. Are the job descriptions, pay levels, contracts, and benefits comparable or dramatically different? What will be the staff needs in the new church entity? What staff will remain in their current position, be redeployed to another area in the church, downsized, or released? What are the severance policies?

Staff of the joining church may be asked to continue to serve in the same capacity or could be redeployed to another area based on need, compatibility and skill set. All salaries at Christ Fellowship are at the industry standard or above. Severance policy of Christ Fellowship is individualized based on performance and length of service.

17. Missionaries. Will funding support for the missionaries, parachurch ministries and organizations supported by the church be continued, phased out over time, or ended upon completion of the merger?

Assuming theological and philosophical congruence, Christ Fellowship will continue to support a joining church's current missionaries, para-church ministries, and organizations ministries for at least one year and will eval-uate the continuing fit of each missionary and organization within the mission, vision, and values of Christ Fellowship.

Legal

18. Lawyer. Do we have legal counsel to guide us through the legal steps of a church merger?

Christ Fellowship has legal counsel to guide through a church merger.

19. Church Name. Will there be a name change of one or both congregations? How will that be decided?

The new name will begin as Christ Fellowship followed with an identifying name with a focus on the local community but may be able to incorporate the joining church name to identify the local campus.

20. Voting. How will the decision to merge be decided and by whom—the denomination, the board, or the congregation? What do the church bylaws require? Will a congregational vote be required? If so, what will be the process and what percentage is required for approval? What is the lowest approval percentage the two churches are willing to accept?

Christ Fellowship's members must vote in the case of acquisition of debt or property, otherwise the Lead Pastor, Leadership Team, and Board of Trustees would approve.

21. Dissolution. What will be the dissolution process of the joining church? Will this be a strict merger, asset purchase by the lead church, or a donation by the joining church? What do the laws of your state dictate?

The legal dissolution and merger process will be determined on an individual church basis.

22. Property/Facility. What will the new church entity do with any property and/or facilities gained in the merger? Will the property and/or facilities be kept or sold? What are the legal requirements and state laws for transfer of church property? What legal counsel do we need?

The property and/or facilities would become part of Christ Fellowship.
The property and/or facilities will most likely be kept, unless there is an
unusual circumstance. Legal counsel would be involved.

23. Assets & Liabilities. What tangible assets do the two churches bring
to the table in terms of property, facilities, and equipment? Is there an
inventory of all property and equipment? Due diligence is a must to
determine what repairs, maintenance costs, and hidden liabilities come
with these items.

Christ Fellowship has full inventory of all property and equipment. Both
churches will bring all property, facilities, and equipment to the merger.

The joining church's property, facilities, and equipment will become a part
of Christ Fellowship. The joining church will enjoy the benefits of all Christ
Fellowship properties, facilities, and equipment post-merger.

24. Debt Management. What debt does either church bring to the
merger? Is it manageable?

Christ Fellowship has no debt.

25. Timeline. When is the earliest possible date a merger could occur
between the two churches? What are the things that need to happen and
by when for a merger to occur?

For the merger to take place, the leadership and congregation of the joining
church must go through the requirements of their constitution and bylaws
and provide full access to their financial data. Mergers can occur in a mat-
ter of months as long as the merger is feasible and desirable.

APPENDIX E: FAQS FROM WOODSIDE BIBLE CHURCH

When the leadership of two churches is ready to recommend a merger to their respective congregations, a helpful communication tool is a Frequently Asked Questions (FAQ) document. We introduce this idea as a part of the Declaration stage in chapter 6, and then chapter 15 offers an FAQ template. Typically, the FAQ is made available to a church's entire constituency, both online and in print. Appendix E showed a denominational example, and below is a nondenominational version. Each highlights the typical questions that a church merger FAQ seeks to address.

What Does a "Merger" Mean?

We will become one congregation known as Woodside Bible Church. The church would become a Woodside Bible Church campus governed by the Woodside elder board. [NAMES] will serve as campus pastors part time to care for the campus. We would be one church meeting at several locations. The campus will use Woodside's current constitution, statement of faith, and missions' policies as its governing documents. All current members of [JOINING CHURCH'S NAME] will be given the opportunity to automatically become members of Woodside.

Who Will Preach Each Sunday?

Like the other campuses, we would have a teaching team that would preach the message. Primarily [NAMES] will comprise the team. The message content is the same across all campuses.

Will There Be Ministry Opportunities at the New Campus?

There will be many opportunities to prayerfully consider. Volunteers will be needed in worship leading, children's ministry, small groups, students, young adults, and so on. We will welcome those who have a desire to be part of building this new campus in [CITY].

What Are the Financial Liabilities?

Members of our finance committee have studied this proposal and are excited about the possibilities of what God can do in the city of [NAME]. The church is debt free and brings approximately $[AMOUNT] in savings. The church also owns a parsonage that is mortgage free. The building is in excellent condition and is located at [ADDRESS]. It is our plan to cover our weekly expenses from the current level of giving.

What Would Happen to [NAME OF JOINING CHURCH'S] Staff and Volunteers?

All paid church staff will be evaluated by the deacons of [NAME OF JOINNG CHURCH] and Woodside elders and, if appropriate, be offered roles within the Woodside team. [NAME OF JOINING CHURCH] ministry leaders will be given the opportunity to serve at the [NAME OF CITY] campus in their areas of passion and giftedness.

Why Are We Doing This Merger?

The merger fits into our vision at Woodside: Helping people belong to Christ, join in Christ, grow in Christ, and reach the world for Christ. Our discussion with the leadership of [JOINING CHURCH'S NAME] began in [DATE] and has involved much prayer and interaction. The merger will allow us to join forces with the wonderful people of [JOINING CHURCH'S NAME] in reaching the [CITY] region for Christ. As leadership, we know that this church is God's and we want to serve Him. Let's together be dependent on God in prayer and express our confidence in Him by boldly acting in faith.

What Are the Steps in Concluding the Merger?

The congregation of [JOINING CHURCH'S NAME] and the congregation of Woodside Bible Church—all its campuses—will vote Saturday and Sunday [DATES]. If the vote passes, the legal work will be completed, launch date selected, and the specifics of campus development will begin. We will be inviting people to join us in developing another Woodside campus, helping us realize our vision of affecting our region with the life-changing message of Jesus Christ. Meetings will take place early in [MONTH] for people to get more information on the service opportunities at [CITY].

APPENDIX F: CHURCHES NAMED

Church Name	City and State	Current Lead Pastor	Website	Chapter
Anthem Church	Broken Arrow, OK	Brad Jenkins	weareanthem.church	4, 15
Bay Hope Church	Lutz, FL	Matthew Hartsfield	bayhope.church	4
Calvary Christian Church	Winchester, KY	Mike McCormick	calvarychristian.net	14
Capstone Church	Anderson, SC	David Barfield	capstonechurch.com	13
Christ Fellowship Miami	Palmetto Bay, FL	Omar Giritli	cfmiami.org	4, 14, Appendix D
Church of the Highlands	Birmingham, AL	Chris Hodges	churchofthehighlands.com	16
Crosspoint Church	Hutchinson, KS	Andy Addis	crosspointnow.net	1
Crossroads Church	Cincinnati, OH	Brian Tome	crossroads.net	1, 13
EastLake Church	Chula Vista, CA	James Grogan	eastlakechurch.com	4, 14
First West	West Monroe, LA	Michael Wood	firstwest.cc	5
Ginghamsburg Church	Tipp City, OH	Rachel Billups	ginghamsburg.org	15
Grace Church	Cape Coral, FL	Jorge Acevedo	egracechurch.com	3

Saddleback Church	Lake Forest, CA	Rick Warren	saddleback.com	2
Sandals Church	Riverside, CA	Matt Brown	sandalschurch.com	1, 2
Silver Creek Fellowship	Silverton, OR	Rob Barnes	scf.tv	14
Southbridge Fellowship	Raleigh, NC	Scott Lehr	sfchurch.com	15
Spirit of Faith Lutheran-Methodist Church	Woonsocket, SD	Rhonda Wellsandt-Zell	no website	12
Sun Valley Community Church	Gilbert, AZ	Chad Moore	sunvalleycc.com	8, 12, 15, Appendix C
Sunrise Church	Rialto, CA	Steve Garcia	sunrisechurch.org	4
The Bridge Community Church	Ruston, LA	Chris Hanchey	thebridge.cc	4
The Chapel	Libertyville, IL	Scott Chapman	chapel.org	3, 4, 14
The Chapel	Akron, OH	Tim Armstrong	thechapel.life	8
The Connection Church	Pelham, AL	Wendy Davis-Lovell	theconnection.cc	9
Village Church	Highland Village, TX	Matt Chandler	thevillagechurch.net	2
Vintage Faith Church	Santa Cruz, CA	Dan Kimball	vintagechurch.org	13
Washington Heights Church	Ogden, UT	Roy Gruber	whc.faith	5
Woodside Bible Church	Troy, MI	Chris Brooks	woodsidebible.org	12, Appendix E

ACKNOWLEDGMENTS

Our list of the world's most supportive people begins with Jim's wife, Deryl, and Warren's wife, Michelle. We love doing life together with you.

We also thank the patient churches that helped us learn how to be pastors. Jim credits Hoffmantown Baptist Church, Albuquerque, New Mexico; Faith Baptist Church, Kaiserslautern, Germany; Woodmen Valley Chapel, Colorado Springs, Colorado; Willow Creek Community Church, Chicago, Illinois, and Christ Fellowship, Miami, Florida. Warren wants to single out three churches that have deeply impacted him: First Baptist, Atlanta, Georgia, Warren's church home during his teenage years; Princeton Alliance Church, Princeton, New Jersey, where Warren was on staff for eleven years; and Liquid Church, where Warren is on the church board.

Jim also expresses appreciation to more than five hundred churches who contracted his consulting services—and who have taught him valuable insights from the front trenches of ministry. In addition, Jim is grateful (Warren as well!) for the support of Tony Morgan and The Unstuck Group in the research of this updated version of *Better Together*. Tony and Jim started their companies about the same time to serve local churches and have been strategic partners with many churches over the years. The formal joining of MultiSite Solutions with The Unstuck Group in 2019 embodies the principles of this book and is a living example of the synergy two companies can experience by coming together under one banner.

Warren likewise appreciates all the pastoral leaders who have welcomed his visits and interviews through Leadership Network and through his previous work with the Charles E. Fuller Institute for Evangelism and Church Growth under Carl George and also the Beeson Institute for Advanced Church Leadership under Dale Galloway. Warren's current employer, ECFA (the Evangelical Council for Financial Accountability) has been tremendously supportive of Warren's merger research, such as cosponsoring the 2019 survey on which so many of the statistics and stories in this edition of *Better Together* are based.

We also are grateful to The Unstuck Group, ECFA, Leadership Network, and David Fletcher and his XPastor.org for sponsoring the 2019 Church Merger Survey in addition to all the networks and organizations that helped get word out about our survey.

Both Jim and Warren are grateful for those who contributed time, expertise, and counsel to both editions of *Better Together*, many helped with both versions.

The first edition would not have happened without Warren's excellent support staff, especially Kelly Kulesza and Stephanie Plagens at Leadership Network, as well as other colleagues there: Dave Travis, Greg Ligon, and Mark Sweeney. Staff at Jossey-Bass who helped improve this book include Sheryl Fullerton, Joanne Clapp Fullagar, Alison Knowles, Lisa Coronado-Morse, and Susan Geraghty.

The second edition would not have happened without the research and graphics expertise of Warren's assistant Dianne Russell. We are most grateful for her Herculean efforts, cheerful spirit and amazing timing.

We also got significant help from several specialists including Marc Glassman, a statistical consultant; Scott Thumma, researcher and statistician; and attorneys Wendi Hodges and David Middlebrook for the legal material that appears in both editions.

Warren's prayer partner for the first edition of this book was Len Kageler and Jim's ministry-long prayer partner is Becky Kennard. For the second edition, Warren's small group at Living Christ Church was his anchor during the year of working on these edits.

Many people read the manuscript and suggested important and helpful improvements. First-edition readers included Ed Bahler, Russ Bredholt, Charlie Boyd, Wade Burnett, Chuck Davis, David Fletcher, Chris Hughes, Kelly Kulesza, Greg Ligon, Tony Morgan, Tom Nebel, Russ Olman, Dan Reiland, Chris Ritter, Dale Roach, Kristy Rutter, Jonathan Schaeffer, J. David Schmidt, Daniel Serdahl, Gary Shockley, Wayne Smith, Dave Travis, and Jon S. Vesely. Those who read drafts of the second edition included Jose Alonso, Pat Colgan, Skipp Mahmer, and Tony Morgan.

We also thank the more than a thousand people who participated in the merger surveys we orchestrated in 2011 and 2019 (described in appendix A). Both editions of the book are titled *Better Together*, and we again want to thank the original brainstormers who helped us "discover" that title. They include Jeff Butler, Marc Curnutt, Peter DiPippo, Taylor Moffitt, David Rudd, Brad Sargent, and Ildefonso Torres.

Finally, the updated and expanded version would not have come together without the unswerving belief that Beth Gaede had in the need for a new version of *Better Together*. Plus, she served as an outstanding editor and project advisor. We're very grateful for her and the entire publishing team, including production editor Claire Vanden Branden.

MEET THE AUTHORS

Jim Tomberlin has served the body of Christ in a variety of ministries from pastoring a church in Germany to growing a megachurch in Colorado Springs, to pioneering the multisite strategy at Willow Creek Community Church in Chicago. He currently serves as the senior executive pastor at Christ Fellowship in Miami. He trained for ministry at Georgia State University (BA) in Atlanta and Dallas Theological Seminary (ThM).

In 2005 Jim founded MultiSite Solutions, a church consulting company that has assisted hundreds of churches in multiplying their impact through intensive multisite, church merger and multiplication consultation.

In 2019 Jim merged MultiSite Solutions with Tony Morgan's The Unstuck Group (TheUnstuckGroup.com) to expand their capacity to assist more churches.

On Twitter and Instagram as the @MultiSiteGuy Jim continues to track multisite developments and has become the nationally recognized expert on multisite church. In addition, on Twitter he has become the @MergerGuru having assisted more than a hundred churches through the church merger process.

Jim resides in Colorado Springs, Colorado. Jim and his wife, Deryl, have three grown children.

Warren Bird, PhD, is a leading researcher of trends in Protestant churches. He graduated from Wheaton College (BA) and Wheaton Graduate School (MA) in Wheaton, Illinois; Alliance Theological Seminary (MDiv), Nyack, New York; and Fordham University (PhD), Bronx, New York. An ordained minister serving on church staff for sixteen years, he pastored churches on the East Coast as lead pastor and as assistant pastor, and during that same period served as an adjunct faculty member at Alliance Theological Seminary, Nyack, New York, for twenty-four years. He has authored or coauthored thirty-two books including *Liquid Church, Hero Maker, Next: Pastoral Succession That Works,* and *How to Break Church Growth Barriers.* Warren is the former director of research and intellectual capital development for Leadership Network, and he now serves as vice president of research and equipping for ECFA (the Evangelical Council for Financial Accountability).